KU-547-283

Prostitution

Prevention and Reform in England, 1860–1914

Paula Bartley

London and New York

First published 2000 in the UK and the USA
by Routledge
11 New Fetter Lane, London EC4P 4EE

Simultaneously published in the USA and Canada by Routledge
29 West 35th Street, New York, NY 10001

Routledge is an imprint of the Taylor & Francis Group

© 2000 Paula Bartley

Typeset in Garamond by Florence Production Ltd,
Stoodleigh, Devon
Printed and bound in Great Britain by TJ International Ltd,
Padstow, Cornwall

All rights reserved. No part of this book may be reprinted
or reproduced or utilised in any form or by any electronic,
mechanical, or other means, now known or hereafter invented,
including photocopying and recording, or in any information
storage or retrieval system, without permission in writing
from the publishers.

British Library Cataloguing in Publication Data
A catalogue record for this book is available from the British
Library

Library of Congress Cataloging in Publication Data
A catalog record for this book has been requested

ISBN 0–415–21456–4 (hbk)
ISBN 0–415–21457–2 (pbk)

For Jonathan Dudley

Contents

PART IV
Purifying the nation

Figures

Table

Acknowledgements

I am indebted to a number of people for helping to improve *Prostitution*. First of all, I would like to thank Lesley Hall for giving me sound historical advice, sharing her considerable expertise, suggesting several lines of enquiry and commenting on the reform section. Robert Pearce acted as unofficial editor and generously read and commented most helpfully on the whole manuscript.

Prostitution is based on my PhD thesis. I was fortunate to have had three excellent supervisors, John Benson (my director of studies), Angela V. John and Roger Leese, to support me through each stage of the thesis. Their combined wealth of knowledge and constructive criticism have been invaluable and I thank them warmly. John Benson, patiently and painstakingly, also helped in transforming the thesis into a book. I am grateful to my two external examiners, Carl Chinn and Jane Rendall, for their constructive suggestions. I would like to thank many colleagues at the University of Wolverhampton. In particular, Mike Cunningham and Martin Durham both offered useful advice; Marie-Clare Balaam generously photocopied relevant articles from *The Lancet* and *British Medical Journal* while engaged in her own research; Jan Broadway helped locate primary sources in Newcastle and Gloucester; Barbara Gwinnett not only read a number of chapters but also allowed me to include some of our joint thinking in the conclusion of this book; and Malcolm Wanklyn gave me continuous support throughout. My third year undergraduate students were always willing to discuss my research and made my teaching of this topic a delight. Ian Grosvenor, University of Birmingham, offered useful advice on the 'feeble-minded', as did Helen Self, who helped me with the legal aspects, so I would like to thank them too. The anonymous reader made many useful comments which I have incorporated into the book. Thanks are also due to June Purvis and Heather McCallum for their patience and perseverance, to Christine Firth for her meticulous copy-editing and to Sally Carter.

I visited numerous local history libraries, record offices and other institutions for this research and would especially like to thank the staff of Camden Local History Library and the Metropolitan Records Office, London, as well as staff at Leeds, Nottingham and Plymouth Record Offices for their friendly and encouraging assistance. The staff at Manchester, Chris Upton at Birmingham and Sheila Gopualen at the Public Records Office, Kew, took an active interest in my research and were exceptionally helpful, and I would like to give them special thanks. I should also like to thank the reservation staff at the Bodleian Library, Oxford, and the British Library telephone reservations staff for their efforts in locating material. Daphne Glick at the National Council of Women, David Doughan at the Fawcett, Captain John Smith at the Church Army, the staff and volunteers at the Society of Friends, the Galton Institute, the Wellcome Institute and the archivists at the Salvation Army and Birmingham Police Museum all provided me with information. I thank them all. I am also indebted to the librarians at the Dudley Campus of the University of Wolverhampton, who obtained numerous articles, theses and books for me, and to Cham Patel and Graham Taggart for their technical support.

My greatest thanks are to my husband, Jonathan Dudley, who commented on numerous drafts, made endless cups of tea, poured the odd glass of wine and shared in my enthusiasm for this topic over the years. The book is dedicated to him with gratitude and with love.

Introduction

'O 'Melia, my dear, this does everything crown!
Who could have supposed I should meet you in Town?
And whence such fair garments, such prosperity?'
'O didn't you know I'd been ruined?' said she.

'You left us in tatters, without shoes or socks,
Tired of digging potatoes, and spudding up docks;
And now you've got bracelets and bright feathers three!'
'Yes, that's how we dress when we're ruined,' said she.

'Your hands were like paws then, your face blue and bleak
But now I'm bewitched by your delicate cheek,
And your little gloves fit as on any lady!'
'We never do work when we're ruined,' said she.

'I wish I had feathers, a fine sweeping gown,
And a delicate face, and could strut about Town!'
'My dear – a raw country girl, such as you be,
Cannot quite expect that. You ain't ruined,' said she.

These verses from *The Ruined Maid* by Thomas Hardy are an ironic comment on the lives of both respectable and not-so-respectable young working-class women. Amelia, the 'ruined maid', displays, in material terms at least, every sign of upward social mobility whereas her interlocutor, although unimpeachably moral, remains locked in the poverty of her class. Virtue may be its own reward but in Hardy's terms it is a poor prize.

For the most part Victorian and Edwardian reformers preferred the image of Hardy's other heroine, Tess, rather than Amelia. In his novel, *Tess of the D'Urbervilles*, Hardy paints a different picture of a 'ruined maid' where Tess, seduced and betrayed by an aristocratic libertine, is inevitably driven towards her ultimate destruction. Sexual impurity and its corollary, prostitution, certainly caused concern. Considered a 'social evil', prostitution commanded attention from the church, the state, the medical profession, philanthropists, feminists and others, each of which offered a range of solutions to control and ultimately to end it. Fears that it would infect the respectable world, destroy marriages, the home, the family and ultimately the nation led to attempts to regulate and reform the prostitute and to prevent and suppress prostitution. The Contagious Diseases Acts (CD Acts) were passed to make paid sex safe for the armed forces, institutions were founded to reform individual prostitutes and preventive organisations were set up to tackle what was considered the underlying causes of prostitution. This book focuses on the reform of prostitutes and the prevention of prostitution. It examines the variety of reform institutions, ranging from large penitentiaries to small homes, all of which attempted to make former prostitutes into morally virtuous women. The book surveys the changes in the reform of prostitutes and argues that the prevention movement emerged as a result of the failure of these reform initiatives. One of the important preventive organisations discussed, the Ladies' Association for the Care of Friendless Girls, aimed to eliminate the causes of prostitution. It was founded to train and educate young women perceived to be at moral risk, to help single mothers in their first confinement and to pass laws to protect female virtue. By the late nineteenth century, prostitution came to be associated with 'feeble-mindedness', and the book explains this shift by analysing a number of changes in attitude within Victorian society – attitudes to the provision of care for mentally ill people, to female madness, to the development of eugenics and to charitable work itself. When it became evident that both the reform and preventive movements had failed to curb prostitution, social purity workers attempted to suppress prostitution and to create a moral climate in which prostitution would finally disappear. The last part of the book explores the contradictions within the social purity movement and concludes that moves to prevent prostitution ultimately failed.

Reformers may have expressed alarm about prostitution but there are numerical inconsistencies regarding its extent in England during this period.[1] Mid-century figures for London fluctuate between 5,000 and 220,000 (which made 7 per cent of the population). In the 1860s some suggested that there were up to half a million prostitutes in England yet police statistics maintained that numbers were in the region of 30,000. The figures for those prosecuted for prostitution were even less: in 1860 only 7,119 women were actually tried for prostitution offences.[2] Police prosecution statistics remained remarkably consistent throughout the nineteenth and early twentieth centuries; in 1896, for example, 7,537 women were put on trial for prostitution. The discrepancies in the range of figures occur because of the ways in which statistics were collected and by whom. Some sources included courtesans, single mothers and women who cohabited with men as prostitutes: broad definitions such as these will obviously explain high numbers. In contrast, other sources quote police figures which included only women prosecuted for prostitution. This will often account for the allegedly low numbers of prostitutes. Moreover, even police figures varied significantly. In the late nineteenth century, the Liverpool Chief Constable believed that prostitution in Liverpool was rampant, stating that there were between thirty and fifty known brothels in one street alone. In contrast, the Chief Constable of Sheffield confidently asserted that there were no brothels at all in his patch, leading the Chief Constable of Liverpool to comment that it was 'farcical and ridiculous' to believe that there was no prostitution in a city with 350,000 inhabitants.[3] One notoriously corrupt superintendent, who maintained that prostitution had diminished in Manchester, had produced the result by doctoring the evidence.[4]

Nonetheless, it was commonly accepted that London, ports (such as Liverpool) and army towns (such as Colchester) held the highest number of prostitutes, followed by cities (such as Manchester) and resort towns (such as Brighton). For example, in 1881 police sent for trial 5,942 women in London, 4,615 in Liverpool, 2,091 in Manchester and 477 in Birmingham.[5] Country fairs, particularly 'hiring fairs', were also thought to be utilised by 'vicious' people for the systematised demoralisation of the young.[6] Interestingly, prostitution was believed to be less rife in mill and factory towns: in Oldham, for example, only 66 prostitutes were prosecuted in 1881.[7] On the whole, prostitution was contained within certain areas in these towns and cities. In London, Charing Cross, the Haymarket, Regent Street and the West End were notorious; in Manchester, Oxford Street (known as the 'Dirty Mile') was infamous; in Liverpool the amphitheatre, where 'unrebuked Acts of gross indecency were committed in the refreshment area', the Domville Dance Hall in Lime Street, where 'vice ran riot; abandoned wretches in the form of women, demons in the shape of men, held their orgies there',[8] and the Zoological Gardens were among the most well known. Of course, women may have also worked elsewhere and there may well have been a larger number of discreet brothels which did not come to the attention of the police or social reformers.

In 1857 William Acton, referring to prostitutes, inquired 'who are those fair creatures, neither chaperones nor chaperoned, "those somebodies whom nobody knows"?'[9] Prostitutes, of course, were never a homogeneous group. In common with the social stratification prevalent at this time, prostitutes were classified according to a hierarchy.[10] Henry Mayhew identifies six main categories: kept mistresses; demi-mondains; low lodging house women; sailors and soldiers' women; park women; and thieves' women. This, as with most categorisations, oversimplifies the composition of the nineteenth-century prostitute population even though it does indicate the diversity of the male social groups they serviced. Moreover, Henry Mayhew defines the prostitutes in relation to the men who used them rather than to their own social class. Those involved with the rescue and reform of prostitutes believed that dressmakers, seamstresses, milliners, bonnet makers, shop girls, agricultural labourers, barmaids, flower girls, shop girls and above all domestic servants made up the majority of the prostitute population. Frederick Merrick, chaplain of London's Millbank Prison, found that out of 16,000 prostitutes he interviewed, 40 per cent had been domestic servants. Similarly,

LIVERPOOL
JOHN MOORES UNIVERSITY
AVRIL ROBARTS LRC
TEL. 0151 231 4022

rescue workers noted that most prostitutes had, at one time in their lives, been employed in domestic service: a Salvation Army register showed that as many as 88 per cent of reclaimed prostitutes were former servants. Undoubtedly, prostitutes who came into contact with either prison officials or reformers were overwhelmingly working class.

Prostitution was not illegal but it was a stigmatised activity, socially unacceptable and surrounded by so many legal restrictions as to be illegal in all but name. In fact prostitutes were penalised by the legal system simply because they were prostitutes. Actions which would not constitute an infringement of the law by 'respectable' women were illegal if committed by known prostitutes: loitering for example was not in itself a criminal offence and became so only if practised by women thought to be prostitutes.[11]

Causes of prostitution

In his novel, *The New Magdalen*, Wilkie Collins endows his heroine Mercy Merrick (alias Grace Roseberry) with a personal history little short of parody.[12] Abandoned by her father and brought up by her immoral mother among acrobats and actors, Mercy Merrick is falsely accused of stealing a pocket handkerchief and sent to prison. On release she is drugged senseless before being seduced (i.e. raped) by 'gentlemen'. Orphaned, penniless and friendless, Mercy Merrick resorts to the only occupation available to women deprived of their 'reputation' and without references: prostitution.

Some reformers sympathised with Collins' interpretation and liked to regard prostitutes as victims who, seduced by upper-class men, had been abandoned to their fate on the streets. The conventional stereotypes were flower girls corrupted by the roués who frequented West End theatres: in Liverpool, flower girls were synonymous with prostitutes.[13] Similar versions of the seduction myth involved seamstresses beguiled by customers and domestic servants violated by younger sons and husbands of the household. Others maintained that men decoyed young girls with bribes of money and toys or else procured them for brothels by pretending that they were to enter domestic service. This white slavery, as it was known, emphasised the innocence of prostitutes at the expense of morally guilty men. Undoubtedly, those involved in the rescue and reform of prostitutes needed to convince themselves, and those whom they asked for financial support, that prostitutes were worth saving. The following quote, from the Society for the Protection of Young Females, may not delineate the real causes of prostitution but it does portray what reformers believed them to be:

> It has been proved that upwards of four hundred individuals procure a livelihood by trepanning females from eleven to fifteen years of age, for the purposes of Prostitution . . . when an innocent child appears in the streets without a protector, she is insidiously watched by one of these merciless wretches and decoyed, under some plausible pretext, to

an abode of infamy and degradation . . . She is stripped of the apparel with which parental care, or friendly solicitude had clothed her, and then decked with the gaudy trappings of her shame, she is compelled to walk the streets; . . . should she attempt to escape from the clutches of her seducers she is threatened with instant punishment, and is often barbarously treated.[14]

Admittedly, such beliefs were not borne out by the evidence as most prostitutes were not seduced by men of the upper classes. Out of Merrick's sample, only 5,000 out of 16,000 said that they 'owed their ruination' to men. Moreover, only a fifth of the 5,000 had been seduced by 'gentlemen'. On the contrary, many had been 'led astray' by other girls who had persuaded them to sell their bodies for money.

In general, reformers were more sophisticated than to embrace the seduction myth unreservedly and accepted that there were a multiplicity of reasons, rather than a monocausal explanation, for the cause and continuation of prostitution. Michael Ryan put forward the causes of prostitution as

seduction; neglect of parents; idleness; the low price of needle and other female work; the employment of young men milliners and drapers in shops in place of women; the facilities of prostitution; prevalence of intemperance; music and dancing in public houses, saloons and theatres; the impression that males are not equally culpable as females; female love of dress and of superior society; the seductive promises of men; the idea that prostitution is indispensable; poverty; want of education; ignorance; misery; innate licentiousness; improper prints, books and obscene weekly publications; and the profligacy of modern civilisation.[15]

Those working for the rescue and reform of prostitutes tended to agree. According to the life histories of between 600 and 700 women collected from rescue workers, missionaries, magistrates, policemen, relieving officers and Poor Law officials, there were many complex causes for prostitution ranging from personal failure through to social inadequacy. The belief that prostitution was caused by numerous psychological, social and economic factors remained a central tenet of moral reform philosophy between 1860 and 1914. Nevertheless, over time there was a gradual, and somewhat imperceptible, shift from holding prostitutes responsible for prostitution to thinking of them as the victims of masculine sexual profligacy and social injustice.

A number of reformers believed that prostitution was a consequence of personal moral weakness and therefore blamed women for prostitution. Rescue workers stressed that prostitutes had a wild impulsive nature, a restlessness and a need for independence which drove them onto the streets. This view was shared by the Labour Leader, Ramsay MacDonald, who held that the 'natural' prostitute was a 'person who is vain, who is vulgar, who is intemperate'.[16] Although such a perspective marks out prostitutes as culprits rather than victims, this type of analysis, according to Judith Walkowitz, views women as acting positively rather than reactively.[17]

Drink was closely associated with prostitution. Alcohol was thought to stimulate the animal passions while lowering the moral so that 'a woman that drinks will do anything'.[18] Former Sunday school scholars who had become prostitutes attributed their first downward step to intemperance.

> Love of drink is the worst enemy these poor girls have to fight, often falling into sin at first when under the influence of alcohol, they drink again from misery, until the craving so gets the mastery over them, that, humanly speaking, they are beyond help.[19]

It was rare to find a sober prostitute since ever increasing amounts of alcohol and narcotics were thought necessary in order for women to prostitute themselves. Public houses were held responsible for much of male sexual incontinence. Not only did the brewing industry expand throughout the nineteenth century but also mid-century licensing laws enabled publicans to keep their premises open all day if they so wished. This, according to some, increased the susceptibility of men. In addition, many landlords encouraged prostitution – indeed some pubs doubled as brothels – because of the additional custom it would bring.

The stock argument for prostitution was that it preserved the virtue of young women. 'But for her the unchallenged purity of countless happy homes would be polluted', wrote William Leckie in 1905.[20] Within marriage too, different rules applied. Monogamy in women was considered essential but men enjoyed greater sexual latitude since the emotional, psychological and physical make-up of the sexes was thought to differ. Sexual desire in men was considered to be overpowering whereas in women it was passive and controllable. Married men, who were willing to pay for the means of satisfying their sexual needs, therefore needed prostitutes to avoid pestering their wives too much. Reformers, however, rejected the doctrine that prostitution was inevitable because of the need to protect the chastity of good and virtuous women from men's insatiable sexual appetite. By the end of the nineteenth century, they had turned the biological explanation upside down, but like an upturned photograph it was nonetheless recognisable. Reformers may well have demanded that men be as chaste as women but their version still rested on the assumption that men were the aggressive sex who, lacking the natural biological urge to remain monogamous and virtuous, needed to curb their passionate tendencies.

By the end of the nineteenth century reformers were generally unanimous that prostitution was founded on the poverty of working-class women and saw a direct causal relationship between the low level of women's wages and the recruitment of prostitutes. Prostitutes were considered the archetypal victims of industrialisation. Many reformers, including the Evangelical and iconoclastic Ellice Hopkins, believed that the lowering of wages below subsistence level led to prostitution. As there was virtually no female equivalent of the prosperous male artisan, prostitution occurred because of the inadequacy of women's wages in relation to their needs.[21] Wealthy people who paid women workers low wages were blamed for causing prostitution. Such exploitation prohibited women from becoming economically independent, thus forcing them to earn their living on the streets. H.M. Richardson, a reformer, complained that

> employers of female labour do not pay their hands sufficient to enable them to live without prostitution. Such employers were morally in the same category as the 'bully' who lives on the earnings of a woman's immorality . . . society, in getting cheap commodities, is actually parasitic upon these women.[22]

Certainly, prostitutes seemed to be recruited from poorly paid employment such as dressmaking, shop work, unskilled farm work, public bar work and domestic service more easily than from others.[23] Each of these occupations was characterised either by intermittent seasonal unemployment or low wages and sometimes both. Technological inventions, such as the increasingly popular sewing machine, which was widely in use by the 1870s, threatened those in the sewing industry by lowering their wages and decreasing job opportunities even further. Shop girls too were perceived to be at risk because of their long hours of tedious toil, the harsh regulations imposed upon them, the necessity for keeping up appearances and the 'general physical, moral and mental unhealthiness of their daily life'.[24] Both agricultural labourers, particularly those who worked in the notorious 'gang system', and barmaids were considered to be at risk not only because their work lay them open to sexual harassment but also because of their alleged acceptance of premarital sex. Domestic service, however, was seen to be the chief recruiting ground for prostitutes as domestic servants were not only as sweated as needlewomen but also thought to be subject to the 'allurements of wealth. The person who lives below stairs and who gets stolen glances of the tinsel and the glitter above stairs.'[25] Even in prosperous times, it was difficult for these working-class women to live on their meagre wages, let alone save towards leaner times. The average woman worker could barely support herself even when she was comparatively well and strong. Wages for such women were so low throughout the nineteenth century that prostitution became an attractive possibility.

Those involved in the reform of prostitutes stressed that the inability of women to find work caused prostitution. Women were certainly among the unemployed in the overstocked labour market of Victorian and Edwardian England: in London alone there was a surplus of 200,000 women with queues of 150–200 applicants for many jobs. Helen Ware suggests that an unemployed woman with no savings or friends to help her had to choose between 'starvation, the workhouse or the streets'.[26] By 1911, some held protective legislation responsible for prostitution because it curtailed women's employment opportunities still further:

> working women stand today with a sea of destitution all around them; their power to labour is like a little strip of sand, on which they crowd together, working with incessant toil for a bare life. And every now and then man's laws sweep away first one bit and then another, while the women crowd closer and work harder. What will become of them? No one knows or cares. More legislation is threatened, which may involve thousands of women in disaster – what wonder that women fall in thousands and win in shame the bread denied to labour![27]

If unemployed women turned to prostitution once their savings had been spent, but before they had pawned all their clothes, they could maintain themselves and their home and return to respectability the following working season.[28]

Women's opportunity for financial independence was further jeopardised when the Poor Law Amendment Act 1834 attempted to abolish outdoor relief (under the old Speenhamland system women, as well as men, could have their wages supplemented if they earned too little), thus making the workhouse a grim alternative to destitution. Seventy-six years later, Beatrice Webb reconfirmed this by alleging that the Poor Law was such a deterrent that it prohibited 'a great many unfortunate women in their hour of need from applying'.[29] Destitution, it was believed, directly produced a certain amount of prostitution and in eliminating its causes prostitution would inevitably diminish.[30] Moreover, workhouses were thought to be excellent recruitment centres for prostitution because young women who were sexually innocent mixed indiscriminately with those who were not. Workhouses also sent young women into domestic service – the occupation most susceptible to prostitution. This economic perspective marked a further shift away from blaming individual women to blaming society, but apart from a few Quakers who urged reformers to concentrate on improving women's wages,[31] and those who recommended women join the Women's Protective and Provident League or a trade union to campaign for better pay, few solutions were offered to end such exploitation by those involved in the reform of prostitutes.

A number of women reformers, probably influenced by the emerging women's movement, believed that the gross inequality between girls and boys was responsible for prostitution. Girls had little educational or job opportunities, making them dependent on men. Until the female sex had financial and economic independence, they argued, prostitution would continue to flourish. Furthermore, at all times, girls were expected to please boys and men. Mrs Bunting, an active moral reformer, complained that girls were always seen as inferior and condemned that habitual under-valuing of all that concerns the girl's life, as compared with the boy's. A girl is expected to be ready to give up engagements, purposes, work of various kinds, if the brother's convenience is thereby interfered with . . . this sort of idea of the general second-rateness of the position of girls runs through all a boy's conceptions . . . We bring our boys up selfishly, and selfishness of the most dastardly kind is the result.[32]

Not all shared this conviction. Another influential reformer, the Revd Arthur Brinckman, suggested that it was the independence of women in 'taking up the positions hitherto held by men, in claiming positions on platforms and Parliament which led to men showing less courtesy towards the weaker sex' that led to sexual immorality.[33]

Poverty and inequality may have been the overwhelming reason for prostitution but inadequate wages did not necessarily drive women onto the streets. For the very impoverished, prostitution was never an alternative. Many women had little contact with men who might pay for prostitutes or else, for various reasons, might be unable to prostitute themselves. Elderly women, desperately poor in this period, rarely became prostitutes, nor did sweated workers like fur pullers, however low their wages might sink. Fur pullers, considered to be one of the lowest places in the ranks of women's labour, worked in an atmosphere thick with hairs and

> tainted with the sickly smell of the skins. Everything around them is coated with fur, and they themselves look scarcely more human than the animals beside them from the thick deposit of fur which covers them from head to foot . . . The women suffer greatly from chronic asthma.[34]

Prostitution may have offered a way out of this degradation but fur pullers rarely took such an opportunity. Other very poorly paid women, who may have had the chance to become prostitutes, accepted low wages as their lot and acquiesced in their near starvation. For instance, home workers, notably shirt makers and matchbox makers, declined to become prostitutes as 'honour or apathy and fondness for their children' kept such women off the streets.[35] Nevertheless, it is perhaps fair to say that prostitution was based on the inequitable distribution of wealth: it needed one section of the community, namely men, to have enough surplus money to be able to afford to pay for the sexual services of another section of the community, namely women, who were financially less well off.

Very poor women, it was believed, were generally not driven to prostitution unless they were single, homeless or without family or friends. Marriage was considered an effective protection against prostitution since a male wage was thought sufficient to keep both individuals. Most prostitutes interviewed by Frederick Merrick had never been married, which implies that husbands provided a safeguard for their wives against the risk of prostitution. In the absence of a welfare state women had to rely upon their families to support them in times of crises. Families could, and did, provide invaluable moral and economic support, as girls who lived at home with caring parents rarely became prostitutes unless the family faced starvation.[36] Employers of tea shop girls and similar trades paid extremely low wages knowing that their young employees lived at home and that parents would subsidise them. Undoubtedly, women became prostitutes because they had no close relative to provide them with moral and financial support. Poor biological parenting was certainly blamed for prostitution: evidence from contemporary records suggests that prostitutes lived with cruel, drunken and uncaring parents or step-parents. Few of the imprisoned prostitutes interviewed by Frederick Merrick enjoyed the support of a united family and large numbers had lost one or both parents.[37] Homeless, without friends, family or funds to support them, the only alternative to the reform institution was the workhouse – or to return to the streets. Certainly, the case books of Southwell House, Nottingham, reveal that most women who entered prostitution did so out of desperation. For example, Lilian Burrows 'was brought up by a woman who ran three bad houses in London ... when only 12 years of age she was ruined while under the influence of chloroform'. Similarly, Elizabeth Woods had 'lived with' a married man since the age of 11, had had a child by him at the age of 12 before being evicted and forced to wander from town to town.[38]

For some, the very existence of urban life made prostitution, if not inevitable, then highly likely. Cities were perceived as centres of vice since they offered too much freedom and anonymity. Overcrowding, endemic in most cities, was put forward as the reason for prostitution countless numbers of times in rescue reports later on in the nineteenth century. In a middle-class inspired tautology, immorality was associated with poverty, which simultaneously was associated with the working class. Prostitution, it was supposed, resulted from the generalised indecency of the working class as large families lived, ate, drank and slept together in one room, which made the cultivation of chastity impracticable. Working-class homes were considered to be breeding grounds for incest since families lived in one room, with several people sharing a bed. Uncles slept with nieces, brothers with sisters, cousins with cousins. Rescue workers thought that it was 'fairly common practice' for mothers either to force their daughters to sleep with male lodgers or to make them solicit on the streets. They certainly believed that prostitutes were drawn from 'depraved' homes in which girls were sexually abused by their own fathers, stepfathers or brothers, uncles or other male adult relatives.

Young girls, brought up in these potentially immoral and degrading homes, naturally became immoral and degraded themselves. Born into the lowest stratum of society, without decent family values, working-class girls were thought to develop bad habits and be without the virtues associated with gentility. The writer in *The Vanguard*, the journal of the Church of England, who remarked that 'fathers and mothers allow their boys and girls to litter down like pigs, and they can hardly wonder if they grow up like pigs', merely reflected a more general lack of sympathy towards the working class.[39] This lack of moral fibre, it was alleged, resulted in their subsequent downfall and entry into a world of vice. The members of the Nottingham Committee who wrote the following extract voiced the opinions of most reformers when they stated that

> we dare not attempt to measure the proportion of these rescue cases who have grown up from infancy in an atmosphere of such baseness that it becomes natural to them to fall into sin whenever it confronts them ... They are so permeated with evil ideas that they flare into vice when exposed to certain opportunity, as inevitably as a ship laden with dynamite explodes when exposed to certain temperature ... Till the homes are transformed and the parents realise the sacred trust which God has given them in their children, these terrible tragedies of the ruin of young lives will continue.[40]

Unsatisfactory home conditions sometimes led to homelessness. Common lodging houses, in which the homeless congregated, were thought to be potential recruiting grounds for prostitutes since men, women and children slept the night, huddled together, often in one bed in these wretched hovels. This led to a laxity in moral standards which in turn contributed towards the growth of prostitution among working-class women. Lodging houses, which were kept open all night, were considered the last resort of the lowest class of prostitute

> who engage a room for the night with the first man she makes the acquaintance of. The man frequently remains for a short period only, and the woman is then free to use the room for the remainder of the night with as many men as she can induce to accompany her.[41]

Older women were thought to encourage younger women, who had happened to stray into the lodging house in a destitute condition, to adopt the same immoral life. It was generally believed that 'many a girl in such a lodging house has been persuaded to sell one article of clothing after another until everything has gone and recourse has had to be made to the streets'.[42] In 1907, in an attempt to stop, or at least limit, prostitution in lodging houses, the London County Council forbade the practice of single men and women sleeping in the same area.[43]

However, Victorian and Edwardian observations that poverty and over-crowding led to immorality need careful scrutiny. Not everyone subscribed to the theory that being underprivileged was an obvious cause of prostitu-tion as some of the richer West End districts of London were considered far more immoral than the poverty-stricken East End.[44] Moreover, sexual licence was accepted in some working-class circles and did not necessarily lead to prostitution. Paradoxically, it was supposedly chaste young women domestic servants of the upper working class who were likely to prostitute themselves rather than brick makers in Tipton, Dudley or the pit-brow workers of Wednesbury who tended to accept premarital sex as natural.[45] Nonetheless, rescue workers held on to the stereotype of impressionable young women who, driven by poverty and already morally corrupted, were led inexorably into prostitution.

Historiography

Feminist historians are indebted to Judith Walkowitz for not only rediscovering this forgotten part of women's history but also for bringing new theoretical insights into the history of prostitution. Her first major contribution, *Prostitution and Victorian Society*, details the moves towards and the campaigns against the three Contagious Diseases Acts of 1864, 1866 and 1869.[46] The CD Acts applied to garrison towns and naval ports such as Portsmouth, Plymouth, Woolwich, Chatham, Sheerness, Aldershot, Colchester and Shorncliffe: at no time did cities without an army or naval base, such as Birmingham, London and Manchester, come under their jurisdiction. Under these Acts, police were given powers to arrest those suspected of being 'common prostitutes', order them to undergo an internal examination at a certified hospital and if found diseased, detain them for a period of treatment or until they were pronounced cured. Not surprisingly, many objected to this curtailment of human rights, and a vigorous campaign movement to repeal the Acts emerged. Eventually, after years of petitioning, leafleting, lobbying, holding meetings, writing articles and going on deputations by those opposed to the CD Acts, they were repealed in 1886.

Victorian and Edwardian moral reformers were critical of the CD Acts because they allegedly sanctioned the existence of prostitution by trying to make it safe. Such reformers rejected the idea that prostitution was inevitable and aimed to eliminate it completely. Not surprisingly, given the broad political and religious composition of those involved in the reform and prevention movement, there emerged several different ways to curtail prostitution. Those who regarded prostitutes as the cause and continuation of prostitution preferred to found a variety of establishments to reform women rather than tackle the problem at source. They established penitentiaries, asylums and homes all over the British Isles to take women off the streets and convert them into decent moral citizens. While there have been a number of books that deal with the regulation of prostitution, there has been limited geographical coverage of the reform of prostitutes.[47] Research on reform has been based on the military town of Windsor, the cathedral city of York, the largely Presbyterian cities of Glasgow and Edinburgh and the Catholic country of Ireland rather than England.

The historiography of reform falls into two main categories: that which views reform work uncritically, and somewhat eulogistically, and that which has been informed by feminist theory. Church historians, such as Valerie Bonham, Penelope Hall and Ismene Howe, typify the eulogistic genre.[48] These writers, whatever their particular focus, maintain that reform work benefited women because it extricated prostitutes from the terror of nineteenth-century streets. Penelope Hall and Ismene Howe, for example, place reform work within the context of the Church of England's social work. Only one chapter of their book deals specifically with reform work – which results in a rather sketchy portrayal – but the authors offer an important contribution to historical knowledge by showing the interrelationship between reform work and religion. Nonetheless, because these authors hold a doctrinal, Christian perspective they tend to justify the repressive nature of penitentiaries. Valerie Bonham's privately published book offers an empirical study of an all-female English institution – the Clewer House of Mercy. Part of a trilogy on the history of the sisters of St John the Baptist, it provides a close examination of a penitentiary run by nuns. Her use of the extensive records at Clewer enables her to paint a detailed picture of penitentiary life which enriches our understanding of the religious nature of these types of institutions. Unfortunately, Valerie Bonham's analysis is weakened by her religious conviction and by her hagiographic rather than critical approach to the history of Clewer. As a consequence, as with Penelope Hall and Ismene Howe, Valerie Bonham justifies the punitive regime of such institutions.[49]

Other historians have preferred to place the reform movement within the context of feminist debate. Frances Finnegan's study,[50] which focuses on York, Maria Luddy's, which charts the Catholic institutions set up in Ireland,[51] and Susan Mumm's,[52] which examines the conventual system in England, are based on well-marshalled primary evidence and offer a major contribution to the literature. In contrast to the former historians, all are critical of penitentiaries. These are largely empirical histories which contrast sharply with Linda Mahood's more theoretically based work on Scotland. According to Linda Mahood,[53] her book is underpinned by Foucauldian discourse, social control theories and feminist historiography and this conceptual framework is used to construct the first ever detailed history of reform institutions in Glasgow and Edinburgh. To a large extent this excellent book breaks new ground by focusing on the 'gendering' of the reform process. Penitentiaries, Linda Mahood argues, produced a gendered regime in which female proletarians were encouraged to take up quite distinctive positions in society. Such institutions were seen to serve 'two social control functions directly: sexual control and vocational control'.[54] Magdalene asylums were designed to socialise women into the social and sexual mores of the middle class as well as to create an industrial workforce of domestic servants. Nonetheless, although Mahood provides new insights into the reform of prostitution, religion, a powerful motivating force in nineteenth-century Britain, remains unexplored.

Despite this burgeoning literature, it is safe to say that there has been no research which has examined approaches to reform throughout England. The first part of this book will therefore focus on the various types of reform organisations founded in England in order to add to our knowledge and to offer a corrective to the picture of reform institutions advanced by other writers. It will use a different interpretative model than that applied by other historians of reform. Historians, it has been shown, use a variety of empirical and analytical frameworks with which to understand reform institutions. Those who focus on religious motivations tend to neglect the influences of gender and class. In contrast, historians who examine the importance of gender and class tend to ignore, or seriously underplay, religious influences. It is the aim of this chapter to draw upon the work of previous scholarship but to demonstrate that the categories of gender, class and religion all help towards an understanding of the process of moral reform.

Reform promised only one of a number of solutions to the problem of prostitution and by the 1880s prevention was used to supplement reform work. When the prevention of prostitution is mentioned, historians are unanimous that Ellice Hopkins was a crucial figure. Largely through her efforts, it is said, Ladies' Associations for the Care and Protection of Young Girls were set up in towns and cities across England in order to prevent young women from becoming prostitutes. This type of preventive work has received even less critical attention than the reform movement and, to date, there is no one book which charts its development. Indeed there are only a few scattered references to the work of the Ladies' Associations with research based largely on Ellice Hopkins' writings rather than their practical application.[55] Furthermore, the few historians who have mentioned Ladies' Associations tend to perceive them, confusingly, as either a prudish force or a progressive one. Edward Bristow, for instance, views Ellice Hopkins as an unfulfilled spinster who sublimated her sexual passions for the movements she created, became ill from neurotic diseases and died regretting that she had not married.[56] In contrast, Sheila Jeffreys believes her to be a prophet of radical feminism.[57] The 'truth' is far less simple. The second part of this book will discuss the seemingly symbiotic, sometimes complementary, and sometimes conflicting relationship between gender and class with reference to the development of Ladies' Associations. The expectation of finding a degree of unity among women that transcended class barriers was undermined by the empirical evidence. Time and time again, it will be argued, the question of class intruded into a notional shared womanhood as middle-class women sought to control the lives of the working class.

Towards the end of the nineteenth century, prostitution became more and more associated with 'feeble-mindedness'. The term 'feeble-minded' was used to describe those with learning difficulties and, though recognised as a derogatory term by today's standards, it is a term which will be used in this book. Those perceived to be 'feeble-minded' were thought to be particularly open to seduction since they were too intellectually challenged to put up any resistance to the demands of unprincipled men. Once seduced, the downward path was thought to be all too slippery – statistics 'proved' that 'feeble-minded' women formed a large proportion of prostitutes found in various institutions. Until the work of Anne Digby and David Wright,[58] Mathew Thomson,[59] and Lucia Zedner,[60] the history of the 'feeble-minded' was largely neglected by historians. Their collective works contribute significantly to the debate but, even so, the connection between prostitution and those perceived to be 'feeble-minded' is never fully explored. The third part of the book will therefore analyse how reformers sought to end prostitution by building homes and campaigning for legal changes for those considered to be at moral risk. It will argue that the focus on the 'feeble-minded' and prostitution must be placed within the context of changes in mental health provision, attitudes towards female madness, the development of eugenics as much as in charitable endeavour.

When it became evident that both the reform and other preventive movements had failed to end prostitution, social purity workers tried to restrain prostitutes and to create a moral climate in which prostitution would inevitably disappear. A number of different organisations, such as the National Vigilance Association, were founded to enforce the law against prostitutes, to encourage male chastity, to end child abuse and to censor obscene literature. To enter the debate about social purity may well be to enter an interpretative labyrinth, but there are three main strands in the historiography to date: historians writing in the 1970s usually present their work empirically – and often uncritically – rather than theoretically. By the 1980s two theoretical polarities become evident: radical feminism and socialist feminism, both of which seek to explain prostitution by reference to their own conceptual frameworks. By the 1990s these two positions are bridged by a new eclecticism which drew on a variety of theoretical paradigms.

The image of imperious middle-class ladies wearing elegant dresses and large flowery hats dispensing moral soup to grateful impoverished women is now, thankfully, a fading one in the historiography of social purity, but elements of it are still present in the work of some of the earlier male historians.[61] Edward Bristow is one of the first historians to write about social purity and his work has contributed to its scholarly development.[62] From today's perspective Edward Bristow's work is curiously dated because his analysis is obviously untouched by the later theoretical insights provided by feminist historians. For instance, he believes that social purity was inspired by religious fanatics and views the movement as an homogeneous repressive entity which sought to curtail sexual expression. Social purity is thus seen as a nineteenth-century version of the Festival of Light, conservative, inhibiting, strait-laced and unworthy of serious consideration. As a result, the work of women involved in social purity is portrayed as being slightly odious to men because they clung to a respectable and moribund morality.[63] Consequently, the radical philosophy of the early social purity groups is ignored. There is therefore little analysis of the concern that women social purity workers expressed about prostitution, white slavery and child sexual abuse. Feminist influence on social purity is thus forgotten and remains unexplored. Judith Walkowitz may not share the same moral and political paradigm as Edward Bristow but she comes to similar conclusions.[64] Ellice Hopkins, acknowledged leader of the social purity movement, is seen to represent a right-wing and reactionary trend. Much of her work, Judith Walkowitz insists, involved the banning of fairs and other working-class leisure pursuits because they were the sites of immorality. In particular, the moral crusades of the social purity movements are considered repressive and hostile to working-class culture. As a consequence, Judith Walkowitz ultimately assumes that the concept of the working-class struggle is intrinsically superior to that of women's, but it must be acknowledged that, in 1980 when her book was written, conceptual models for labour history (which focus on class) were much better developed than feminist ones (which utilise gender).

In contrast, Sheila Jeffreys is critical of the way in which previous historians viewed social purity as an evangelical, anti-sex and repressive movement engendered by moral panic.[65] Instead, she places the feminist contribution to social purity on the moral map by examining the way in which the ideas and personnel of the women's movement shaped its course. Two currents, she claims, flowed into the social purity stream: religious revivalism and the Contagious Diseases Acts. When the CD Acts were repealed in 1886, women involved in the Ladies' National Association joined the social purity movement en masse. From an early stage, the National Vigilance Association was imbued with a feminist consciousness. Social purists, Sheila Jeffreys maintains, believed that men, not women, were responsible for prostitution, which resulted in women being regarded as victims of masculine sexual irresponsibility rather than sinners. Sheila Jeffreys emphasises the positive tendencies of social purists by showing how they prosecuted rapists, child abusers, sexual harassers and men who indecently exposed themselves. They also campaigned to tighten up the law on incest, to raise the age of consent and to make affiliation summonses (whereby men who had fathered 'illegitimate' children were forced to pay for their upkeep) more effective.[66] Although Sheila Jeffreys, in describing the unity of feminists and social purists, provides a refreshing alternative to the claims of Edward Bristow, she glosses over the tensions between them and in writing within the parameters of gender misses out important class issues. Writing from a similar radical feminist perspective as Sheila Jeffreys, Margaret Jackson provides an equally invigorating and provocative alternative to Edward Bristow.[67] Male power, Margaret Jackson asserts, was considerable in Victorian and Edwardian England and was exhibited in sexuality as much as in high politics, economics, war and diplomacy. In this carefully researched book Margaret Jackson charts the history of the feminist challenge to this patriarchal model and examines the ways in which women attempted to construct a female-centred sexual identity. Some of these debates, Margaret Jackson claims, found expression in the social purity movements of the teenth century. However, as with Sheila Jeffreys, Margaret Jacks down the ambiguities and contradictions within the social purity

Both Frank Mort and Lucy Bland recognise the tensions both social purity and between them and the women's movement.[68] acknowledge the middle-class background of social purity workers, the complicated motivations of women like Ellice Hopkins and the contradictions which arose between a radical sexual politics and a repressive political framework. Nonetheless, Frank Mort expresses a deep-seated fear about the growing power of the nineteenth-century state which is perceived as a homogeneous, repressive entity rather than the contradictory instrument it was in practice. In addition, Frank Mort maintains that the coercive legislation proposed by the social purity workers increased, to an alarming extent, the already powerful state. Middle- and upper-class men and women used this increasingly powerful instrument 'for enacting their own class specific demands' whereas the working class viewed the state as a repressive force.[69] Thus when social purity workers liaised with the local police they are criticised for consorting with the working-class enemy. Underlying Frank Mort's ideas is a belief that co-operating with the police is a bad thing – whatever the cause. Frank Mort's political framework resists the fact that the state was utilised to enact and enforce beneficial laws which protected the weaker sections of society. Like Frank Mort, Lucy Bland's meticulously researched book is concerned with the ways in which the state increased its influence over the lives of its citizens but, rather than viewing the state as a monolithic structure, she demonstrates its fragmentary nature. She explores the tensions within social purity by noting that on the one hand, it espoused radical sexual politics: it campaigned against child sexual abuse. On the other hand, it rested within a middle-class framework of repression: it helped to close down brothels and police prostitutes. The class and gender contradictions within the social purity movement, Lucy Bland suggests, are not easily reconciled but are ones which still face feminists campaigning against pornography today.

However, despite these theoretical advances, most research focuses on the publications of the metropolitan branch of the National Vigilance Association. The fourth part of the book will draw on the interpretative frameworks put forward by previous historians but will analyse regional social purity associations too. It will offer an additional perspective on the interrelationship and tensions between gender and class by arguing that, between 1880 and 1914, these associations shifted some of the blame from women to men and sought to question, challenge, curtail and change male sexual behaviour because of a belief that prostitution could be cured only if men behaved responsibly. At the same time, however, social purists advocated a moral orthodoxy that was ultimately repressive for everyone. Perhaps more importantly, social purity failed in its attempt to eliminate prostitution, to end child abuse, to change male sexual behaviour and improve sexual morality in general. Despite the efforts of the reform and preventive movement, prostitution continued.

Primary sources

The evidence used for this book, by the nature of its subject matter alone, is bound to be partial, ambiguous and fragmentary. It is based mainly on official unpublished and published documents ranging from Home Office records through to annual reports and Parliamentary Papers. Annual reports, gathered from a number of towns and cities throughout England, proved particularly useful because they presented an overview of each organisational structure and provided an account of what happened, and because the reports were perceived through the eyes of the managers they provided 'unwitting testimony' to their taken-for-granted values.[70] Obviously there are a number of problems associated with using annual reports as evidence, since only large and middle-sized organisations tended to publish their records, they were written from the perspective of the managers of each organisation, the reports provided only a summary of a year's work and they tended to eulogise success and underplay failure. Moreover, the testimony of the young working-class women whom they hoped to influence was largely absent except when refracted through the words of the managers. Newspapers, journals and pamphlets helped flesh out the skeletal frame of the annual reports but, for the most part, reinforced the substance of the latter. Specialist journals such as *Seeking and Saving,* the *National Union of Women Workers' Quarterly Magazine* and the *Vigilance Record* proved invaluable in providing in-depth coverage of issues and individuals even though, once again, each had its own particular perspective. Reports from parliamentary committees and commissions were particularly useful because many influential moral reformers gave evidence to them. Thus, when women such as Ellen Pinsent reported to the Royal Commission on the Care and Control of the Feeble-Minded, it helped piece together some of the attitudes and assumptions held by such women. Similarly, conference reports and sermons, because speeches were printed in full, reflected some of the values, attitudes and assumptions of the reformers. However, it was impossible to discover the complex motivations of those involved in the reform and prevention movement or to gain much insight into the responses of those who were rescued because they left no written personal records of their own. Manuscript case books and committee minutes may be fraught with the same problems as most source material but they offer an unpublished, and therefore less censored, interpretation of events. Case books, such as that of the Leeds Ladies' Association for the Care of Friendless Girls, may have been written by the managers of the organisation but time after time they revealed the sadness and poverty of the young girls whom they rescued as well as the perspective of the writers. Correspondence could be fascinating: the letters of Miss Stride gave an account of a breakdown in relationship between the Charity Organisation Society, the Executive Committee and the woman who managed a reform home in Tottenham, London.

Home Office records proved invaluable in assessing the response to and the success of reformers' actions. The Metropolitan Police, unlike any other police force, was (and still is) under the jurisdiction of the Home Office and had to report to them directly. As a consequence there was an abundance of records directly relevant to this book. For example, police constable notebooks which reported on the state of prostitution in various London districts could be compared with the literature from social purity workers. Judicial statistics which were collected nationally, by listing the numbers of women actually prosecuted each year for prostitution, clearly challenged the claims of reformers that prostitution had diminished because of their efforts.

Notes

 1 Michael Mason, *The Making of Victorian Sexuality* (Oxford: Oxford University Press, 1995), p. 78.
 2 Figures taken from *Judicial Statistics of England and Wales* 1860.
 3 *The Vigilance Record* (August 15th 1890), p. 79.
 4 Edward Mynott, 'Purity, Prostitution and Politics: Social Purity in Manchester 1880–1900' (PhD thesis, Department of History, University of Manchester, 1995).
 5 *Judicial Statistics* 1882.
 6 *The Southwell Diocesan Magazine* (May 1888), p. 73.
 7 *Judicial Statistics* 1882.
 8 *Society for the Suppression of Vicious Practices, Report of the Annual Meeting* Liverpool, 1868, p. 5.
 9 William Acton, *Prostitution* (London: MacGibbon and Kee, 1968), p. 24.
10 Linda Nead, *Myths of Sexuality* (Oxford: Basil Blackwell, 1988), p. 96.
11 See appendix for details, p. 202.
12 Wilkie Collins, *The New Magdalen* (London: Alan Sutton, 1998, first published 1873).
13 Helen Ware, 'Prostitution and the State: The Recruitment, Regulation, and Role of Prostitution in the Nineteenth and Twentieth Century' (PhD thesis, University of London, 1969), p. 408.
14 *The Society for the Protection of Young Females and Prevention of Juvenile Prostitution, c.* late nineteenth century.
15 Michael Ryan, *Prostitution in London* (London: H. Baillière, 1839), p. 171.
16 Ramsay MacDonald, 'The Social and Economic Causes of Vice', in *The Nation's Morals, Being the Proceedings of the Public Morals Conference* (London: Cassell, 1910), p. 216.
17 Judith Walkowitz, *Prostitution and Victorian Society* (Cambridge: Cambridge University Press, 1980).
18 James Miller, *Prostitution Considered in Relation to its Cause and Cure* (Edinburgh: 1859) (William Acton's newspaper cuttings).
19 *The Southwell Diocesan Magazine* (July 1888), p. 139.
20 William Leckie, *History of European Morals* (1905), p. 283.
21 Helen Ware, 'Prostitution and the State', p. 351.
22 H.M. Richardson, *The Outcasts* (London: National Union of Women's Suffrage Societies, c. 1910), p. 5.
23 Ibid., p. 5.

24 Ibid., p. 5.
25 Ramsay MacDonald, 'The Social and Economic Causes of Vice', p. 215.
26 Helen Ware, 'Prostitution and the State', p. 366.
27 Lady Aberconway, *Votes for Women* (August 11th 1911), p. 734.
28 Helen Ware, 'Prostitution and the State', p. 367.
29 Mrs Sidney Webb, 'The Social and Economic Causes of Vice', in *The Nation's Morals, Being the Proceedings of the Public Morals Conference* (London: Cassell, 1910), p. 208.
30 Ibid., p. 208.
31 *Friends Quarterly Examiner* (1900), p. 183.
32 *National Union of Women Workers' Conference* 1891, p. 187.
33 *Seeking and Saving* (1886), p. 91.
34 *Home Industries of Women in London* 1897, p. 19, cited in Helen Ware, 'Prostitution and the State', p. 363.
35 Helen Ware, 'Prostitution and the State', p. 356.
36 Ibid., p. 410.
37 This was corroborated by reform statistics: in 1862, 345 out of 487 women who entered Rescue Societies' homes had lost one or both parents, and in the House of Mercy at Bovey Tracey in 1881 three-quarters of the inmates were orphans (*Seeking and Saving*, August 1881, p. 74).
38 Case Books, Southwell House, Nottingham.
39 *The Vanguard* (October 1887), p. 74.
40 *Southwell House, Nottingham, Annual Report* 1886, p. 7.
41 Memo from Metropolitan Police Executive Department, March 7th 1913 (MEPO 2/287).
42 *Manchester and Salford Wesleyan Mission Annual Report* 1896, p. 43.
43 London County Council, Common Lodging Houses, 1903 (MEPO 2/1287).
44 Bishop of Stepney, *The Vigilance Record* (August 1908), p. 63.
45 Helen Ware, 'Prostitution and the State', p. 421.
46 Judith Walkowitz, *Prostitution and Victorian Society*.
47 Ibid. See also P. McHugh, *Prostitution and Victorian Social Reform* (London: Croom Helm, 1980).
48 Valerie Bonham, *A Place in Life* (Windsor: privately published, 1992); M. Penelope Hall and Ismene V. Howe, *The Church in Social Work* (London: Routledge and Kegan Paul, 1965).
49 Valerie Bonham, *A Place in Life*, pp. 204–205.
50 Frances Finnegan, *Poverty and Prostitution* (Cambridge: Cambridge University Press, 1979).
51 Maria Luddy, 'An Outcast Community: The "Wrens" of the Curragh', *Women's History Review*, 3, 1992; Maria Luddy, '"Abandoned Women and Bad Characters": Prostitution in Nineteenth Century Ireland', *Women's History Review*, 6, 1998; Maria Luddy and Cliona Murphy (eds), *Women Surviving* (Dublin: Poolbeg Press, 1990).
52 Susan Mumm, '"Not Worse than Other Girls": The Convent-Based Rehabilitation of Fallen Women in Victorian Britain', *Journal of Social History,* 29(3), 1996. This article draws largely on the work of Valerie Bonham. Susan Mumm's excellent book *Stolen Daughters, Virgin Mothers* (London: Leicester University Press, 1999) places reform work within the context of Anglican sisterhoods.
53 Linda Mahood, *The Magdalenes* (London: Routledge, 1990), p. 7.
54 B. Littlewood and L. Mahood, 'Prostitutes, Magdalenes and Wayward Girls', *Gender and History,* 3, 1991, p. 163.
55 See Paula Bartley, 'Preventing Prostitution: The Ladies' Association for the Care and Protection of Young Girls in Birmingham, 1887–1914', *Women's History Review*, 7(1), 1998.

56 Edward Bristow, *Vice and Vigilance* (Dublin: Gill and Macmillan, 1978).
57 Sheila Jeffreys, *The Spinster and her Enemies* (London: Pandora Press, 1985).
58 David Wright and Anne Digby (eds), *From Idiocy to Mental Deficiency* (London: Routledge, 1996).
59 Mathew Thomson, *The Problem of Mental Deficiency* (Oxford: Clarendon Press, 1998).
60 Lucia Zedner, *Women, Crime, and Custody in Victorian England* (Oxford: Clarendon Press, 1991).
61 In particular, Edward Bristow's *Vice and Vigilance* and Frank Prochaska's *Women and Philanthropy in Nineteenth Century England* (Oxford: Clarendon Press, 1980) typify this genre.
62 Edward Bristow, *Vice and Vigilance*.
63 Ibid., pp. 96–100.
64 Judith Walkowitz, *Prostitution and Victorian Society*.
65 See Sheila Jeffreys, *The Spinster and her Enemies*; Sheila Jeffreys, '"Free from All Invited Touch of Man": Women's Campaigns around Sexuality, 1880–1914', in L. Coveney (ed.) *Explorations in Feminism: The Sexuality Papers* (London: Hutchinson, 1984).
66 Sheila Jeffreys, *The Spinster and her Enemies*, pp. 6–26.
67 Margaret Jackson, *The Real Facts of Life* (London: Taylor and Francis, 1994), pp. 22–31.
68 Frank Mort, *Dangerous Sexualities* (London: Routledge and Kegan Paul, 1987); Frank Mort, 'Purity, Feminism and the State: Sexuality and Moral Politics, 1880–1914', in M. Langan and B. Schwarz (eds) *Crises in the British State 1880–1930* (London: Hutchinson, 1985); Lucy Bland, *Banishing the Beast* (London: Penguin, 1995).
69 Frank Mort, *Dangerous Sexualities*, p. 141.
70 Arthur Marwick, *The Nature of History* (London: Macmillan, 1970).

Part I

From sinners to Cinderellas

The reform of prostitutes

1   Reform institutions

Prostitution, it was believed, would be eliminated if there were no prostitutes. Reformers therefore founded a variety of institutions, ranging from large penitentiaries and asylums to smaller homes, to rehabilitate prostitutes and make them respectable once more. These establishments can be considered part of a Christian 'archipelago' of reform which stretched all over England:[1] most cities and large towns had at least one institution dedicated to the reform of female prostitutes. Men, who used prostitutes or were prostitutes themselves, were never singled out in this way. It is the concern of this chapter to show that although the penitentiary system of reform was favoured in late-eighteenth- and early-nineteenth-century England there was an increasing diversification of institutions from the mid-nineteenth century onwards as a result of the establishment of several sisterhoods, an Evangelical revival and the development of the women's movement. Nevertheless, it will be argued that these institutions shared much in common. Reform was entirely about working-class women being saved by their middle-class 'superiors' since it was generally working-class women who were sought out, stigmatised and ultimately rescued by women and men who had the time, money, social connections and the desire or conscience to achieve this. Chapter 1 examines the various types of reform institutions, their belief systems and their entrance procedures while Chapter 2 focuses on the daily lives of the inmates incarcerated within them.

Types of reform institutions

Unquestionably, reformers believed that there were distinct differences between the institutions they founded: they called them particular names, created various management structures and built different sized institutions. The first method of reform, the penitentiary system, was the hallmark of both the established Church of England and the Roman Catholic Church. The earliest penitentiary, the Magdalen Hospital, was opened in Whitechapel, London, in 1758. Its 'success' – alongside developments in social welfare policies – led to the establishment of other institutions, particularly in the first two decades of the nineteenth century.[2] The mid-nineteenth century witnessed a further increase in the numbers of penitentiaries as a result of the formation of the Church Penitentiary Association (CPA)[3] and, inspired by the Oxford Movement, the establishment of several sisterhoods devoted to the rescue and reform of prostitutes.[4] By 1885 there were said to be fifty-three penitentiaries connected with the Church of England. However, this estimated number is probably low,[5] since only the ones which sent in returns to the official journal of the Church of England reform movement, *Seeking and Saving,* were included. By the end of the nineteenth century, there were also thirteen Roman Catholic institutions for the reformation of upwards of 886 women.[6]

Historians, on the whole, have tended to focus on the penitentiary system of reform,[7] but the Evangelical Church of England religious revival of the mid-nineteenth century provided a new impetus for reform work. Evangelicals advocated an alternative system of reform and tried to establish a family home system rather than a penitential one. The leading Evangelical Tory, Lord Shaftesbury, was patron of the first society, named the London Female Dormitory, which founded its first home in Camden Town, London, in 1850.[8] Others swiftly followed.[9] Evangelicals formed their own co-ordinating society in 1856, the Reformatory and Refuge Union, but this body dealt more with prevention than with reform, targeting young women perceived to be in moral danger rather than those who had 'fallen'. By 1908 the Reformatory and Refuge Union was managing approximately 320 Magdalen Institutions. The Salvation Army, the Church Army and the Jewish Ladies' Association, possibly influenced by their opposition to the Contagious Diseases Acts, also set up their own institutions. Mrs Catherine Booth opened the first English Salvation Army home in Whitechapel, East London, in 1884 and several small homes were founded subsequently elsewhere. The Jewish Ladies' Association set up a rescue home for young Jewish girls in Shepherd's Bush in 1885, which was thought to be the only one of its kind in Britain.[10]

Not all institutions were connected so formally with religious organisations. Lock hospitals[11] and hospitals with lock wards[12] tried to reform unmarried female patients being treated for venereal disease.[13] The Metropolitan Police and Cambridge Undergraduates founded reform institutions within their locality.[14] Individuals, famous and otherwise, set up their own establishments or looked after prostitutes privately: Josephine Butler brought ailing prostitutes back to her home; Angela Burdett-Coutts provided the money for Charles Dickens to supervise Urania Cottage; Adeline, Duchess of Bedford founded and helped manage her own institution.[15] Even the Prime Minister, William Gladstone, was a fervent rescuer of prostitutes. Many other, much less famous, individuals set up their own small, privately managed homes too.[16] By the end of the nineteenth century, women, working in all kinds of institutional settings, met once a year at the National Union of Women Workers' (NUWW) Rescue Work Conference to discuss strategies and compare practice.

Not surprisingly, given the varied nature of reform institutions, there were several different managerial structures but all, without question, were managed by the upper or middle class. There were three main methods of running reform institutions: some were managed by men who employed female workers as matrons and laundry workers;[17] some were managed jointly by men and women; some were managed by women only. By the end of the nineteenth century, men-only-managed institutions were criticised:

> This work among fallen women is distinctly women's work ... I do not believe that this work among women can or ought to be done by men; not only is it contrary to our own sense of modesty and refinement that men should engage in it, but those most experienced know well that to these over-excited and wrongly-directed natures the very fact of being the subject of kindly interest to a man is in itself disturbing and prejudicial.[18]

Institutions set up by the Church of England tended to be governed by a mixture of clergy and lay men and women. Men remained in overall charge, acting as managing directors and public relations officers, representing the institution at annual meetings, writing the annual reports, administering the finances and talking to the press. The CPA, the co-ordinating body of the penitential movement, was certainly male dominated. The Archbishops of York and Canterbury were joint presidents with approximately twenty-eight other bishops acting as vice-presidents. The CPA might have stated that it did not interfere with the internal management of their institutions but in practice it maintained a powerful presence. All institutions remained under the spiritual guidance of the Church of England, which gave grants to the institutions they favoured,[19] and encouraged the bishopric to take an active role in the reform work of their diocese. Moreover each institution had a bishop as titular head: for example, the Archbishop of Canterbury was nominally president of the Dartford Penitentiary. Women, on the other hand, acted as middle managers, supervising the internal affairs of the establishment, purchasing the necessary articles and goods, superintending the employment, diet and dress of the inmates, and organising any leisure activities. At the Manchester and Salford Asylum for Female Penitents, as in many others, female committee members visited the institution daily, talked to all the inmates, inspected every department and entered their daily reports in an official book. As a rule, the CPA preferred nuns to run institutions, not only because they devoted their entire lives to the cause, but also because it was felt that none were so fit to redeem the prostitute than the 'unfallen, upright, pure sisterhood' who were without moral blemish.[20] Susan Mumm suggests that ordinary women, who were either married or who were expected to marry, were thought unsuited to reform work because it might decrease their respect for men and thus undermine marital harmony.[21] Nuns, generally recruited from the higher ranks of society, were thought more

LIVERPOOL JOHN MOORES UNIVERSITY
LEARNING SERVICES

capable (because of their education and 'habits of self-command') of exercising authority than paid workers who were usually from an 'inferior'
class.[22] Of course, nuns, like paid workers from other institutions, still came
under the authority of male clergy.

In female-managed institutions, which were not linked to religious foun-
dations, women were responsible for both the public and the private work
involved in running them and thus were not answerable directly to any
man. From such work many female reformers – like Josephine Butler and
the Duchess of Bedford – gained experience in public speaking, expertise
in running organisations, a measure of financial acumen, administrative,
marketing and social welfare skills. They attended regular committee meetings to discuss policy and practice, organised and spoke at annual meetings,
collected and managed subscriptions and spent time in the homes that they
had set up dispensing advice.

Not surprisingly, given the great diversity between institutions, there
was a degree of rivalry within the reform movement, as each believed that
their particular system was the most appropriate.[23] Women who founded
their own establishments thought that institutions managed by nuns were
inadequate.[24] One of the chief critics of the convent system, Ellice Hopkins,
complained that

> the fundamental principle of a sisterhood being life in community, and
> that of the Cottage Home being family life . . . I question the domestic
> character of Sisters . . . especially when their tastes have led them to
> adopt a dress borrowed from the dead-house to represent joyous conse-
> cration to God.[25]

In response, homes run by individual women were criticised by the Church
Penitentiary Association because they were free from official constraints and
were not sufficiently disciplined or controlled. This, it was believed, led to
gross negligence and sometimes corruption. In the case of Miss Stride, who
managed a number of homes in Tottenham, London, this criticism was
perhaps warranted. After enduring a libellous attack by an anonymous
member of the Charity Organisation Society, Miss Stride was accused of
gross financial mismanagement and became a *cause célèbre* in the local
Haringey press. Apparently, Miss Stride had been declared bankrupt in
1863 and had used charitable donations for her own personal consumption
rather than for the comfort of the women in her charge. As a consequence,
committee members like Lord Shaftesbury withdrew their support, Miss
Stride became ill, her home closed down and she eventually died in 1879
at the age of 51.[26]

Occasionally there was friction between the male executive and the female
managers in institutions with a sexually mixed management structure. Revd
Micklethwaite, the chaplain of the House of Mercy at Horbury, believed
that a close financial watch should be kept over women workers. Account

books, he stressed, should 'always be open to inspection, and should be duly audited from time to time by some experienced hand, or the waste will be enormous, as women are generally extravagant in spending money which is not their own'.[27] On one occasion the Gentlemen's Committee of the Liverpool Penitentiary were 'deeply concerned at the unsatisfactory nature of the proceedings of the Ladies' Committee' when the Ladies' Committee were thought to exceed their powers.[28] The female managers may not have appreciated such views but they seemed to have little redress – there were never any comments from women about the men – because men not only wrote the reports but also held the more senior positions.

Reformers may have shared a common objective but they disagreed over the means to that end. There was even dissent over the most suitable size for a reform institution so the number of women in these various institutions fluctuated between as low as five and as high as two hundred. Figure 1.1, based on an analysis of the available statistics of reform institutions, shows that most institutions which recorded their figures held between ten and thirty inmates.[29] The Anglican penitentiary at Clewer held large numbers of women but those which held over a hundred inmates tended to be Roman Catholic institutions where inmates were sometimes encouraged to remain for life.

The Anglican nuns at Clewer believed that reform should be carried on within the large institutional atmosphere of a penitentiary. It was supposed that women could be more easily disciplined and controlled within a penitentiary because they were able to classify penitents and divide them into those who had recently fallen and those perceived to be hardened in vice.[30] In contrast, Evangelicals and other reformers wanted to keep numbers small so they could bestow individual care on the inmates. They set up smaller establishments, often called homes – which they often stressed was a home

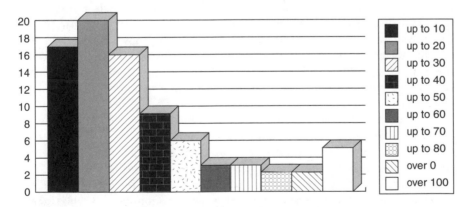

Figure 1.1 Average numbers in reform institutions in the 1880s
Source: collated from *Guide to Schools, Homes and Refuges in England for the Benefit of Girls and Women* (London: Longmans, Green, 1888)

with a small 'h' rather than a capital 'H' – based on the family principle and allegedly indistinguishable from private residences.[31] The naming of the institution, 'Home', a highly persuasive symbol of contented domesticity, was supposed to be greatly significant: homes were not only considered the natural habitat of women but also places, allegedly, of comfort and support. However, the name 'Home' was full of ambivalent meaning as inmates enjoyed an enforced family existence. Reform may have taken place within a less punitive context than a penitentiary but the language of love was rhetorical and disguised real relationships of power. The maternalist approach favoured by the smaller institutions was still based upon inequality since mothering was not only a bond of affection but also a bond of control. The association between the lady and the inmate was an association between the parent (the older philanthropist) and the child (the younger inmate). Mothers, albeit often kind and gentle, disciplined, controlled and regulated the lives of their children even when those children accepted their restrictions.[32] In effect, the relationship between the committee members remained one between adult and child, middle and working class, superior and underling. As a consequence, women were reduced to the status of dependant – the status of children – when they entered the institutions. The young age of the inmate and the older age of the committee members undoubtedly helped establish a parental relationship based on authority and submission. There was thus only a marginal difference between the larger and smaller institutions as although the smaller homes may have been benign institutions they were, like the penitentiaries, ultimately coercive.

Attitudes towards prostitutes and prostitution

Prostitutes, not the men who used them, were the objects of moral scrutiny. All of the institutions studied, whatever their religious foundation or composition, mainly viewed prostitution as a female profession: male prostitution was rarely discussed or considered even in the 1890s, when the Oscar Wilde trials were widely reported elsewhere. Nonetheless, those involved in the reform movement held different opinions of prostitutes. In many ways the attitudes, values and assumptions held by the committees of the various institutions were framed within a particular gendered, religious and class context.

The established wing of the Church of England in particular considered prostitution to be a female problem which undermined the principles of female sexual propriety. Women were held to be either virgins or wives and mothers, not free and independent sexual beings. Illicit sex, one can assume, was considered to be a natural biological urge for men but not for women. Prostitutes were often perceived as sexual contaminators who threatened the institution of marriage, the sanctity of the family and ultimately the sexual and moral order of the time. They were considered to be ruinous to civilisation.[33] It was commonly supposed that female prostitution affected and contaminated the whole of society, ruined health, destroyed spiritual life, undermined mental power and ate, like a canker, at the heart of English life.[34] Prostitution was seen to tarnish the minds of the innocent as 'it flaunts about the streets, it meets our sons and our daughters, and it taints the atmosphere in which it moves'.[35] Prostitutes, defined as the human agent of depravity and vice, were seen to be dangerous to their communities since 'they prowled about our streets, corrupting the morals, infecting the bodies and ruining the souls of our youth'.[36] Consequently, these institutions curtailed the activities of those who threatened it. If the individual prostitute was reformed, prostitution would be eliminated and sons – and ultimately society – saved from moral danger.

Not everyone blamed women for the sins of prostitution and argued that prostitutes should not be seen as a class apart. Ellice Hopkins believed that 'men divide us women into two classes: us pure women, from whom nothing is too good, and those others for whom nothing is too bad. But let us prove by our actions that our womanhood is ONE.'[37] Josephine Butler questioned why penitentiaries should only cater for women: 'Why not men who have been immoral, as well as women, be confined to a Penitentiary?'[38] A few other radical individuals expressed concern that men who paid for sex had also fallen and asked 'why not erect Homes for the men, who are leading just as evil lives, and who at least are as bad as the women they help to degrade?'[39] However, these objections remained at a rhetorical level since no attempts were made to build male asylums, penitentiaries or homes for those men who had strayed from the Christian path of virtue and had fallen from moral grace.

Religious conviction shaped attitudes towards the prostitute. Unquestionably, the names used for these institutions reflected the variety of religious thinking in this period. Penitentiaries, for example, evoked images of a triple fusion of sin, punishment and penitence. In contrast, Magdalen Asylums not only were blessed with the name of that most famous of all female sinners, Mary Magdalen (who makes her first appearance in the Bible as a prostitute and ends it at Christ's feet when he lay dying on the Cross), but also aimed to offer sanctuary and forgiveness rather than reproach. Yet, Magdalen Asylums remained punitive in practice as, like Mary Magdalen, inmates were encouraged to repent their past life, ask forgiveness for their sins and make a fresh start so that they could be assured entry to future Paradise. Furthermore, even though most of those involved in the reform of prostitutes believed that prostitution was a sin they differed in the way they perceived the individual prostitute. The established Church of England initially held a rather punitive attitude towards prostitutes whereas Evangelicals, though similarly believing prostitution to be sinful, were more sympathetic towards them. By the end of the nineteenth century, although the sinful version still had its adherents, the emphasis on punishment had generally shifted to one of forgiveness. 'Neither do I condemn thee; go and sin no more', a comment made by Jesus Christ to a woman accused of adultery, became a phrase commonly used by the committees of various institutions.

The established Church, undoubtedly sharpened by its belief that prostitution was a grievous sin, considered prostitutes to be sinners who would be excluded from the Kingdom of Heaven and condemned to everlasting fire. Precious souls, it was argued, would be damned eternally in hell,[40] since 'we are dealing with a sin which more than any other sin hardens the heart and petrifies the feeling'.[41] Parallels were drawn between prostitution in England and Sodom and Gomorrah with similar inevitable consequences. Both the language and the sentiments expressed in sermons, annual reports and conferences, in keeping with Anglican belief, convey images of sin, damnation and a punitive God. The rhetorical style of such records testifies to the obsession that the organisers of these institutions had with the punishment of souls. The language used in this sermon was certainly resonant with religious fervour:

> How are the corruptions and horrors of the pit seething loathsomely within them, even as they glide here and there, with hollow cough and the ghastly counterfeit of mirth, along our midnight streets to their sudden and almost inevitable end . . . if they dare to look inward, a crushing sense of utter degradation – hell already in the first gnawing of the undying worm, and the near bellowing of the unquenchable fire; while close before them, and with its smoke and flames cast already in their face, is the inevitable, with its outer darkness, its gnashing of teeth, and its endless wailing.[42]

Prostitutes were regarded as moral criminals – as well as civil criminals – by some in the CPA. Comparisons were made between the laws of England and the commandments of God. Whereas it was thought to be the duty of the state to prosecute those who broke the civil law, it was the duty of the Church to fight sin vigorously and condemn those who transgressed the moral code.[43] Prostitutes who were found soliciting were charged in the civil courts but others were reminded that they had sinned, not only against the world, but also against God and therefore, like similar wrongdoers, they needed to be punished.[44] Those who exonerated prostitutes, by viewing them as either victims or martyrs rather than sinners, were criticised: 'this sentimental placing of prostitutes on an ideal pedestal . . . and not at all as objects for condemnation, is one of the most disastrous things in all this flabby age'.[45]

In *The Making of Victorian Sexual Attitudes*, Michael Mason argues that the Evangelical wing of the Church of England was less repressive than the established Church.[46] Certainly, in Evangelical and other institutions a forgiving God often replaced the punishing hand of God. Reformers drew parallels between their work and the compassionate approach of Jesus Christ, God's only son, towards sinners. Luke's story of the prostitute who washed Christ's feet with her tears, wiped them with her long hair and anointed them before being forgiven was often referred to as an example to be followed. Prostitution was still considered to be a sin but prostitutes were viewed less as sinners and more as victims of social injustice, with the result that the emphasis was placed on forgiveness rather than on punishment. To a large extent women were considered to be the perennial prey of wicked, debauched men who led them astray and who abandoned them when they had lost their first flush of youth. As a consequence, women were regarded as feeble, passive and pathetic and, like children, incapable of exercising moral judgement.

Whatever the attitude towards the individual prostitute, most of those involved in reform shared a redemptive approach. To reclaim a single individual soul from eternal spiritual damnation was considered to be an important offering to God as His son had died on the Cross in order to save humanity. The personal redemption of a single prostitute accorded with notions of personal faith for just as Christ had laid down his life for the sins of humanity, and thus redeemed the world, so reformers expected to lay theirs down by working hard to save souls, and thus redeem themselves. Rescue work was accordingly done for Jesus Christ and 'for the souls he loves'.[47] In addition, Evangelical Christians believed that the temporal world was a preparation for the spiritual which meant that they should devote their entire lives to good works in order to be worthy of Heaven.[48] The parable of the lost sheep was used constantly as a comparison between rescue work, prostitution and religion. Significantly, the privilege and responsibility of seeking to bring those termed wandering sheep home to the Good Shepherd's flock was seen to be immeasurable. By returning the lost sheep (i.e. the prostitute) to the heavenly fold the redeemers not only saved a soul but also notched up a point for themselves on some heavenly tally. Volunteers were therefore encouraged to do all in their power to help the fallen to 'return to the ways of happiness and peace and holiness'.[49] There was 'joy in the presence of the angels of God over one sinner that repenteth'.[50] Prostitutes were encouraged to repent their past life, ask forgiveness for their sins and make a fresh start so that they could be assured entry to future Paradise. Christians, in establishing reform institutions, were therefore acting according to Christ's will and by the inspiration of the Holy Spirit.

> It is only when we are constantly reminding ourselves that we are taking part in the hand to hand contest between our Master and the Great Enemy, that we are fighting on our Lord's side for the souls that He died to save, only then shall we have the strength and the courage to persevere.[51]

Of course, many men and women involved in the reform of prostitutes may have done so for personal as much as religious reasons. Female reformers continually complained about women (other than themselves) who worked with prostitutes for salacious reasons – they recognised that rescuing women from the streets was an exciting experience, and almost as attractive in terms of Christian adventuring as being a missionary among 'savages'. For other respectable middle-class women it may have been the way to project and deal with their own 'dark' side vicariously yet safely.[52] All women engaged in reform work became knowledgeable about impurity, talked about sexual matters generally considered inappropriate and associated with women far below them in the moral scale but allegedly religious conviction and faith kept them pure.

The religiosity, which dominated early thinking, softened from the 1880s and was modified by a class analysis which focused on poverty but the transition was gradual and sometimes imperceptible. As a result, prostitutes were viewed less as sinners and more as 'Cinderellas' and archetypal victims. Many reformers, including Ellice Hopkins, argued that prostitutes were the casualties of economic injustice rather than of natural wickedness. Those who paid women workers low wages were blamed for prostitution since it prohibited women from becoming economically independent, thus forcing them to earn their living on the streets. This new perspective marked a shift away from blaming individual women to blaming society, but few solutions were offered to end such exploitation. Moreover, the view that working-class women were to be pitied rather than condemned was undermined by assumptions held about the working class. Prostitution, as mentioned in the introduction, was believed to result from the low moral standard which existed among sections of the working class as much as poverty. Nonetheless, attitudes were not always coherent – at one and the same time women were viewed as victims, sinners and sexual contaminators.

Selection procedures and admission policies

Not surprisingly, given the varied nature of reform institutions, reformers differed over the efficacy of recruitment procedures. There were a number of ways in which potential inmates could enter reform institutions: some came on their own initiative, some were recommended by subscribers or magistrates, clergymen, police visitors or missionaries brought others. Some managers disliked the idea of prostitutes entering of their own accord since they believed these prostitutes used the institution to escape from the police, as a temporary rest home when they were 'weary of the town', were ill or came in for a quick 'wash and brush up'.[53] Such prostitutes were seen as manipulative sinners who did not deserve to be reformed. Others welcomed everyone since 'few know the pain and effort it must cost a girl covered with her shame to present herself voluntarily at the door of an asylum, and none can know the agony of being rejected under circumstances so humiliating'.[54] Rigid entrance procedures, they argued, stopped those who were genuinely penitent and in need from applying. It was also believed that even when women were insincere, kind treatment, 'disentanglement from their companions, opportunity for reflection, spiritual ministry, strike sparks from a smouldering conscience, and in some cases create a desire to stay and reform, though no repentance was in their heart when they crossed the threshold'.[55]

Reform institutions, in a number of respects, can be seen as an informal extension of the prison system.[56] Some managers, from across the religious spectrum, exerted their class power by utilising magistrates and police as recruitment officers. By working so closely with those who apprehended, prosecuted and sentenced prostitutes, reformers were identified with the authorities rather than its casualties. Prostitutes, of course, may well have been unable to distinguish between the informal policing of the reformers and that used by officials. The liaison which took place between the magistrates, the police and the managers of homes could be viewed as a form of class control whereby charitable enterprises colluded with the local authority to deny the rights of working-class women. Magistrates, particularly after the Probation of Offenders' Act 1897, sometimes gave young women convicted of soliciting the choice of either a prison sentence or residence for two years in a reform institution.[57] In some towns and cities, women operated a semi-legal scheme whereby they visited the courts regularly to ensure that magistrates handed young first offenders over to their keeping rather than send them to prison.[58] However, a few Evangelical reformers were critical of this approach in case they were seen as a vigilance or police agent. 'No one who goes in for rescue work should have anything, directly or indirectly, to do with getting either prostitutes or their abettors and harbourers prosecuted and punished.'[59] Some penitentiary managers worked closely with lock hospitals or hospitals with lock wards which implemented the Contagious Diseases Acts.[60] Once again, such reformers were identified with a legal system which, by arresting and detaining women suspected of being common prostitutes, was considered ultimately coercive and punitive. Not all rescue societies would accept women from government lock hospitals: the Society for the Rescue of Women and Children refused to take such cases because it was opposed to the CD Acts and did not wish to be associated with any establishment that did.

Other Evangelicals and Nonconformists preferred to select their own candidates for admission more directly and often recruited prostitutes through street work, midnight meetings or brothel visiting.[61] The London Female Mission to the Fallen employed eight paid missionaries, each of whom was responsible for a particular area of London: one missionary was solely responsible for the bridges of London. Late night meetings were also held in towns and cities across England. At these events, the prostitutes attending were invited not to return to work but to enter a reform institution. Ellice Hopkins and her supporters were critical of midnight meetings, because the prostitutes who attended were generally drunk and disagreeable, so they went straight to the brothels during the daytime to recruit. Volunteers who visited brothels were encouraged to wear elegant clothes, clean gloves and a pleasing hat so that prostitutes could see that virtue was not always dowdy and disagreeable.

All institutions operated selection procedures of some kind. Prostitutes, unlike the lost sheep of parable fame, were rarely seen as a homogeneous group but were, in effect, categorised into those worth saving and those who were not – often the women's age was the determining factor in this. A sliding scale of morality operated in most institutions: at one end of the sexually dissolute spectrum stood the older, irredeemable prostitute whereas at the other stood a much younger, impressionable and compliant woman who could be saved. Not every woman who wanted to enter a reform institution was allowed to do so. In general, women were categorised by age, health, class and sincerity. There were a few institutions who accepted any woman who wished to enter, whatever her age, 'who is anything like sober',[62] but these were the exceptions as most institutions had little interest in the professional or 'hardened' prostitute who may have been 'down on her luck'.[63] Management committees tended to accept younger women in preference to those who had been on the streets for some time as 'they had come to the conclusion that it was useless to receive any woman over 30 years of age',[64] not only because they were thought irreclaimable but because they allegedly had an adverse influence on younger inmates.[65] Most institutions therefore recruited women in their twenties but a few focused on those of a much younger age.[66] Ellice Hopkins feared that very young girls were increasingly found in reform institutions,[67] such as the Highgate Penitentiary, which 'twenty-five years ago, was a Home for fallen women, fifteen years ago it was a Home for fallen girls, now it is also a Home for fallen children'.[68] By the late 1880s, however, attitudes had softened and the Church of England tried to establish an institution purely for older 'hardened women, deep in sin and drink',[69] but it seems, according to Susan Mumm, that only one community ever offered permanent provision for such women.[70] Nonetheless, in 1907, the London Female Preventive and Reformatory Institution continued to refuse those thought incorrigible and past reformation.[71]

In addition, presumably for reasons of prudence, only healthy women were generally admitted. In theory doors were wide open to receive the penitent fallen but no one who was pregnant or diseased was generally accepted.[72] In the small-pox outbreak in Liverpool in 1902–3 the committee felt that it had to exercise great care in admitting women who might have come from infected districts.[73] Even the Salvation Army, who advocated an open-door policy, were concerned that 'some girls who are ill and starving, throw themselves on us, not to get saved – but for food, rest, and bodily strength. When they are better they go away again to the old life.'[74] Potential inmates submitted to a physical examination by a male surgeon or physician to ensure that they were physically fit to enter: those who did not fit this rigid age and health criterion were generally referred to the workhouse or the lock hospital. Factory inspectors noted that strong girls who could do laundry work were all too readily admitted to reform institutions whereas poor and weakly girls were rejected because they could not help to make a profit.[75] However, not all institutions selected their applicants quite so cynically as some larger institutions had a separate infirmary for those too ill to work.[76]

It was evident that a number of reformers held on to their class convictions by categorising women by social rank. Middle-class women were sent to different institutions from working-class women or else were contained within separate sections within them. Even though potential inmates were all considered 'morally degraded',[77] the 'birth, manners and education' of middle-class women were still thought to make them superior to the working class.[78] Middle-class women therefore entered institutions such as St Monica's Home in Brighton,[79] or St James Diocesan Home in Fulham, London, which held 'the wife and daughter of a clergyman, the widow of an officer of rank, the near relative of a late eminent artist, the daughter of a solicitor, an assistant in a ladies' school and several daughters of respectable tradesmen'.[80] Larger penitentiaries, such as Wantage and Clewer,[81] had a separate division for upper-class penitents, who were kept apart from the rest of the inmates.[82] Of course, such women were rather atypical subgroups who were more likely cast-off mistresses or single mothers than ex-prostitutes.

Potential inmates, of whatever class, generally had to convince reformers of their sincerity before they were admitted into their respective institutions. Nothing was left on trust. In the larger institutions inmates either came directly from a refuge,[83] which acted as a feeder and selection home, or entered a probationary ward where they were kept apart from the rest of the penitents for approximately three months.[84] It was thought that the first three months of seclusion tested the resolve of those who wanted to be admitted for those unable to bear the monotony left during that period. If admitted straightaway it was thought that they might unsettle the minds of those who had only just settled in to the two-year incarceration.[85] Some even tested the genuineness of potential inmates by

> asking them if they are willing to go to the workhouse till a vacancy is open ... It is a severe test of their repentance to be willing to go under workhouse discipline ... but it is effectual, and saves our dear Rescue officers much trouble, expense, and sorrow in the end.[86]

Obviously in the smaller institutions, young women were admitted directly but even so they were not admitted until their past had been investigated.[87] Working-class young women were not considered to be reliable witnesses to their own past: only when their history had been verified by parents, friends or employers was it believed.

Reform institutions, of whatever religious persuasion, subjected inmates to ritual humiliation, took away their personal identity and with it their femininity. The matrons of Evangelical institutions were instructed to receive each inmate kindly and were urged to let their manner be as bright and winning as possible:[88]

> I myself have often been struck with the cold reception of the girl when she enters these Homes. She is made to feel herself something of an outcast; the first greeting is too often 'Sit down, and then you must go and take bath' which is not a very warm welcome when a girl is just beginning a fresh and better life. No doubt, in time it becomes a business to receive new girls to the matron; but she also needs to be taught that when a girl is starting on so new a life things should not be made too strict and penitential for her; her good resolutions should be strengthened by sympathy and kindness.[89]

This must have been a difficult task when the inmate was about to be physically belittled. Advice manuals suggested that inmates were washed with carbolic soap and examined to see if their heads were quite clean. Methylated spirits were used to 'remove anything alive' and ointment rubbed in. In bad cases it was sometimes felt necessary to cut off the hair.[90] At the beginning of the nineteenth century short hair was compulsory in many institutions but by mid-nineteenth century most had abandoned this. It was even argued that short hair was contrary to Christianity as Christ had encouraged at least one fallen woman to wipe his feet with her long hair. Certainly, in cutting their hair very short, the inmates — just like nuns — lost some of their sexual allure and thus were no longer perceived as a moral danger to themselves and to others.

Reformers tried to obliterate all signs of the inmate's physical past by getting rid of their personal belongings. On full admission clothing was taken away, sometimes converted into suitable garments for the use of others or else 'disposed of under the direction of the Ladies' Committee',[91] either because it was unsuitable attire or because it was verminous and dirty. A distinctive dress, which marked out the penitent from other women, was a characteristic of most penitentiaries: people in York easily recognised penitentiary inmates by their grey cloaks and bonnets.[92] In the first Magdalen Hospital at Streatham the uniform, which consisted of a blue print for every day and a light brown dress with a white tippet for best, remained the same for 150 years.[93] Criticism was made of the utter plainness, ugliness and uniformity of this type of penitential garb,[94] so a few managers of institutions provided 'plain and neat dresses', rather than uniforms, for the use of penitents, but rather than pay out for new dresses, they favoured second-hand clothing in case inmates ran away with their recently acquired clothes. Nevertheless, institutions which discarded penitential dress remained in the minority as even as late as 1907 Miss Tracey, a factory inspector, complained that only one or two homes 'have gone so far as to let them wear the garb of everyday life, discarding the hideous clothes so often adopted'.[95] Clothing helps to give us our identity so, on wearing such garments, young women not only were marked out by the community as reforming penitents but also gave out the message that they had relinquished their past lives, and with it their sexuality, entirely.

Reform managers thought it reasonable to intern women who had not been convicted of a crime, so before being accepted into most reform institutions inmates had to agree to stay for two years. For those reformers who supported a long incarceration, two years was seen to be the right amount of time: in the first year they settled in while towards the end of the second year they were seen to be growing in 'spiritual awareness'. The committees of most institutions believed, like those of the Worcester Diocese in the following quote, that it took a long time for women to re-establish a moral character and to be truly reformed:

> it is the shortest time in which anything like reformation of character can ordinarily be effected and the Penitent sufficiently trained to face again the temptations of the world, and earn an honest livelihood. The wreckage of the moral fabric is in most cases so far reaching that its reparation must needs be slow and gradual, depending upon God's blessing upon daily and hourly discipline, untiring vigilance on the part of those who watch for the souls of the penitents.[96]

Apparently, two years gave sufficient time for inmates to learn how middle-class managers expected working-class women to think and behave and for inmates to learn new habits associated with the class and gendered order of the nineteenth and early twentieth centuries. A long stay also removed inmates from the influence of friends and family, as it was a self-contained community where the only contact with the rest of the world was through the committee and staff. It was believed that if inmates were not distracted by corrupt (i.e. working-class) outside influences they might more easily internalise the cultural values of the institution. More importantly, the institution protected society from the malevolent influence of the fallen women since prostitutes, as contaminated women, needed to be kept separate from the clean and morally healthy. Reformers hoped to preserve public morals by the temporary withdrawal out of society of those who were its corrupters.[97] In contrast, men who used the prostitutes did not have their freedom curtailed since there is no evidence of men being treated in this way.

Of course, there were no statutory powers to compel inmates to remain for two years but the doors in many institutions were kept firmly locked. If inmates wished to leave the asylum they were legally free to do so and could not be forcibly kept against their will. Whether these human rights were known by the inmates, who may well have viewed the asylum rules and regulations as legally binding, particularly as many would have faced a gaol sentence if they had not 'volunteered' for a reform institution, one will never know. It may not have been compulsory to stay for two years but inmates were often persuaded not to leave. If women wished to leave before this time they had to give a few days' notice during which time efforts were made to dissuade them. Anyone wishing to leave had to undergo several interviews with the matron, the superintendent and the chaplain before they were allowed to go, which proved to be a fairly effective weapon. Even so, many women refused to stay for such a long time and to encourage them to remain, a number of institutions introduced a scale of progressive payments for good behaviour which increased each month.

Others disagreed about the efficacy of a two-year incarceration and believed that reformative treatment should be lengthened or decreased in duration as the special circumstances of each inmate demanded. Moreover, institutions which insisted on a two-year stay were thought incapable of testing young women's capacity to remain chaste: when inmates were confined and enclosed for two years they remained 'pure' but when let out in the world and free from restraint they 'strayed' because 'they have no opportunity of exercising their individual powers, consequently their moral courage is latent, and their characters not as much strengthened as they might be'.[98] Smaller reform homes managed by individuals often kept women for much less time than the recommended two years, but it was still middle-class reformers who judged whether or not inmates were ready to leave, often persuading them to stay if it was thought desirable:

> before she goes I see her, talk to her plainly, ask where she is going to sleep, and give her two shillings; nine times out of ten she will not go . . . but if the doors were locked, and she was bound in writing to stay two years, she would run away.

Homes such as these in turn faced criticism from those who favoured the two-year system. Short-stay homes, as they were called, were condemned because inmates were seen to 'go out as ignorant as they came in' and fell back into the same wicked ways.[99] By the end of the nineteenth century, with the exception of the Salvation Army, all the representatives of the Preventive and Rescue Committee of the National Union of Women Workers supported a two-year period of reform.[100] Older penitents incarcerated in the Convent of the Good Shepherd sometimes remained there for life.

In some respects, reform institutions in England varied considerably. An ex-prostitute could undergo widely different experiences, depending on which institution she was referred to. In some she might be made welcome whereas in others she might even be refused entry. Once admitted, she might find herself sharing accommodation with just a few women in a small home or with hundreds of others in a large institution. In the smaller homes, she might be given second-hand or new clothing, space of her own and be treated humanely, whereas in larger institutions she might be put in uniform and be expected to conform to rigidly enforced rules and a strict disciplinary code. Despite this variance, it is perhaps safe to assume that, apart from a few exceptions, institutions in England shared much in common with those found in Ireland and Scotland. Although there were significant denominational differences between English institutions, which in turn led to different perceptions of prostitutes, there were equally striking similarities. Indeed, Chapter 2 will argue that the seemingly more compassionate approach of the later reform movement, even though it may have benefited certain individual inmates, did not mark a new stage in the structure of reform.

Notes

1 Alexander Solzhenitsyn named the system of work camps in the former Soviet Union the Gulag archipelago and others have described the prison system of Britain in a similar vein. See M. Ignatieff, 'State, Civil Society and Total Institutions: A Critique of Recent Social Histories of Punishment', in S. Cohen and A. Scull (eds) *Social Control and the State* (Oxford: Martin Robertson, 1983), p. 92.

2 For instance, the penitentiaries at Bristol, Leeds, Liverpool and Norwich were all founded at this time: *Bristol Female Penitentiary Annual Reports*; *Leeds House of Rescue Annual Reports*; *Liverpool Female Penitentiary Annual Reports*; James Hooper, *Norwich Charities: Short Sketches of their Origin and History* (Norwich: Norfolk News, 1898), p. 199.

3 The Church Penitentiary Association was founded in 1852: see Edward Trenholme, *Rescue Work* (London: Society for Promoting Christian Knowledge, 1927), p. 3.

4 By the late nineteenth century there were supposedly ten important Anglican sisterhoods and twelve smaller sisterhoods, many of whom were devoted to the rescue and reform of prostitutes (*NUWW Conference* 1893, pp. 6–7). For example, the famous Clewer Sisterhood and the convents at Wantage and Bussage, Gloucester, were founded purely to work with ex-prostitutes (*Stroud News*, November 12th 1948). In 1898 Mrs Ruspini founded the Order of Divine Compassion which also focused on rescue and preventive work: see J.M. Cole and F.C. Bacon, *Christian Guidance of the Social Instincts* (London: Faith Press, 1928), p. 14.

5 *Seeking and Saving* (July 1885), p. 3.

6 *The Guide to Schools, Homes and Refuges in England for the Benefit of Girls and Women* (London: Longmans, Green, 1888).

7 For example, Valerie Bonham, Frances Finnegan, Maria Luddy, Linda Mahood and Susan Mumm all focus on the penitentiaries. See the introductory chapter for an overview of the historiography.

8 William J. Taylor, *The Story of the Homes* (London: London Female Preventive and Reformatory Institution, 1907), p. 31.

9 The Albion Hill Home was founded in Brighton in 1851, the Society for the Rescue of Young Women and Children in 1853, the London Female Preventive and Reformatory Institute in 1857, the Female Mission in 1858, and the Homes of Hope in 1860.

10 *Seeking and Saving* (1888), p. 193.

11 Both London and Liverpool lock hospitals set up reform wards.

12 For example, the Royal Albert Hospital in Plymouth, which had a separate lock ward, also established a reform ward.

13 The London Lock Hospital opened a home because it believed that there was no other provision for women who had just left the hospital but who could not yet find work (letter from Lock Asylum, July 1876).

14 The Undergraduates' House of Rescue was founded in 1886 (*The Guide to Schools, Homes and Refuges in England*).
15 *Lady's Pictorial* (October 19th 1895), p. 620.
16 For example, Mrs Hampson's House in Tollington Park, London, Mrs Sessions' Home in Gloucester and Lady Sitwell's Home in Scarborough were all privately managed (*The Guide to Schools, Homes and Refuges in England*).
17 Some, like the London Society for the Rescue of Young Women and Children, St Mary's Home of Refuge and Penitentiary in Manchester and the London Female Preventive and Reformatory Institution, were managed by the clergy and were therefore men only. The Home for Penitent Females in Derby, the Diocesan Home at Frieston, Lincolnshire, and the Anchorage Mission near Regent's Park, London, were run by a 'committee of gentlemen'. *The Vigilance Record* noted that there were at least fifteen reform institutions in the London district with only men on their governing body. These consisted of the Society for the Rescue of Young Women and Children; Magdalen Hospital, Streatham; Home of the Good Shepherd, Middlesex; the Midnight Meeting Movement for the Rescue and Reclamation of Fallen Women, Red Lion Square, London; London Diocesan Penitentiary, Highgate; Female Mission to the Fallen; Church Mission to the Fallen; London Lock Hospital; House of Refuge, Pimlico; St James' Diocesan Home, Fulham; St Mary Magdalene's, Paddington; St Martin's, Hereford; Church of England Penitentiary in Kent; Good Shepherd's Home, Leytonstone (*The Vigilance Record*, June 15th 1887, p. 36).
18 Mrs Goodenough, *NUWW Conference* 1893.
19 *Seeking and Saving* (July 1885), p. 3.
20 Worcester Diocesan Church Penitentiary Association reported in *The Worcester-shire Chronicle* (October 3rd 1885), p. 6.
21 Susan Mumm, *Stolen Daughters, Virgin Mothers* (London: Leicester University Press, 1999), p. 100.
22 Sisterhoods such as the Sisters of St John the Baptist, who were responsible for the management of homes in Clewer in Berkshire, Leamington Spa in Warwickshire and Bovey Tracey in Devon, the Order of Divine Compassion, which ran the Magdalen Hospital at Streatham, and the Sisters of St Michael at Bussage were three of the most well known (Some Account of the House of Mercy for Penitent Women at Bussage, in Two Letters by the Lord Bishop of Graham's Town and by the Revd T. Keble, Gloucester, 1865, p. 3).
23 *Seeking and Saving* (June 1882), p. 125.
24 For example, the Liverpool Rescue Society and House of Mercy, Mrs Rogers' Memorial Home in Birmingham, the Manchester and Salford Asylum for Female Penitents and the Nottingham Home for Fallen Women all had female presidents, vice-presidents and committees (*The Southwell Diocesan Magazine*, April 1888, p. 41). Yet others were small homes such as that run by Mrs Andrew Johnson in Walthamstow, London, Anna Wilkes in Poplar, London, and Emma Sheppard at Frome (*Minutes of Evidence taken before the Select Committee, House of Lords, State of Law Relating to the Protection of Young Girls* 1882, p. 40).
25 Ellice Hopkins, *Notes on Penitentiary Work* (London: Hatchards, 1879), p. 14.
26 Correspondence and papers of Miss Stride.
27 *Seeking and Saving* (February 1882), p. 30.
28 Liverpool Female Penitentiary Minute Books, October 1852.
29 Figure 1.1 is collated from *The Guide to Schools, Homes and Refuges in England for the Benefit of Girls and Women*.
30 Revd Carter, *The First Ten Years of the House of Mercy* (London: Joseph Masters, 1861), p. 15.
31 *Society for the Rescue of Young Women and Children Annual Report* 1899, p. 6.

32 See Carroll Smith-Rosenburg's *Disorderly Conduct* (New York: Alfred A. Knopf, 1985) for a discussion of mother–daughter relationships in Victorian America.

33 *Penitentiary Work in the Church of England, Papers for Discussion at the Anniversary Meeting of the Church Penitentiary Association, 1873* (London: Harrison and Sons, 1873).

34 *Birmingham Daily Gazette* (March 13th 1877).

35 *Birmingham Magdalen Asylum Annual Report* 1861.

36 *Introductory Report of the Society for the Establishment of a Magdalen Society in Liverpool* 1809, p. 12.

37 Ellice Hopkins, *Notes on Penitentiary Work*, p. 9.

38 Josephine Butler: J.M. Cole and F.C. Bacon, *Christian Guidance of the Social Instincts*, p. 7.

39 Letter to *The Woman's Herald* (January 24th 1891).

40 *Leeds Guardian Society Annual Report* 1864, p. 3.

41 *Bristol Female Penitentiary Annual Report* 1877, p. 5.

42 A sermon preached at St James' Church, Piccadilly, before the Church Penitentiary Association, April 26th 1853, by Samuel Lord Bishop of Oxford (London: Spottiswoode and Shaw, 1853).

43 *The Worcestershire Chronicle* (October 4th 1884), p. 6.

44 *Bristol Female Penitentiary Annual Report* 1879.

45 *The Pioneer* (August 1888), p. 8.

46 Michael Mason, *The Making of Victorian Sexual Attitudes* (Oxford: Oxford University Press, 1994).

47 Edward Trenholme, *Rescue Work*, p. 4.

48 David Englander, 'The Word and the World: Evangelicalism in the Victorian City', in G. Parsons (ed.) *Religion in Victorian Britain* (Manchester: Manchester University Press, 1988), p. 18.

49 *Birmingham Daily Gazette* (March 14th 1876).

50 *St Mary's Home, Manchester Annual Report* 1884, p. 9.

51 Mrs James Goodenough, 'Mission Work Among the Fallen in England', *NUWW Conference* 1893, p. 11.

52 I am indebted to Lesley Hall for this insight.

53 Harriet Nokes, *Twenty-Three Years in a House of Mercy* (London: Swan, Sonnenschein, 1888), p. 24.

54 *The Magdalen's Friend* (1860), p. 162.

55 Ibid., p. 163.

56 See Linda Mahood, *The Magdalenes* (London: Routledge, 1990).

57 In Nottingham, the magistrates and Chief Constable were considered to be 'very kind in placing girls in the hands of Southwell House Committee, instead of convicting them' (*The Southwell Diocesan Magazine*, September 1889, p. 179) whereas Liverpool police frequently directed women to the home there (*The Southwell Diocesan Magazine*, September 1889, p. 179).

58 For example, in towns and cities such as Birmingham (*The Friend*, 1890, p. 170) and in Brighton and Nottingham (*Brighton Police Court and Rescue Mission Annual Report* 1896) reformers preferred this method.

59 Arthur Brinkman, *Notes on Rescue Work* (1885).

60 For example, the Royal Hospital at Devonport, Plymouth, sent young women to the Devon and Exeter Penitentiary, the House of Mercy at Bovey Tracey and homes in Plymouth itself (Select Committee on Contagious Diseases Acts 1882).

61 For example, Nottingham reformers sought out women at the Goose Fair held annually in Nottingham (*The Southwell Diocesan Magazine*, May 1888, p. 72).

62 The Roman Catholic Convent of the Good Shepherd, the Penitentiaries at Stone in Kent and the Salvation Army were among them. The Mayfair Union stated

that 'No girl who is anything like sober is ever refused admittance': Edward
Trenholme, *Rescue Work*, p. 45.

63 *NUWW Conference* 1898, p. 5.

64 *St Mary's Home of Refuge and Penitentiary, Manchester, Annual Report* 1885, p. 6.

65 *Liverpool Female Penitentiary Annual Report* 1905.

66 Indeed, concern was expressed that out of twenty-six young women in the
Plymouth Penitentiary, six were 15 and one was 14 years of age (*Seeking and
Saving*, June 1884). As a consequence both the Society for the Rescue of Women
and Children and the London Society for the Protection of Young Females built
homes for teenagers and young children.The Society for the Rescue of Women
and Children had a special home for children under 12 years which held about
fourteen young women who were 'fallen' or what they termed 'outraged'; the
London Society for the Protection of Young Females had a home for over eighty
young women between the ages of 9 and 15; and a home was built in
Monmouthshire for children under 12 years old. In these institutions the children were not treated as penitents but as children who 'must have fallen into
evil, not knowing it to be evil' (*Seeking and Saving*, November 1881, p. 151).

67 Ellice Hopkins, *Select Committee on Law Relating to the Protection of Young Girls*
1882, p. 8.

68 *Seeking and Saving* (June 1882), p. 122.

69 *Seeking and Saving* (July 1889), p. 154.

70 Susan Mumm, *Stolen Daughters, Virgin Mothers*, p. 103.

71 London Female Preventive and Reformatory Institution, correspondence and
papers, April 13th 1887.

72 *Rules and By Laws of the Manchester and Salford Asylum for Female Penitents*
(December 23rd 1822).

73 *Liverpool Female Penitentiary Annual Report* 1903, p. 4.

74 *The Vigilance Record* (November 1889), p. 118.

75 Arthur J. Maddison, *Hints on Rescue Work* (London: Reformatory and Refuge
Union, *c.*1895), p. 105.

76 In St Mary's Home, Wantage, the sisters cared for penitents dying of consump-
tion (*Seeking and Saving*, September 1881, p. 98). Similarly the Magdalen
Hospital at Streatham and the Leeds Guardian Society had a separate infirmary
with which to treat and care for convalescent and sick inmates: H.F.B.
Compston, *The Magdalen Hospital* (London: Society for Promoting Christian
Knowledge, 1917), p. 179; *Leeds Guardian Society Rules* 1821, p. 11.

77 *St James' Home Annual Report* 1857.

78 Ibid., 1858, p. 1.

79 *The Guide to Schools, Homes and Refuges in England for the Benefit of Girls and
Women*, p. 119.

80 *St James' Home Annual Report* 1858, p. 3.

81 Evelyn Villiers, 'Classification in Penitentiary Work', *NUWW Conference* 1912,
p. 12. At Clewer, the 'ladies' paid £50 per annum towards their keep. See
Valerie Bonham, *A Place in Life* (London: privately published 1992), p. 220.

82 Upper-class penitents tended to be single mothers rather than ex-prostitutes
(*NUWW Conference* 1912, p. 12).

83 In 1885 there were approximately eighty-three refuges in England which acted
as receiving houses and/or probationary houses for penitentiaries and longer
homes: *The Guide to Schools, Homes and Refuges in England for the Benefit of Girls
and Women*, pp.108–115.

84 In the Leeds House of Rescue young girls remained in the house for a probationary period of three weeks before being sent on to other institutions for two
years (*Leeds House of Rescue Annual Report* 1895, p. 6). At the House of Mercy
in Horbury, penitents were divided into two classes: the raised girls and the

probationer girls. During the first month of their stay, the probationers, like those in Leeds, were kept apart from the rest until proven fit to be received into the main house where the 'raised' girls lived (*Seeking and Saving*, July 1881, p. 49).

85 *Seeking and Saving* (January 1882), p. 4.
86 *The Vigilance Record* (November 1889), p. 118.
87 Arthur J. Maddison, *Hints on Rescue Work*.
88 *NUWW Conference* 1898, p. 9.
89 Ibid., p. 8.
90 Arthur J. Maddison, *Hints on Rescue Work*, p. 113.
91 *Rules and By Laws of the Manchester and Salford Asylum for Female Penitents* (December 23rd 1822).
92 Frances Finnegan, *Poverty and Prostitution* (Cambridge: Cambridge University Press, 1979).
93 H.F.B. Compston, *The Magdalen Hospital*, p. 172.
94 *Seeking and Saving* (June 1882), p. 177.
95 *Annual Report of Chief Inspector of Factories and Workshops* 1907, p. 203.
96 *Worcester Diocesan Council Annual Report* 1892, p. 6.
97 *Leeds Guardian Society Annual Report* 1868, p. 3.
98 *Seeking and Saving* (March 1888), p. 198.
99 *Seeking and Saving* (June 1882), p. 175.
100 *NUWW Occasional Paper* February 1912, p. 18.

2   Daily life inside reform institutions

Whether prostitutes were viewed as sinners or victims, all the managers of reform institutions, whatever their religious affiliation or managerial structure, held similar long-term objectives. Reformers shared an identical rehabilitative goal of reshaping young working-class women into honest, reliable, compliant, morally upright and hard-working domestic servants who would lead a future life of unblemished decency. With only minor variations, they set about doing it in a comparable way. This chapter will argue that the working patterns, leisure facilities and general lifestyle on offer at reform institutions, despite new developments in the process of reform, remained markedly alike.

Rules and regulations

Reform institutions were, like other punitive institutions, bound by rules and regulations because, as Linda Mahood points out, reformers thought that inmates could be reformed only if their daily lives were fully structured.[1] Moreover, young, female, working-class inmates were assumed incapable of exercising moral judgement without a strict regulatory framework in place. Rules and regulations not only established order but also were believed to be essential in the maintenance of authority. Obeying rules certainly must have encouraged submissive behaviour – an essential ingredient for a working-class woman. Nevertheless, rules were enforced in different ways. The reform journal, *Seeking and Saving*, suggested that there were four main methods of disciplining inmates and keeping order in institutions. The first was a military or prison discipline where everything was done to a signal; the second was silent discipline 'where all creep about silently';[2] the third was unrestrained discipline where inmates were allowed to 'laugh and talk and sing about the Home in perfect freedom';[3] and the fourth was the discipline of force where inmates were carried off forcibly to their room if they refused to obey.

The Church Penitentiary Association maintained that lax discipline did not prepare inmates for the tough life of domestic service. It was also believed that good order and Christian conduct could be fostered and sustained only by the strictest supervision.[4] And so, in the penitentiary at Clewer, inmates were taught to bow low before the sisters and to speak only when spoken to.[5] In other places, especially Evangelical homes, a 'mixture of love and wisdom, gentleness and firmness, sympathy and discretion' ruled inmates.[6] This approach, in theory at least, controlled by kindness rather than restraint but the aim was the same, because the managers of these institutions still wished to remould their inmates.

The details of actual rules and regulations differed between institutions but punctuality, industriousness and modesty were expected in most places. Talking at meals and in the bedrooms was often forbidden, and inmates were not permitted to enter any bedroom other than their own. Noisy behaviour, loud talking, swearing and conversation about improper matters were also frowned upon.[7] So too was carelessness and rudeness. Moreover, most institutions employed the 'eloquence of silence' whereby inmates were forbidden to allude to their past lives.[8] Some institutions managed by nuns forbade any talking at all outside recreation time but this was criticised because it placed too much of a strain on 'wild and untrained' girls.

In larger institutions rules were hung on the walls as a constant reminder for the inmates to obey. The House of Mercy at Horbury kept a report book in which all breaches of rule, bad language and poor work were entered. Each Monday these report books were sent to the Sister Superior of the penitentiary, who deducted a half-penny from weekly earnings of four pence for misconduct.[9] These weekly statements were posted up on the notice board as a reminder to all inmates of the need to behave. Withdrawal of food was a common punishment. If inmates came down late at breakfast, they went hungry, and if girls were sent to their rooms for disobedience or other misdemeanours they were given bread and water rather than a hot meal.[10] In some penitentiaries inmates were hit or kept in a punishment room.[11] Other institutions tried to encourage good behaviour by financial enticements rather than punishments.[12] Liverpool inmates were able to draw small sums of money to buy 'innocent indulgences' such as sweets and fruits if they behaved well all week.[13] Strict rules and regulations were thought inappropriate for smaller institutions where inmates were known personally to the management. Some smaller homes therefore had few or no rules but this may have been because inmates were controlled more directly through personal knowledge and influence. In the Salvation Army homes no one was imprisoned or restricted in diet for any offence.[14] These homes had less formal discipline, restraint and control and no rule of silence,[15] but if women misbehaved consistently they were admonished and publicly expelled before the rest of the inmates, whatever the nature of the institution.

On entry, freedom in the larger institutions was generally curtailed. Inmates were denied access to the ordinary daily pattern of life: they could not shop, visit friends or go for a leisurely walk unaccompanied. As penitent sinners, and as working-class women, inmates were assumed incapable of exercising moral judgement when outside the confines of the asylum. It was a total institution, shielded from external influences whereby inmates' only contacts with the outside world were the committee members and the staff of the institution. According to Linda Mahood this was because of a belief that inmates might internalise the mores of the institution if they were not distracted by material concerns.[16] However, there was a religious, as well as a pragmatic, reason for this approach. Comparisons were drawn between prostitutes and the Israelites who had fled from oppression in Egypt: 'The principle was complete separation from the people, the customs, the locality, and from everything that could by any means tend to allure them back to or cause them to dwell on the place of their sojourn amidst the abominations of Egypt.'[17] And so prostitutes, like the Israelites, were to be completely cut off from their past in order to forget their own previous personal 'abominations' and to avoid being contaminated by the outside world. In most institutions penitents were not allowed to receive a letter or message without it previously being inspected by the matron or allowed to leave the premises except on urgent business and only then accompanied by a trustworthy female. Visiting was also circumscribed: in Norwich mothers or other female relatives were allowed to visit inmates only on the first Saturday in every month between 9a.m. and 12p.m.[18] At one home in Finsbury Park inmates were not allowed a postage stamp in case they communicated with friends who might entice them away.[19] The London Lock Asylum even built an upstairs kitchen so that inmates would not have the 'opportunity for gossip with tradesmen that would be given downstairs'.[20]

This strategy of containment was condemned by many. In a letter to the Reformatory and Refuge Union one critic pleaded that

> I hope there may be a strong pronouncement against the practice of *never* letting girls go outside the walls of the Home ... I know some Homes where this conventual and to my mind most objectionable, custom is carried out. Anything worse, from every point of view, I cannot imagine. Fancy *two years* of such confinement![21]

At Emma Sheppard's Home at Frome, inmates were free to leave the home during the day, and sometimes worked outside the home, coming back at night. She disapproved of institutions which took away the freedom of their inmates, arguing that they were, 'I think, misnamed, being more a system for criminals than for penitents'.[22]

Eating and sleeping

It is difficult to discern the true diets of inmates as these were rarely published but evidence suggests that the food on offer was not dissimilar to another punitive establishment for the working class, the workhouses. To be fair the average single woman worker would have fared much worse.

Needlewomen, for example, were considered to be the worst-fed class of all and rarely ate meat save sheep's brains or black pudding.[23] By 1900 workhouse food was more nutritious than the food consumed by the working class, reported in Rowntree's survey of poverty in York since the authorised workhouse diet included 22 ounces of meat and 8 ounces of fish per adult a week.[24] However, even if workhouse food was superior it was still regarded, as M.A. Crowther points out, as 'one of the privations of institutional life' because it was unrelentingly monotonous.[25] At no time did meals of reform institutions include delicious and tempting food or food favoured by the working class such as kippers, bloaters, pickles and cockles, a lack which must have sent out a message to inmates that they were being penalised for their past lives. The recommended diet of the CPA included meat five times a week, fish one day and bread and cheese on Friday. Currant puddings were supposed to be supplied on Sundays. The rest of the meals were to consist of bread and butter with tea or coffee.[26] Similarly, an Evangelical advice manual recommended the meals shown in the box.[27]

> Sunday: Cold boiled beef with plain pudding
> Monday: Pea soup with bread
> Tuesday: Roast meat with veg
> Wednesday: Plum pudding
> Thursday: Stewed beef with veg
> Friday: Roast meat with veg
> Saturday: Boiled rice with sweets
> Supper: Bread and cheese

Of course these were ideal, if somewhat monotonous, diets, which many institutions might not have adhered to. Even when diets were published and seemed to include wholesome and plentiful food, inmates did not always receive it, as in the case of the Magdalen Hospital in the early years of the nineteenth century. When wheat was scarce or perhaps meat was expensive these were excluded from the menus.[28] Certainly, Ellice Hopkins condemned the insufficient diet of penitentiaries: 'In one the girls were so fearfully hungry that one poor child used to pick the potato-peelings out of the sut-hole, furtively frizzle them in the fire, and eat them to stay the cravings of her healthy young appetite.'[29] In the early twentieth century, lady factory inspectors noted that in one House of Mercy not only was the diet poor but also inmates did not eat their main meal until 3 or 4p.m. even though they had risen early and had been doing physically demanding work.[30] Moreover, when the institution needed to economise the diet of the inmates suffered: in Leeds the committee cut the amount spent on food in a desperate attempt to balance the books – in 1862 the average cost per head of food was 3s weekly but this decreased two years later to 2s 7d.[31]

Young women usually slept in dormitories, sometimes with beds so crammed together that there was no space to move between them.[32] Situations such as these prompted Ellice Hopkins to complain that such dormitories, often without private washing arrangements, curtains or supervision, allowed for the 'mass of corrupt humanity [to be kept] together at night under circumstances which simply ensure the most corrupt infecting all the others'.[33] As a result, some establishments gave inmates either a cubicle to themselves or a separate bedroom. The smaller the home the more privacy inmates seemed to enjoy but this may equally have as much to do with morality and control than with kindness.

For two years, in whatever institution they inhabited, women were rarely alone. Like the inmates of many prisons and convents, they lived, worked and prayed alongside others: it was an enforced communal existence. Penitents were supervised by sisters during meal-times, work and recreation and were even watched over when they slept. However, once again, women in smaller homes did not experience such authoritative treatment but this may have been because managers could exert a more personal influence.

Work

All the unpaid work, from scrubbing floors, cleaning windows, making beds, sweeping carpets and mending clothes, the preparing and cooking of food and washing of the household linen, was performed by the inmates under supervision. By the nineteenth century laundry work, which was a money-making enterprise, had become the leitmotiv of most reform institutions, whatever their religious affiliation. This had not always been the case. In the Magdalen Hospital at Streatham in the eighteenth century inmates were employed in a variety of tasks – lace making, making artificial flowers, gloves, garters and children's toys, spinning, embroidering and weaving hair for wigs.[34] Reservations were expressed about the suitability of laundry work but other working-class women's jobs were rejected as unsuitable. Needlework was dismissed because it was too poorly paid; fruit picking, dairy work and other agricultural work were thought inappropriate because such work took place in harsh and coarse surroundings; knitting was criticised by medical men as too sedentary; and factory work gave women too much freedom in the evening.[35] As a consequence, laundry work eclipsed other work especially when the physical exercise involved meant that 'the wild restlessness, the lawlessness, the animal passions and excitement of the old street life, are worked off by muscular exertion'.[36]

Linda Mahood argues that reform institutions depended on the work of the inmates for its material reproduction. Certainly, laundry work embodied the principles of good capitalist enterprise as it became more and more a competitive business. In some penitentiaries there was even a temptation to admit women known to be good laundresses in preference to those who were in greater need. Laundry work was probably favoured because it was more profitable than other kinds of female work, had the advantage of requiring only a small capital outlay in the first instance and was immediately remunerative.[37] It was, unlike agricultural work, non-seasonal and therefore had no slack time. Laundry work made each institution financially viable and cut the cost of the inmates' confinement. Eton, the prestigious public school, paid the Clewer House of Mercy £270 per annum to wash the household linen and personal laundry of some seventy boys.[38] Nonetheless, the financial position of institutional laundries remained precarious. Most were plagued by financial difficulties since the earnings from the laundry were never sufficient to cover the running costs;[39] in practice, organisers relied on subscriptions, congregational collections, legacies and other charitable donations to support their institution.

In the first half of the nineteenth century most inmates did not receive any wages for their labour and so had little desire to work hard making the financial situation of institutions even more uncertain. Various incentives were offered in an attempt to overcome this problem. Many reform institutions adopted the practice of giving small bonuses to inmates who had worked hard in order to encourage habits of industry and self-respect.[40] There is no doubt that this system enjoyed some success as discipline and work allegedly improved in institutions which introduced similar reward systems. This scheme served many purposes: it encouraged women to work hard because they were anxious to earn money; it helped discipline through the judicious use of financial reward and it encouraged good middle-class virtues of thrift.

> Discipline and diligence are consequently much more easily maintained. Take one result: no one has absconded; or in other words, left the Institution without leave. No doubt the fear of losing her earnings, which would be forfeited, has had its influence in this matter.[41]

Work reinforced not only thrift but also class and gender conformity. These institutions replicated the work pattern of the 'real' world by preparing inmates for a similar job outside. It trained women in what was considered to be the only fitting occupation for working-class young women: domestic service. As a consequence, no encouragement was ever given for young women to transcend either their class background or their gender role. Increased job opportunities, particularly in the latter part of the century, opened up employment prospects for women but training was never offered in the newer occupations such as typing and clerking.

Linda Mahood maintains that inmates relearnt their lost feminine skills through laundry work since it re-educated them into correct female attitudes and modes of behaviour and to a feminine role that was their expected future. However, laundry work was hard, rough and physical labour usually undertaken by an equivalent female type and could hardly have prepared inmates for domestic service in a 'genteel' middle-class home. Certainly factory inspectors questioned whether laundry work actually did exercise the 'refining influence' demanded by reformers.[42]

> The statement that laundry work is beneficial for the formation, amelioration and development of character, is one which should not be accepted without grave consideration. We feel that it should be considered whether laundry work exercises the refining influence which is essential for the upraising of those degraded characters so often found in Penitentiaries. To anyone who has seen wash-house work in full swing, with its damp, oppressive heat, its heavy odour, it must appear at least questionable how far such work is the most suitable for the reformation and education of the kind of girl committed to a Reformatory or a Penitentiary. Laundry work is undoubtedly hard labour.[43]

Laundry work, and its associated occupation, domestic service – more so than other working-class women's work such as factory work – encouraged feminine dependency rather than independence. Women were reduced to the status of dependants in institutions and remained so when employed as a domestic servant. Domestic servants lived in the rather enclosed world of a private house and were under constant supervision by their employers both in their work and free time. In addition, domestic servants lived in close proximity to their middle-class employers so it may have been presumed that ex-inmates might have the correct moral values, learnt in the institution, reinforced by their social superiors.[44] Employment in a middle-class home, allegedly, gave women a foothold on the ladder of female respectability.

Linda Mahood[45] and Frank Prochaska[46] suggest that laundry work prepared inmates as domestic servants to the growing middle class. This may have been the case in Scotland and other areas of Britain but it did not apply to the English towns and cities studied in this research. The numbers of women who left the institutions each year to enter domestic service hardly made a difference to the insatiable middle-class demand for servants. In 1880, for example, 11 inmates left the Birmingham Magdalen Asylum for domestic service to add to an approximate number of 13,827 women employed as domestic servants in the city.[47] Moreover, ex-inmates were not always considered suitable servants for established middle-class families who may well have preferred to employ young women from rural backgrounds rather than someone who was once thought of as a social evil. Certainly, Wilkie Collins' heroine, Mercy Merrick, found it impossible to remain in a respectable home as soon as the family discovered she was a reformed ex-prostitute. Indeed, the low wages received by ex-inmates suggests that they were often engaged by families lower down the social scale who did not need a decorative servant but one who could accomplish heavy work.[48]

Laundry work acted as much a mechanism for penitence as it did for economic and social reform.[49] Religious ideas were certainly important – cleanliness was the grand metaphor of religious purity ranking 'next to godliness'. In eliminating physical dirt, order was established in the spiritual world of the inmates. It is also a highly persuasive metaphor of absolution. In scrubbing sheets white as the purest snow, inmates washed away their sins and regained their shining soul.[50] In addition, laundry work may have been favoured because hard physical labour acted as a penance. In working hard in primitive conditions, inmates atoned for their sins and, like Lady Macbeth, tried to wash away their contaminated past.

Laundry work at reform institutions was definitely harsh, involving a long working day in hot, damp and steamy rooms.[51] Before the Factories and Workshops Act 1907, which regulated the hours and conditions of work in charitable laundries, most young women experienced a long working day. In a scribbled note found in the pages of the minutes of the Liverpool Penitentiary, a committee member recorded the hours shown in the box.[52]

> *Work at 7a.m.*
> *Breakfast 7.30a.m.*
> *Work 8–10.30a.m.*
> *Rest 10.30–10.45a.m.*
> *Work 10.45–1p.m.*
> *Lunch 1–2p.m.*
> *Work 2–5p.m.*
> *Tea 5–5.30p.m.*
> *Work 5.30–8p.m.*

Some inmates began work as early as 4a.m. in order to prepare and light the laundry fires for the day ahead.[53] When the occasion demanded, even longer hours were worked. Ship washing in the penitentiaries of port towns was particularly demanding because of the amount of laundry to be washed within a short time: sometimes the laundry comprised over 9,000 sheets and towels which had to be washed, dried and ironed before the ship set sail. Not surprisingly, this led to greater abuse, especially when a ship had been delayed and came into port for only a few hours.[54] In such emergencies, inmates were forced to work through the night. One lady factory inspector reported that she had received a complaint of nineteen hours per day being worked in a laundry managed by nuns.[55] Indeed, a petition was sent to the Home Office arguing that the proposed Factory Act 1907 (which aimed to restrict hours and improve conditions in charitable laundries) would be detrimental to the efficient working of their respective institutions.[56] However, by the time the Act was passed, factory inspectors reported that most charitable institutions restricted their hours of work to fewer than the statutory twelve hours.[57]

Laundry work, whether performed in reform institutions or in public laundries, took place in poor sanitary conditions. There were usually three processes involved: washing, folding and ironing. Laundry workers in public laundries, Malcolmson stresses, suffered from rheumatism, ulcerated legs, bronchitis and other allied complaints as a result of standing for long hours in ill-ventilated damp rooms.[58] According to factory inspectors, public laundries were

> very narrow in space, ill ventilated, continually filled with steam and fumes, wet underfoot on the ill-laid stones, between which stand pools of dirty water, terribly over-heated with the stores on which the irons are heating and by which the clothes are drying, conditions more destructive of health would be hard to find. The women are scarcely ever free from colds and coughs.[59]

It is hard to believe that institutional inmates were healthier than laundry workers were elsewhere, especially when the annual inspectors' reports for 1907 spoke of poor ventilation, hard and long hours, inadequate fencing, steam and the dirty walls of institutional laundries. A 'solid block of steamy fog' filled wash houses,[60] so that inspectors were unable to see across the room and where unfenced ironing stoves in ironing rooms created unbearable heat so that 'the girls are almost "melted"'.[61]

It was believed that laundry work should be done manually and often in harsh conditions to encourage obedience and subservience. In some institutions women used cold water, either pumped by hand from a spring or rainwater, to wash the laundry. Wet washing in most institutions was usually dried in open drying grounds when the weather was fine or in hot air closets when the weather was inclement.[62] It was certainly a punishing schedule for even strong, healthy young women. Some institutions reacted to the criticism that laundry work was hard. At St Mary's, Dartford, it was believed that any preconceived notion as to the dreariness of penitentiary life would be dispelled 'by a visit to the bright airy laundry, where the girls . . . look out on the distant Thames with its ever changing view of passing ships, while piles of snowy linen . . . stand ready to be dispatched',[63] a comment which can be considered only as romantic delusion! Nonetheless there were periodical technical improvements especially if they improved the quality and quantity of the laundry output. New machinery installed in the Liverpool Magdalen Home enabled the institution to take in large amounts of washing from ships, steamers, factories, hotels, cafés and hospitals instead of the rather smaller laundry generated by private individuals.

The following extract, depicting the various reasons why one Evangelical institution favoured laundry work, suggests the importance of absolution and submission, the virtue of industry above indolence and the necessity of remoulding inmates rather than enjoyment of a task well done:

> Its aim is not merely to wash off the taint of the past, but to infuse into her new ideas of life, and of the way in which a happier life may

be attained: to inspire willingness to work into the indolent, self-control into the emotional, self-respect into the passionate: to eradicate the deeply rooted evil habits of the past and to infuse a spirit of order, virtue, propriety and submission: and above all things to bring her to the knowledge of God.[64]

Not all institutions, however, engaged in laundry work. Smaller institutions managed by private individuals trained women in a range of domestic skills rather than just laundry work.[65] In one Barnet home, inmates sewed clothing for the parish orphan school, worked in the kitchen, looked after poultry and tended the vegetable garden.[66] These were the exceptions, however, which proved the rule and even then horizons remained limited to traditional female occupations.

Leisure

Leisure activity provides an excellent example of the ways in which concepts of class and gender shifted according to circumstances. At one and the same time the institutions reinforced gendered class roles in limiting job opportunities while expanding horizons and offering alternatives in leisure. Working-class work was considered appropriate for working-class women whereas working-class leisure was not. Alcohol, fairs, gambling, riotous entertainments and other working-class amusements were discouraged possibly because, as Robert Storch suggests, these types of activities led to indiscipline, potential immorality and ultimately social chaos.[67] Throughout the nineteenth century parks, libraries and museums were built in cities and large towns in an attempt to persuade a potentially disorderly working class to use their spare time improving themselves. Not surprisingly, the leisure pursuits organised for the inmates of reform establishments were similarly respectable, middle class, subdued and – above all – morally elevating. And so the traditional gender roles expected of reputable middle-class women were reinforced in the working class. It can only be assumed that through middle-class leisure pursuits, young women might aspire to the cultural values of the middle class but not to their jobs, their homes or their general lifestyle.

In the early part of the nineteenth century few institutions provided recreational facilities, apart from religious services, because the real object was to bring women to real penitence through work and prayer alone. By the 1880s there had been, if not a softening of attitudes, then a recognition by some of the benefits of providing some respite from laundry work.[68] Supervised leisure, it was believed, eliminated the vices of ignorance, restiveness and uncontrolled, unrestrained behaviour, which had been fostered by an alleged life of self-indulgence. To enable inmates to eradicate these vices it was necessary to imbue the right attitudes not only through work but also through recreation and prayer. Leisure activities may have given inmates a break from the laundry but the amusements on offer were limited.[69] Recreation acted as yet another mechanism for moral reform and a means whereby the cultural and moral gendered mores of the middle class were inculcated. The chief value of recreations to the managers of the reform establishments was 'that they bring the women into personal contact with the ladies who teach them. By this means the ladies come to know the women individually, and in many ways gain an influence over them'.[70] Not surprisingly, recreation was always educative in some way and was always supervised:

> A spirit of lawlessness and impatience of restraint fostered by a life of self-indulgence is ever ready to manifest itself. While even in those who do sincerely desire and strive after what is right, there are frequent failures because the power for good has been so weakened by evil habits that they are unable to carry out the good purposes they may have formed. Hence, it is not so much instruction that is needed as training. And to this end a constant, careful supervision is exercised even during the periods of recreation so as to check the first indication of wrong and prevent the bad influence of one from injuring others.[71]

Religious observance was an important part of every inmate's life.[72] In the church penitentiaries and asylums, paid chaplains conducted a formal service each Sunday, daily prayers were organised by the matrons,[73] while regular Bible classes were held by committee members.[74] Reformers generally disliked inmates going outside the institution because they feared 'the impertinent stare, and the jaunty recognition, in ways one could feel, but could not define, of knots of idle boys and men at the street corners' if the easily recognisable and uniformed inmates were taken to church.[75] Some reformers thought it a mistake to place too much of an emphasis on religion: a few believed that daily religious classes were an excuse for idleness and put too heavy a burden on teachers; others argued that many inmates were sceptical of religion since many Christian men had used prostitutes and churches were often convenient places for assignations; yet others claimed that the Church of England acted as a veneer of respectability on a corrupt and rotten morality.[76] As a consequence, it was urged that too many 'goody-goody' principles be avoided in favour of religious instruction which was related to the experiences and lives of inmates.[77]

Other regular recreational facilities were little more than what would be expected of a respectable middle-class philanthropist rather than working-class or indeed middle-class entertainment. Emphasis was placed on doing good works rather than aping the gentry. This provides yet another example of the ways in which the class and religious assumptions of the managers attempted to modify the behaviour of the female inmates. In particular, penitentiaries encouraged inmates to either read or listen to works from the Church Missionary Society, both of which reinforced humility, obedience and servility – deemed to be proper gender, class and religious virtues. In the rest of their 'spare' time the women were encouraged to be engaged in 'voluntary' work. Inmates were often 'invited' to make garments for the Church Missionary Society as gifts, and while sewing, their thoughts were generally drawn, by reading and conversation, to the good done by other benevolent societies. It is hard to judge how voluntary this missionary work actually was. At one Nonconformist home, similar activities, divided into half-hourly slots, were organised each evening: every other Monday cutting out, needlework and maths; on Tuesdays texts read by some philanthropic lady (books that were read to the inmates were always of a moral and uplifting nature or dealt with household management and domestic service); on Wednesdays domestic drill, musical drill and lessons in physiology; on Thursdays domestic economy and reading; on Fridays darning and patching. Not all institutions gave as much weight to 'useful' activities. At Norwich in winter the inmates played indoor games such as dominoes and draughts while in summer they played outdoor games in the grounds.[78] Most institutions in the latter part of the nineteenth century organised musical and other drills. Of course, such games acted as a mechanism for control in that inappropriate energy was redirected into positive channels. 'A good game affords a healthy vent for their animal spirits, and I may add the animal passions. These poor girls when they first come into our hands are generally afflicted with all sorts of morbid fantasies.'[79] In addition leisure relieved the monotony of inmates' lives, neutralised the irksomeness of the daily routine and compensated for a loss of liberty. Regular leisure activities were organised for pragmatic and humanitarian reasons as well as controlling and reforming ones. When inmates were relaxing in non-conventional institutions they were supervised by volunteers which as a consequence lightened the load of matrons and other workers by giving them a much needed rest.

There were occasional treats. Magic lantern slides were especially popular in the 1890s,[80] but these too were generally of an educational nature: typical slides demonstrated the evils of drink and feckless behaviour or showed missionaries working in other countries. Outside visits were organised by many institutions. Usually this involved a tour of the surrounding countryside, a walk in a park, a country ramble, boating on a lake or a walk by the seashore.[81] Invitations to tea, or garden parties, at the homes of local philanthropists were common. Special events were often celebrated. At Queen Victoria's Jubilee and King Edward VII's Coronation the inmates of many institutions were provided with tea and an afternoon out to watch the celebrations which reinforced loyalty not only to authority in general but more especially to the reigning monarch.

Most inmates did not enjoy any long periods of time off save that of Christmas and Easter and, in Roman Catholic institutions, the holy days of obligation when inmates spent most of the time in church. At the Albion Hill Home in Brighton, inmates were given a half day off on Boxing Day. Occasionally inmates had an odd day off in the year. Factory inspectors noted that the managers of some institutions complained about the statutory six holidays a year enforced by the 1907 Act and tried to avoid them. One factory inspector sardonically remarked that the ladies in charge of one institution had assured her that their inmates loved the work so much that a holiday was a misfortune![82]

Success of reform institutions

Reformers not only perceived themselves as a force for tremendous good but also believed that the reform institutions they managed had contributed to a significant decline in prostitution.[83] 'I think the rescue societies and those co-operating with them, . . . are entitled to a very large share, the largest share I may say, of the credit of these results.'[84] Of course, such optimism was unrealistic. Not only did prostitution remain firmly in place but also the success rate of the institutions was not high: the majority of those who entered reform institutions did not become domestic servants. Figures 2.1 and 2.2, compiled from the *Rescue Society Annual Reports* between 1853 and 1881 and the Church Penitentiary Association records between 1860 and 1873 demonstrate the limited success of the reform movement.[85] The number of women in the Rescue Society, from both the 'fallen' and 'unfallen' category, who eventually became domestic servants remained just under half of all those admitted. Similarly, those who were designated 'favourable' (that is those who became servants) by the Church Penitentiary movement were in the minority.

The records of individual institutions confirm this limited 'success': between 1758 and 1915 the Magdalen Hospital at Streatham discharged 4,580 out of 14,057 women 'at their own request' or for 'improper conduct', which was more than a quarter of those admitted. One home in Paddington, which had seven admissions and seven discharges in one year, managed to have only two become domestic servants.[86] One is therefore led to question

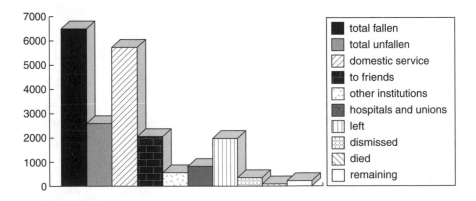

Figure 2.1 Rescue Society Annual Reports 1853–1881

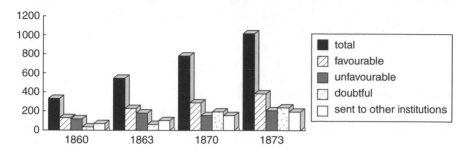

Figure 2.2 Church Penitentiary Association records 1860–1873

the overall competence of the reform movement, especially since admission policies were so exacting.

Certainly, not all inmates welcomed the opportunity to embody virtuous, middle-class, upper-working-class and feminine values. Women, as Linda Mahood has demonstrated in Scottish institutions, rejected the class and gender role allotted to them and the alleged imposition of a middle-class moral ethos. The literature indicates that there was sporadic unrest in the institutions even though it was not always recorded in the annual reports. For example, there were often indirect allusions to unrest rather than direct ones. It was often reported that the homes were much more settled;[87] that harmonious conditions prevailed;[88] that the inmates fell in with the rules and arrangements of the home;[89] that they did not have to expel that year for misconduct;[90] that 'never before has there reigned through-out the House such a universal spirit of obedience';[91] that there had been no serious disturbance or case of gross insubordination;[92] nor conduct demanding severe punishment;[93] that conduct had improved and was marked by more steadiness and gentleness than had been observed in some previous years;[94] that the general tone and conduct of the inmates during the year have been good.[95] One can only assume from reports such as these that life was far from settled, harmonious and peaceful within the institutions.

Occasionally the literature was more candid and reported that there were 'some troublesome cases of insubordination to deal with',[96] or that the 'obscene language and doings at this Hospital are very terrible'.[97] Certain individuals were thought too excitable, mischievous and prone to inventing the 'most wonderful romances'.[98] Case books from Southwell House, Nottingham, reveal that women sent to reform institutions elsewhere were often sent back to Nottingham because of inappropriate conduct. Clara Boggington was dismissed from an Edmonton home in 1887 for 'trouble-some behaviour, fighting and using bad language'; in the same year, Annie Poppel was dismissed from Lincoln House for threatening to throw a hot iron at another girl and 'was a most troublesome girl, her temper at times unbearable. She is very mischievous and not the least industrious.' The

LIVERPOOL
JOHN MOORES UNIVERSITY
AVRIL ROBARTS LRC
TITHEBARN STREET
LIVERPOOL L2 2ER
TEL. 0151 231 4022

Convent of the Good Shepherd dismissed one girl in April 1893 with a violent temper because she hit another;[99] in 1899 Ellen Hensby was dismissed from St Mary's, Rusholme, for being a shocking influence over the younger girls; and Fanny Hopkins was sent back from Horbury 'on account of extremely insubordinate conduct. She persisted in disturbing the girls in the dormitory at night and when removed to a room by herself, she tore her clothing, unravelled her stockings and broke crockery.'[100] A number of times discipline broke down completely because of wild and unruly inmates. In Bristol in 1886 the matron in charge was physically unable to cope, suffered a mental breakdown and left the institution in a state of disorganisation. In a letter to the Charity Organisation, Elizabeth Blackwell complained of the obscene language and terrible doings at the London Lock Asylum.[101] Even middle-class women incarcerated in St James' were perceived to be difficult to control because they were unused to discipline and regular hours. The lady superintendent complained of 'frequent quarrels, outbreaks of waywardness and insubordination' among them.[102] The inmates of these institutions were hardly sweet docile young women who meekly obeyed rigid rules and regulations but more a recalcitrant group of individuals 'with a great variety of tempers and dispositions, more or less habituated to licentiousness, and become impatient to restraint and rule',[103] and most certainly not the victims of popular belief.

Other less obvious forms of rebellion occurred. Laundry work was often beset with problems and complaints about the standard of work were commonplace. It was believed that the standard was low because the laundry was washed and ironed by unskilled, untrained, often unsupervised and unpaid inmates. Of course another reason could be that laundry work permitted inmates some small degree of resistance. Going slow, washing half-heartedly or ironing inadequately were perhaps some of the less obvious ways that young women could register their discontent. Indeed in penitentiaries the refusal to work was a recognised method by which a woman who wished to leave secured her discharge.[104] Certainly, when inmates were too disruptive they were dismissed for poor conduct because to retain them was seen to lead to general disorder.[105] Even so, most institutions were reluctant to do so because it reflected badly on the management.[106]

There were numerous occasions when inmates left the institutions.[107] Some inmates had permission whereas others absconded. Many skipped over the walls even though those who dared to run away were sometimes charged with the theft of their uniform and sentenced to periods of punishment.[108] At one time the Manchester and Salford Asylum was forced to raise the walls of the penitentiary by several feet to prevent the escape of some of the inmates and in order to protect the girls from the curious stares of omnibus passengers who peered over the walls.[109] In 1902 in Liverpool five young women broke open the locks on the doors and escaped over the walls at 10p.m.[110] The managers of institutions always tried to justify a high departure rate because it reflected personal failure:

It is recorded that five of the inmates have escaped over the wall during the year. Some, who do not know the character of the discipline in the Institution, may deem this a proof that it is so strict and severe as to drive some to this step; whereas, all who know the habits of the house are satisfied that, while there is of necessity firmness in maintaining order and decorum, yet that kindness is so blended with authority as to win confidence and love wherever the heart is capable of responding to it. It is easy to account for the cases of escape, when it is considered that most of those who seek refuge come in rags and deepest poverty, and, when they are provided with decent and comfortable clothing, there is a strong temptation to the essentially vicious to abscond with the clothes they have received. It is not surprising, therefore, that four out of the five women had robbed the institution.[111]

Sometimes annual reports recorded running away euphemistically as 'having left of their own accord' rather than be seen to have failed to keep inmates within their institution.

However, it is important not to reify institutions. Inmates' responses may have more to do with the people who ran the institution on a day-to-day basis than a reaction to the rules and regulations of the institution or because the inmates were by nature disruptive. In conventual institutions, such as at Clewer, sisters supervised the work of cooking, laundry and cleaning of the inmates but most managers of most institutions had a more remote role. These institutions may have been financed, administered and managed by the aristocracy, clerics and middle-class female philanthropists but paid, generally working-class, women were in control of the daily supervision and moral welfare of the predominantly working-class inmates. Although the committee appointed and dismissed all the paid staff, the daily routine was not in their hands but in that of the paid female employees.

Paid staff made a significant impact on the lives of the inmates for they could support or undermine the aims and objectives of the managers of the institutions. Good staff were considered essential for the smooth organisation of the institutions and the reformation of the inmates. Poor staff achieved the opposite. It was believed that those who worked in it often set the tone of an institution.[112] The selection of matrons was considered to be a matter of some consideration as it was believed that 'living with refined Christian matrons will do more to develop the stirrings of good in these girls than any amount of direct teaching'.[113] It was considered important for the person in charge to be consistently firm and authoritative but kind. 'The first duty of a Sister is to see that the rules are duly and fairly put in force, and that her assistants know what they have to do. She must always uphold their authority with the penitents.'[114] Yet

penitents should be ruled with a woman's sympathy not with a schoolmistress's rod . . . Never should any loving workers . . . indulge in taunts or sneers against those under her care, the voice should be pleasant, the gesture peaceful, the manner lady-like and not scornful.[115]

As a consequence, great care was taken in recruiting staff:

> the ideal worker is one who has been purified by sorrow and sufferings, which shall have elevated, not have crushed her; young enough in heart to sympathise with the young; old enough to let judgement, not caprice or favouritism guide her actions; patient enough to bear with the waywardness of those around her; orderly enough to keep rules herself, and firm enough to make those under her keep them also.[116]

This ideal, unfortunately, was rarely achieved. For instance, in 1865 both the laundry matron and work matron of the Liverpool Female Penitentiary were charged with theft from the institution and imprisoned. Concern was often expressed that the staff in some institutions exercised their authority in an inappropriate tyrannical manner and managers were urged 'not to imagine that the dulcet tones used to them (by the matrons and other staff) are the same as the penitents experience'.[117] Indeed inmates were thought to be rebellious because of staff intolerance and incompetence as much as natural inclination.

Unquestionably, inmates rebelled or ran away more at certain times than others, which suggests that individuals made a marked difference to the running of any institution. Far from rebelling against the imposition of a class and gender order, inmates might just have rebelled against an unjust, weak or new matron. When a new matron was appointed at St Mary's in Dartford, she faced open disrespect, disobedience, open defiance and rebellion. In this instance, the inmates refused to come into the home for evening prayer, preferring to stay out in the summer house in the garden. The further refusal of inmates to obey any request eventually led the matron to call the police to restore order and induce them all to good behaviour.[118] In 1892, Mrs Rogers' Memorial Home in Birmingham was considered disorganised, undisciplined and ill-managed because of the turnover of staff, the drunkenness of the workers and the loss of a particularly good laundry matron. Matrons also played a large part in the financial stability of the institution as laundry work suffered when supervision and discipline was lax. Under an incompetent laundry matron, standards declined and receipts diminished, leaving an already financially precarious institution even more so.

On the other hand, matrons often made a positive contribution. In Liverpool, after a few years of unrest, calm was restored by Miss McNaughten, who transformed the atmosphere in the institution: 'never before has there reigned throughout the House such a universal spirit of obedience and earnest desire for thorough reformation . . . we attribute the well-being of the House to the unwearied prayerful zeal of our excellent Matron'.[119] In Plymouth too the penitentiary was thought to be fortunate in having a thoroughly efficient matron who by her kindness and firmness, her diligence and faithfulness and her earnest Christian character was seen to be a helpful influence on the inmates.[120] Of course a competent matron made for an efficient laundry and improved finances: as a result of a particularly good matron at Mrs Rogers' Memorial Home in Birmingham, laundry receipts rose from £3 10s to £10 a head over a period of approximately ten years.[121]

Consequently, even though these institutions could be seen as 'total' institutions in that the inmates were severely curtailed at work, rest and play, there were considerable differences both between them and within them at various times. Although the management committees wrote the rules and regulations, they depended on paid staff to implement them. Where these staff were effective, the institution ran smoothly, but when the paid staff were incompetent, the aims of the institution were subverted and problems occurred. Nevertheless, despite being fairly autonomous the matron and other staff were on the payroll of the committee who created the philosophy of the institution – the staff were free only to bend the rules, not to change them.

When the inmates had proved themselves to be morally and spiritually fit, they were either restored to their friends, if respectably inclined, or placed in a situation. On leaving the institution young women were given an outfit which they had paid for out of their meagre earnings in the laundry or else would have to pay for at a later date. In 1904 the outfits cost the Bristol Penitentiary about £5. Many of these outfits were second-hand clothes donated by the committee members or other women. Second-hand clothes were preferred, not only because inmates were not thought good enough to receive new clothes, but also because others often taunted ex-inmates if they wore new clothes. New clothes were considered to be the mark of those who had been institutionalised in one form or another.

Some of the managers of reform institutions sincerely believed that they had succeeded in changing inmates into respectable hard-working and morally upright citizens who found it easy to find employment. Many declared that they enjoyed a good reputation among local employers. The literature stressed that former inmates who had been placed in service proved reliable and hard working. However, such comments originate from official sources and there was no other evidence to either refute or support these claims of success. Another factor for the popularity of employing ex-inmates may well have been the low wages that ex-inmates received. Other institutions, however, stressed the difficulty of finding situations for inmates and expressed anxiety that the choice of situation was limited because 'comparatively few people will talk to a girl from a Penitentiary'.[122] Significantly, some ex-inmates went to work in other institutions. In 1886 Pansy Ratcliffe was sent to the House of Mercy, Wakefield, then in 1889 worked in St Mary's, Rusholme, as kitchen matron and later in 1893 was said to be doing well as a sub-matron in another home.[123] Some were encouraged to emigrate to Australia and Canada, first, because it helped inmates make a fresh start, second, because there were greater job opportunities and plenty of work in the colonies and a desperate shortage of servants and third, because it removed them from English shores to be a trouble elsewhere. Life was seen to be different in the colonies and not 'so much is expected of servants; life is freer, rougher and therefore more suited to them'.[124]

Even when they had left the institution ex-inmates were supervised. To ensure they worked hard and remained morally upright, their new employers carefully monitored those who entered domestic service. Housekeepers gave each institution accounts of ex-inmates' conduct and informed them when they left. Many institutions rewarded ex-inmates with a guinea if they stayed in their positions longer than a year.[125] However, there were few guineas ever given away each year, indicating that few girls remained long in the position allocated to them. Letters published in the annual reports, gifts sent to the institution and regular visits all testified, according to official sources, to the success of reform institutions. In 1880 ex-inmates from the Liverpool Female Penitentiary saved up to buy a large clock which they donated to the institution. A religious order, the Order of Penitents, was also established. At the House of Clewer former inmates joined the Magdalen branch of the order, called Servants of the Cross, and devoted themselves to the care of sick and incurable people. Once again, these accounts emanate from official sources and must be viewed with caution, especially since there were many instances of women absconding from their position, often robbing their mistress before they left, or else proving unsatisfactory in their new situation.[126]

By the beginning of the twentieth century, many of these institutions were in decline. Fewer women applied to the various reform institutions, and the growing distaste by girls and women to enter the penitentiaries, asylums and homes was explained by a number of factors: the length of time they were expected to stay, the severe discipline, the monotonous work and the general lack of individual sympathy. Moreover, the founders and subscribers of these institutions were ageing and thus losing their enthusiasm for the reform of prostitutes.[127] In the Liverpool Female Penitentiary, for example, subscribers were dying off just as the premises needed drastic renovation such as a new roof, outside paint, drains and drain pipes. By 1921 there were only two inmates left in the Liverpool Female Penitentiary and not surprisingly it closed in 1922. More importantly, reform institutions were superseded by new initiatives as prevention rather than cure was considered to be the new way forward. Increasingly, many institutions either accepted women other than prostitutes into their establishments,[128] or changed into homes for single mothers.[129]

Unquestionably, each institution aimed to transform young working-class women into modest, respectable, hard-working and reliable domestics. Nonetheless, it is perhaps safe to say that penitentiaries, on the whole, tended to be less appealing than other institutions. The newer establishments of asylums and homes may have had little impact on the reformatory process in general but they may have had great significance to the individuals concerned. For those incarcerated in a benign institution rather than a punitive one, it might have made a whole world of difference; tantalisingly we can never know more because most of those voices have either been lost or been refracted through the middle-class lens.[130] Consequently, the reasons why certain institutions were perceived as more congenial than others remain hidden.

Notes

1 Linda Mahood, *The Magdalenes* (London: Routledge, 1990), p. 78.
2 *Seeking and Saving* (1867–1872), p. 231.
3 Ibid., p. 231.
4 *St Mary's Home of Refuge and Penitentiary Annual Report* 1882, p. 5.
5 Martha Vicinus (ed.), *Independent Women* (London: Virago, 1985), p. 78.
6 Revd Lee, *Birmingham Daily Gazette* (March 14th 1876).
7 *Liverpool Magdalen Institution Annual Report* 1906.
8 *NUWW Conference* 1890, p. 137.
9 *Seeking and Saving* (July 1881), p. 52.
10 *Seeking and Saving* (January 1882), p. 9.
11 *Seeking and Saving* (June 1882), p. 125.
12 At the oldest penitentiary, the Magdalen Hospital at Streatham, inmates could earn up to ten marks a day for hard work but this was liable to deduction for misconduct (*Seeking and Saving*, February 1882, p. 26).
13 *Liverpool Female Penitentiary Annual Report* 1898.
14 Rider Haggard, *Regeneration* (London: Longmans, Green, 1910), p. 88.
15 *NUWW Handbook and Report* 1912, p. 146.
16 Linda Mahood, *The Magdalenes*.
17 *The Magdalen's Friend* (1861–1862), p. 146.
18 James Hooper, *Norwich Charities: Short Sketches of their Origin and History* (Norwich: Norfolk News, 1898), p. 201.
19 *The Vigilance Record* (March 15th 1889), p. 46.
20 Memo, London Lock Hospital in Miscellaneous Papers.
21 Revd C. Goldney, chaplain of H M Prison, Stafford, in a letter to the secretary of the Reformatory and Refuge Union, June 1894, in Arthur J. Maddison, *Hints on Rescue Work* (London: Reformatory and Refuge Union, c. 1888).
22 *The Magdalen's Friend* (1861–1862), p. 108.
23 John Burnett, *Plenty and Want* (London: Methuen, 1966), p. 193.
24 M.A. Crowther, *The Workhouse System, 1834–1929* (London: Methuen, 1981), p. 217.
25 Ibid., p. 217.
26 *Penitentiary Work in the Church of England, Papers for Discussion at the Anniversary Meeting of the Church Penitentiary Association, 1873* (London: Harrison and Sons, 1873), p. 18.
27 Arthur J. Maddison, *Hints on Rescue Work*, p. 217.
28 H.F.B. Compston, *The Magdalen Hospital* (London: Society for Promoting Christian Knowledge, 1917).
29 Ellice Hopkins, *Notes on Penitentiary Work* (London: Hatchards, 1879), p. 27.
30 *Lady Inspectors' Factories and Workshops Annual Report* 1905, p. 261, in *Annual Report of Chief Inspector of Factories and Workshops* 1905.
31 *Leeds Guardian Society Annual Report* 1862, p. 9; *Leeds Guardian Society Annual Report* 1864, p. 9.

32 Correspondence of London Female Preventive and Reformatory Institution 1907–1914.
33 Ellice Hopkins, *Notes on Penitentiary Work*, p. 15.
34 H.F.B. Compston, *The Magdalen Hospital*, p. 180.
35 Arthur J. Maddison, *Hints on Rescue Work*, p. 120; *The Magdalen's Friend* (1861), p. 267.
36 Ellice Hopkins, *Notes on Penitentiary Work*, p. 20.
37 *Annual Report of Chief Inspector of Factories and Workshops* 1907, pp. 203–204.
38 Valerie Bonham, *A Place in Life* (Windsor: privately published, 1992), p. 205.
39 Correspondence and Papers of Miss Stride 1872–1880 (Metropolitan Records Office).
40 *Birmingham Daily Gazette* (March 12th 1878).
41 *Birmingham Magdalen Asylum Annual Report* 1878.
42 *Lady Inspectors' Factories and Workshops Annual Report* 1905, p. 259.
43 Ibid., p. 259.
44 The subtle irony that many of the asylum's inmates were former domestic servants escaped the asylum committee. Of course it is not known whether the majority of prostitutes were former domestic servants. Domestic servants tended to predominate in rescue and reform institutions.
45 Linda Mahood, *The Magdalenes*, p. 163.
46 Frank Prochaska, *Women and Philanthropy in Nineteenth Century England* (Oxford: Clarendon Press, 1980), p. 148.
47 Census of England and Wales 1881.
48 Even the Charity Organisation Society (COS) was concerned that laundry work might lower the wages of traditional laundry workers because the labour of those in charitable institutions was so cheap (Letter from COS to National Society for the Protection of Young Girls, February 2nd 1893).
49 Edward Bristow, *Vice and Vigilance* (Dublin: Gill and Macmillan, 1978), p. 71; Linda Mahood, *The Magdalenes*, p. 91; and Judith Walkowitz, *Prostitution and Victorian Society* (Cambridge: Cambridge University Press, 1980), p. 71, have all demonstrated the links between penance and laundry work.
50 See Mary Douglas, *Purity and Danger* (London: Routledge and Kegan Paul, 1976) for a discussion of the relationship between cleanliness and religion.
51 Until the Factory Act 1895, laundresses in public laundries sometimes worked ninety hours a week: asylums, homes and other charitable institutions were free from legal restraints until 1907.
52 Note found in Minutes of the Gentlemen's Committee, Liverpool Female Penitentiary, July 1897.
53 *Lady Inspectors' Factories and Workshops Annual Report* 1908, p. 149, in *Annual Report of Chief Inspector of Factories and Workshops* 1908.
54 *Lady Inspectors' Factories and Workshops Annual Report* 1907, p. 153, in *Annual Report of Chief Inspector of Factories and Workshops* 1907.
55 *NUWW Quarterly Magazine* (December 1890).
56 This view was corroborated by the warden of the Magdalen Hospital who wrote to Asquith arguing that factory regulations were inappropriate for reform institutions. She claimed 'that the Holiday Clauses of the Factory Acts are quite inapplicable to the discipline of a Home. It would not be practicable for the women or children in Homes to claim particular days or particular hours as holidays.'
57 *Annual Report of Chief Inspector of Factories and Workshops* 1907, p. 204.
58 Patricia Malcolmson, *English Laundresses* (Chicago: University of Illinois Press, 1986), pp. 93–94.
59 *The Laundry Maid* (September 30th 1893), p. 146.
60 *Lady Inspectors' Factories and Workshops Annual Report* 1907, p. 204.

61 Ibid., p. 203.
62 *Bristol Female Penitentiary Annual Report* 1901.
63 *Seeking and Saving* (January 1882), p. 5.
64 *Birmingham Magdalen Asylum Annual Report* 1898.
65 For instance, in one Aldershot home the inmates did needlework rather than laundry.
66 *The Magdalen's Friend* (1861), p. 153.
67 Robert Storch, 'The Problem of Working-Class Leisure: Some Roots of Middle-Class Moral Reform in the Industrial North, 1825–1850', in A.P. Donajgrodzki (ed.) *Social Control in Nineteenth Century Britain* (London: Croom Helm, 1977).
68 Not all agreed. One particular vicar believed that strong exercise stirred up the passions, arguing too that the institution was a penitentiary and the object was to bring them to penitence (*Seeking and Saving*, April 1888, p. 301).
69 Some reformers believed that recreation came under three headings: educative, useful and purely recreative. Educative included religious worship; useful was recreation which involved the making of children's clothes; and leisure which was rest and entertainment: Arthur J. Maddison, *Hints on Rescue Work*, p. 159.
70 *Liverpool Female Penitentiary Annual Report* 1894, p. 6.
71 *Birmingham Magdalen Asylum Annual Report* 1887.
72 Martha Vicinus (ed.), *Independent Women*.
73 *Birmingham Magdalen Asylum Annual Report* 1870.
74 *Bristol Female Penitentiary Annual Report* 1879.
75 Harriet Nokes, *Twenty-Three Years in a House of Mercy* (London: Swan, Sonnen-schein, 1888), p. 16.
76 *Seeking and Saving* (May 1882), p. 102.
77 Even within religious practice, a religious hierarchy was established. Not all inmates were considered responsible enough to become communicants or to attend church. Admission to the sacraments was regarded as a privilege and so inmates were carefully selected for confirmation in the church. Only those who were considered sufficiently penitent, whose demeanour was 'holy' (which probably meant subservient), who recognised the religious importance of worship, who understood the church services and who had fully imbibed the cultural, religious and gendered mores were accepted as communicants.
78 James Hooper, *Norwich Charities*, p. 201.
79 Ellice Hopkins, *Notes on Penitentiary Work*, p. 24.
80 *St Mary's Home of Refuge and Penitentiary, Manchester, Annual Report* 1896, p. 7.
81 Birmingham inmates visited nearby places such as Sutton Park, the Botanical Gardens and the Lickey Hills during the summer months. Once a year inmates of the Plymouth Penitentiary were taken to Bere Ferrers and in Bristol they were taken to the seaside.
82 *Lady Inspectors' Factories and Workshops Annual Report* 1908, p. 149.
83 The number of prostitutes was said to have diminished from 29,956 in 1862 to 25,627 prostitutes in 1868 as a result of the intervention of reformers (*Minutes of Evidence taken before the Select Committee on Contagious Diseases Acts, 1882*, p. 148). There were no official figures since 1869 but it was believed that prostitution had continued to decline.
84 *Minutes of Evidence taken before the Select Committee on Contagious Diseases Acts, 1882*, p. 150.
85 The Rescue Society claimed a 70 per cent success rate but even its own committee challenged this result because the statistics included those who had been 'returned to friends' among the 9,205 women deemed to have been reformed: H.F.B. Compston, *The Magdalen Hospital*, p. 224.
86 *Seeking and Saving* (1867–1872), p. 231.
87 *Birmingham Daily Gazette* (March 17th 1863), p. 8.

88 *Birmingham Daily Gazette* (March 11th 1883), p. 8.
89 *Birmingham Daily Gazette* (March 10th 1874), p. 6.
90 *Birmingham Daily Gazette* (April 13th 1886), p. 3.
91 *Liverpool Female Penitentiary Annual Report* 1869, p. 6.
92 *Birmingham Daily Gazette* (March 29th 1890), p. 3.
93 *Birmingham Daily Gazette* (May 29th 1891), p. 6.
94 *Liverpool Female Penitentiary Annual Report* 1888.
95 *Bristol Female Penitentiary Annual Report* 1875.
96 *Liverpool Female Penitentiary Annual Report* 1887.
97 Letter from the COS to Elizabeth Blackwell (April 1886) concerning the London Lock Hospital.
98 Harriet Nokes, *Twenty-Three Years in a House of Mercy*, p. 11.
99 The Bristol Penitentiary complained that 'Evil temper, especially, is a source of great difficulty. Passion and jealousy seem often excited by the very slightest cause, and self-will, long unchecked, has in many cases become so thoroughly the ruling principle that self-restraint can only be taught by very slow degrees' (*Bristol Penitentiary Annual Report* 1884, p. 6).
100 Case Books, Southwell House, Nottingham.
101 Letter from Elizabeth Blackwell to COS (April 1886).
102 *St James' Home Annual Report* 1858, p. 4.
103 *Bristol Female Penitentiary Annual Report* 1879, p. 9.
104 *Lady Inspectors' Factories and Workshops Annual Report* 1905, p. 259.
105 Some Account of the House of Mercy for Penitent Women at Bussage, in Two Letters by the Lord Bishop of Graham's Town and by the Revd T. Keble, Gloucester, 1865, p. 14.
106 *Bristol Female Penitentiary Annual Report* 1879.
107 Harriet Nokes, *Twenty-Three Years in a House of Mercy*, p. 26.
108 *Manchester and Salford Asylum Annual Report* 1866, p. 7. See also Frances Finnegan, *Poverty and Prostitution* (Cambridge: Cambridge University Press, 1979).
109 *Manchester and Salford Asylum Annual Report* 1876, p. 7.
110 In this case, the police were told of the escape and searched for the inmates during the day. The head matron went looking for them on three consecutive nights and found two of them in the 'worst lodging house' in the city (*Liverpool Female Penitentiary Annual Report* 1902).
111 *Manchester and Salford Asylum Annual Report* 1889, p. 7.
112 Arthur J. Maddison, *Hints on Rescue Work*, p. 67.
113 *Leeds Guardian Society Annual Report* 1862, p. 3.
114 *Seeking and Saving* (February 1882), p. 30.
115 *Seeking and Saving* (March 1882), p. 57.
116 Harriet Nokes, *Twenty-Three Years in a House of Mercy*, p. 65.
117 *Seeking and Saving* (February 1882), p. 30.
118 Harriet Nokes, *Twenty-Three Years in a House of Mercy*, pp. 9–10.
119 *Liverpool Female Penitentiary Annual Report* 1869.
120 *Plymouth, Devonport and Stonehouse Female Penitentiary and Home Annual Report* 1908, p. 10.
121 *Birmingham Ladies' Association for the Care of Friendless Girls Annual Reports* 1895–1911.
122 *Worcester Diocesan Annual Report* 1885, p. 6.
123 Case Books, Southwell House, Nottingham 1885–1914.
124 Harriet Nokes, *Twenty-Three Years in a House of Mercy*, p. 54.
125 For example, Liverpool Penitentiary gave a guinea to all those who remained in their position for over a year.
126 In 1888 two Birmingham young women absconded under very discreditable

circumstances, one left after three days while the other robbed her mistress before leaving (*Birmingham Magdalen Asylum Annual Report* 1888). In Liverpool one ex-inmate was suspected of stealing the money box containing donations and weekly contributions by breaking in through a window (*Liverpool Rescue Society and House of Help Annual Report* 1896).

127 *Liverpool Rescue Society and House of Help Annual Report* 1896.
128 In Leeds the penitentiary trained young girls committed by the magistrates under the Industrial Schools Act (*Leeds Guardian Society Annual Report* 1866, p. 9).
129 In Birmingham, two reform institutions combined in 1920 to become the Association for the Care and Training of Unmarried Mothers and their babies.
130 See Wilkie Collins' novel, *The New Magdalen* (1873), for an account of an ex-prostitute who remained grateful for her time in a reform institution.

Part II

Prevention is better than cure
Ladies' Associations for the Care of Friendless Girls

3 Moral education and protective legislation

When it became evident that the reform movement had failed to eliminate prostitution, a number of philanthropists attempted to stop the problem at source.[1] In the inimitable words of Ellice Hopkins, a fence at the top of the cliff was perceived to be more effective than an ambulance at the bottom.[2] Preventive work[3] was thought to comprise 'the various means of saving the girls most likely to lose their purity, before it is too late and they have gone over the precipice'.[4] Ladies' Associations for the Care of Friendless Girls, it was believed, made an important contribution to preventive work: by 1885 there were 106 Ladies' Organisations set up in most of the major towns of England,[5] with the Church of England journal, *Seeking and Saving*, used to promote its work. This part of the book demonstrates the complexities within preventive work by examining how Ellice Hopkins' ideas were put into practice in various towns and cities across England and will argue that the motivations of those involved in the Ladies' Associations were a complex mixture of class prejudice and gender solidarity. Chapter 3 examines the educational and legal work of the Ladies' Associations and Chapter 4 focuses on the ways in which they cared for (and controlled) 'wayward and troublesome girls'.

All over England, Ladies' Associations for the Care of Friendless Girls were founded to prevent prostitution and to promote chastity and purity.[6] The fact that there were a number of other organisations set up in England with similar aims raises questions about the duplication of women's charitable work in general and of preventive organisations in particular. Side by side, the Metropolitan Association for the Befriending of Young Servants (MABYS), the Girls' Guild of Good Life and the Girls' Friendly Society (GFS) attempted to promote social purity by focusing on respectable working-class young women. By the 1890s MABYS was established in almost all the London Poor Law Unions,[7] the Girls' Guild was operative in the East End of London,[8] while the GFS enjoyed a strong network of support in the provinces.[9] Each of these organisations concentrated on providing a 'friendly face' to young women moving away from home to take up positions in domestic service, helped them to find jobs in respectable households and organised lodgings when they were between situations. The

Ladies' Associations can therefore be considered as part of a nation-wide middle-class women's movement which aimed to influence young working-class women. But although the Ladies' Associations grew out of the work of MABYS,[10] they were founded specifically to confront the alleged inadequacy of the reform movement in curbing prostitution. It was feared that England was fast becoming a country in which young children were forced into prostitution because they lacked the necessary skills for domestic service and were without any form of moral training.[11] As the Paddington and Marylebone Ladies' Association's prospectus stated:

> Penitentiaries and Refuges do not touch the causes of the evil; they only endeavour to save its victims. But associations like this direct their utmost force towards grappling with the first causes of the present miserable state of things; they would bring succour, not after, but before shipwreck; they would snatch back child-victims, straying with unconscious feet upon the very brink of destruction. The terrible fact that not girls only, but children – little children – are taken, or driven forth into the streets at night, to earn the wages of sin.[12]

Similarly, the Leeds Ladies' Association was equally explicit, if less linguistically emotive, and wished to 'help young girls to gain an honest livelihood and lead virtuous lives, who from poverty, neglect or evil example, are peculiarly liable to be led astray'.[13]

In England prevention and women's rights were, if not inextricably linked, then certainly intimately connected.[14] In contrast to the reform movement, Ladies' Associations were all-female with women playing leadership roles as presidents, vice-presidents and committee members. The leaders of Ladies' Associations belonged to networks which allowed them to carve out a role for themselves within a context that was essentially female centred.[15] There is certainly strong evidence to suggest the existence of a cohesive women's group within cities like Birmingham: most of the committee of this particular Ladies' Association lived within the same local area, met socially and participated in a variety of women's charities. Female networking may well have underpinned the structures of Ladies' Associations and helped to formalise and develop this charitable work more generally. In addition, a female identity, if not feminism, provided the justification, momentum and support for women who wished to participate in preventive politics. Many women, in the same way as Philippa Levine has demonstrated for women elsewhere,[16] saw feminism as central to their lives. Those who belonged to the Birmingham Ladies' Association supported equal rights feminism to the extent that they at least subscribed to the suffrage movement. Indeed, some were prominent members.[17] Many supported and even campaigned for the repeal of the Contagious Diseases Acts even though the Acts did not operate in their own town or city.[18]

Furthermore, Ladies' Associations, although led by the Evangelical Anglican, Ellice Hopkins, embraced women of every shade of Christian belief who wished to help girls and young women perceived to be in moral danger. As with those involved in reform work, they were perhaps influenced by incarnational theology and by Christ's Sermon on the Mount. At the same time they may have viewed Christ as a great revolutionary concerned with the redemption of the temporal as well as of the spiritual world,[19] thus making it a Christian imperative to improve the lives of the poor. As the Ladies' Association in Nottingham stated, 'Never forget the MASTER'S declaration, "I came *not* to call the righteous, but sinners to repentance"'.[20] Men were to clean up the country by tackling the pressing problems of physical disease and squalor through a combination of philanthropy and legal reform whereas women maintained responsibility for curing moral pollution. The members of Ladies' Associations were thus motivated by a strong Christian impulse which, influenced by Christ's forgiveness and sympathetic treatment of Mary Magdalen, in turn gave religious respectability to women working with those vulnerable to prostitution.[21]

The beliefs held by the various committees of the Ladies' Associations encouraged them to try to unite middle-class and working-class women in a Christian campaign against prostitution. Even so, notions of female solidarity were located within a well-regulated class context: the woman-centred approach of Ladies' Associations was framed within a window of power and authority. After all, it was middle-class women who founded Ladies' Associations and working-class women who were rescued. The naming of the association 'Ladies' and those who were rescued 'girls' was more than a linguistic device, for it simultaneously mirrored a class and age prejudice. Most, if not all, of the women who managed Ladies' Associations belonged to upper- and middle-class families.[22] Of course, the fact that their husbands or fathers were upper or middle class was important in the process of moral reform, for these men were prosperous enough to enable their wives and daughters to have sufficient time to engage in charitable enterprises. Such women were not restricted by the economic restraints faced by working-class women and indeed many lower-middle-class women: they did not have to seek waged work. Certainly, lower-middle-class women were seen unable 'through their daily avocations to attend the monthly daily meeting',[23] and were enrolled under a slightly different name as associates rather than as full members. The Ladies' Associations depended upon the unpaid work of middle-class women, because, unlike their working-class contemporaries, they had time as well as money. A band of servants, nannies and governesses, often paid for by husbands and fathers, freed these middle-class women from domestic responsibilities at home. Moreover, charitable work was done at the whim of the women, and perhaps with the blessing of the husband or father, but could equally be dropped without any economic impact on the immediate family. Furthermore, charitable work was seen in, if not paternalistic ways, then certainly in 'maternalistic' ones bearing a similar mixture of humanitarianism and class domination. It was a one-way power relationship whereby middle-class women exerted their own definition of what was considered to be correct forms of behaviour and attempted to appropriate the moral selves of the less respectable of the working class. Female unity was therefore illusory as middle- and working-class women shared little in common.

Nevertheless, the relationship was a complex one, and sometimes based on class guilt as much as class control or perceived female unity. A writer in *Seeking and Saving* once asked working-class women for forgiveness for the immoral conduct of men of the middle and upper classes.

> We really must remember that we have not succeeded so admirably with our sons that we can afford to sit in judgement on them in the far more difficult conditions of their life. The mere fact that in that almost purely upper class Assembly, the House of Commons, while the Criminal Law Amendment Bill was passing, there was banded about in the Lobby a coarse, jocular, slang nickname for the men who degrade children.[24]

The Ladies' Associations may have enjoyed a corporate identity but each local group adapted the essentials of Ellice Hopkins' proposals to suit their own local conditions or perhaps the interests of their organisers. Ideally, these associations were divided into four sections: a Moral Educational Branch, a petitioning branch, a preventive branch and the Workhouse Magdalen Branch.[25] However, the ways in which these associations were organised differed across England; some, like Norwich and Rochester, concentrated on the practical aspects of preventive work and ignored the educational and petitioning side, whereas others, like Leeds, embraced Ellice Hopkins' philosophy wholeheartedly.

Moral Educational Branch

As the ideological wing of the Ladies' Associations, the Moral Educational Branch saw itself as preventing prostitution through an educational programme which would attack the cause of immorality at a fundamental level. More and more, the root of all evil was seen to be the absence of good moral teaching.[26] At times, Ladies' Associations appeared to be a progressive force as, like other women-only organisations such as Josephine Butler's Ladies' National Association, it rejected the double standard of morality in favour of a single standard for both sexes and aimed to promote stringent standards for each in order to eradicate immorality.

Superficially, perhaps, this provides an example of how feminist politics defied and undermined moral orthodoxy. Moral reform could be viewed as empowering women because it gave them control over vital areas of human behaviour but it was a false empowerment since the challenge to the double standard was still set within the parameters of orthodox gender assumptions. What is more, although both men and women were expected to adopt high moral standards, it was still women who were expected to make them work. Impure thoughts, words and deeds were considered equally reprehensible in men and women but the responsibility for ensuring chastity lay with the latter. This may have been because middle-class women perceived working-class young women, especially those who were employed by them as domestic servants, as a sexual threat to their own households. If so, preventive work neutralised this threat by making young women responsible for immoral conduct. In the process, Ladies' Associations subscribed to a moral code which demanded more of women than men because they expected women to regulate behaviour. Chastity and purity depended on young women rather than their male partners: it was up to the young women to refuse sexual overtures rather than the responsibility of the male to practise restraint. Moreover, as women were given responsibility for high moral standards they were held accountable if those standards dropped. Thus the abandonment of the sexual double standard by Ladies' Associations did not liberate women but merely changed the nature of their sexual oppression.

Moreover, its decision to emphasise women's domestic role reaffirmed traditional ideas about female sexuality, attitudes and behaviour. It was assumed that the majority of women would be, and would wish to be, wives and mothers. Women, as the primary carers of children, supervised the intellectual, emotional, spiritual and most importantly moral education of the young. As women were perceived to be the moral guardians of the nation it was thought essential that their help be secured in promoting sexual responsibility. As a result, the Moral Educational Branch of the Ladies' Association founded quite distinct all-women organisations: the Mothers' Union and the Woman's League for married women, Snowdrop Bands and other societies for young single women to promote these ideas.

The Mothers' Union and the Woman's League

Both the Mothers' Union and the Woman's League targeted older women.[27] One of the earliest Mothers' Unions was founded by Elizabeth Twining in the mid-nineteenth century but they were later expanded by Ellen Ranyard and Mary Sumner. By 1920 membership of the Mothers' Union rose to over 400,000.[28] The Woman's League was started in London on July 7th 1888 by 120 female representative women workers and was supported by a number of bishops.[29] Although both organisations were supposed to be managed by the Church of England they, like Ladies' Associations overall, welcomed Nonconformists and other religious persuasions. Each union and league was, like each Ladies' Association, independently organised but all believed the way 'towards stemming the tide of crime and vice, of cruelty and misery was by training the children under their charge in habits of obedience and self control from earliest infancy'.[30]

Frank Prochaska argues that the Mothers' Union[31] was part of a maternal culture in which middle-class women with a strong parochial duty attempted to break down class barriers.[32] Certainly, middle-class women were convinced that their concerns converged with those of the working class: Ellice Hopkins insisted that the upper-middle class should avoid 'the irresistible tendency to preach to the poor, that seems to me to have well nigh destroyed all sweet human relationships between us'.[33] In theory, the Mothers' Union wished to include women from all social classes in their sphere of influence:

> Such a Union if conducted on the highest lines, may do much to help Mothers of all classes to recognise more fully their God-given respon-sibility, and to give intelligent care to the training of their families. This is no class matter, and a Mothers' Union will fail of its full measure of usefulness, unless it embraces Mothers of every social grade in a common bond of work, and of prayer.[34]

Mothers' Union members were constantly exhorted to widen their social network for if not 'you are creating divisions and destroying the sisterhood that it is the aim of the Union to encourage. We Members of the Mothers' Union cross out the word patronage from our dictionaries.'[35] Similarly, the Woman's League wanted to bring women of every class into mutual co-operation and to make mothers of every class aware of the sense of their great responsibility as 'divinely appointed guardians of their children's purity'.[36]

In practice, the unity envisaged between women of different classes was illusory. There were different types of members in the Mothers' Union: the presiding member in overall charge; enrolling members, who controlled the local branches; subscribing members, who paid subscriptions; and ordinary members, who were educated by the others. Different kinds of meetings were arranged for the social groups since it was believed impossible to talk to both classes at the same time. 'As a rule, and rightly so, the speaker generally addresses the mother who is a nurse, and avoids addressing the mother who keeps a nurse.'[37] In some places, distinctly different groups were founded for the middle and working class. 'Drawing Room' meetings were arranged for the middle and upper classes. Working-class women did not have 'drawing rooms' – it was a middle-class expression and a middle-class place – so both the terminology and the venue suggest that working-class women were excluded.[38] In contrast, 'ordinary Mothers' Meetings' were founded for the working class and held in working-class districts, often in 'difficult' neighbourhoods – 'the mothers' meeting held once a week in a street where the police almost fear to go'[39] – which suggests that the less 'respectable' of the working class were singled out as an object of attention.[40]

Perhaps not surprisingly, the talks given and topics discussed at meetings, consistent with the formality of meetings more generally at this time, were co-ordinated by the middle-class managers, not by the working-class women who attended. Underlying middle-class women's direction of meetings was an assumption that working-class women were incapable of organising their own groups.[41] Middle-class women attempted, in language that was often patronising,[42] to impose their own economic, sexual and moral agenda on the working class. At the 'ordinary Mothers' Meetings', dressmaking was thought to encourage self-help,[43] while baby classes taught proper child-care. Thrift and economy were established as positive virtues to be inculcated at every opportunity because it was thought 'most astonishing how the poor get into debt and run up bills and pay more for what they buy than it is worth through ignorance'.[44]

The Ladies' Associations adhered to the principles of chastity and moderation rather than sexual autonomy, so there was an emphasis on a rather conformist sexual theory and practice. At no time did Ladies' Associations offer a critique of marriage and the family. Feminists were questioning the nature of marriage at this time: Elizabeth Wolstenholme Elmy, for example, argued that marriage was legalised prostitution but the Ladies' Associations were unsympathetic to these ideas.[45] The Woman's League exhorted middle-class women to influence the women and girls with whom they came into contact by maintaining the Christian law of purity, the sanctity of the marriage vows and to 'discountenance unsuitable amusements and immodest fashions, literature and conversation'.[46] At all times, it was stressed, moral values should be emphasised 'in very clear language, going fully into the great need there is for a higher, purer standard of morality in the towns and villages; the terrible sin and misery entailed by its absence; the causes of the evil; and the means of remedying it'.[47]

Subjects covered in the Mothers' Union centred on social purity; talks on 'How best to train and guard our sons and daughters in the paths of purity', 'Moral Training of Children' and 'How best to protect our daughters' formed the basis of meetings.[48] On every appropriate occasion working-class mothers were encouraged to bring up their children in modesty and purity. Each mother who joined signed a pledge which, judging by the rules below, seemed targeted at working-class rather than middle-class women:

1   To pray for the children once every day
2   Never to allow coarse jests, bad words, or low talk before the children
3   Never to send the girls to public houses or to work at houses of bad character
4   To keep the boys and girls apart at night
5   To try and get the children early to bed, and not to allow our girls to keep late hours in the street
6   Never to speak of sin as a misfortune
7   To try and train the children to be truthful, honest, obedient and pure.[49]

Of course, the consequence of equating home with morality, and home with women, meant that women were inextricably linked to the moral code. There was an implicit acceptance that moral values were embedded in the private sphere of the family. The word 'parents' slipped imperceptibly into a new meaning: women. Women, viewed as the formative influence on young children, were held responsible for inculcating morality.[50] It was the responsibility of mothers to ensure that their children were taught to withstand the 'contaminating and immoral influences' under which so many of them were thrown.[51] Consequently, women bore a disproportionate share of the blame when they failed to impress the appropriate values on to their children.[52] Even the hiring and firing of suitable domestic staff was seen to be women's responsibility, not men's: 'They must see to it that the nurse to whom they entrust their children is not only of sound moral character, but also of a pure and healthy mind . . . She was astonished to find how often children were committed to the care of girls who were most unfit to have charge of them.'[53]

Snowdrop Bands and Evening Clubs

At the younger end of the age spectrum, Snowdrop Bands, begun in Sheffield, were created for working-class young women over the age of 11.[54] There is no evidence that Snowdrop Bands ever targeted middle-class young girls, presumably because they were considered to be less likely to 'fall' from moral grace. These Bands, just like the Mothers' Union, aimed to promote honesty, chastity, civility and to uphold the moral principles favoured by the middle class and by many of the upper classes (and indeed a significant percentage of the working class). Heavy symbolic meaning was attached to the snowdrop, which became an emblem of purity and chastity. Snowdrops were displayed in abundance at all Band meetings and drawn on every leaflet and journal. The Bands had their own journal *The Snowdrop*, which contained innumerable stories of young women who successfully resisted sexual temptation, as well as articles advising members to report any indecent literature and pictures to the Chief Constable of their district. Potting nights, where young girl members planted their own snowdrop bulbs, were also organised.[55] Most Bands held 'brown' (where members potted snowdrop bulbs) and 'white' suppers (when the snowdrops were fully grown) to celebrate these events. For example, in Burnley one 'white' supper consisted of pale-coloured food: stewed apples with custard, lemon and pineapple jellies and a large white iced cake as a culinary metaphor of purity.[56] Each young woman was issued with a membership card on which a picture of a snowdrop was drawn as an artistic representation of chastity and on the back of which was printed a promise that reflected the sexual politics of the Snowdrop leaders:

> We the Members of the Snowdrop Band, sign our names to show that we have agreed that wherever we are, and in whatever company, we will, with God's help, earnestly try, both by our **example** and **influence** to discourage all wrong conversation, light and immodest conduct, and the reading of foolish and bad books.[57]

Beneath the pledge, which encapsulated the aims of the Snowdrop Band, was a space for the owner's signature as a symbol of personal acceptance. The signed membership card acted as an official reminder to its owner of the obligations attached to membership. Nevertheless, these events did not always go according to plan – a celebration promoted by the Nottingham Snowdrop Band to plant bulbs could not take place because no one had thought to bring any.[58]

Women philanthropists throughout England believed that young working-class women benefited from contact with the middle class because the latter would serve as models of moral conduct. Certainly, Ladies' Associations wanted working-class young women to internalise the social mores of the middle class:

> Our aim is to raise the whole standard of life of our working girls, especially with regard to purity of thought and conversation, while they are still young enough to be led and helped. We want to give them some nobler, gentler idea of conduct and character, and to awaken in them some clear perception of what God meant a woman's life and influence to be. We want to get them to make a brave stand against the kind of conversation so freely carried on in many kitchens, work rooms, etc. and against the low tone of mind, and contentment with unclean surroundings, too prevalent amongst them.[59]

Such advice and education – if it ever worked – may have created tensions within the working-class community as the acceptance of middle-class standards of morality could have engendered conflict with colleagues at work and family at home, even though many of the working class may have subscribed to these values.[60] As a consequence of conforming to the Snowdrop Band's pledge, one section of the working class would be set against another. If class loyalties did emerge at work they may have been swiftly undermined by competing moralities. Snowdrop Band young women were supposed to show their distaste when colleagues talked in 'unseemly' ways or tried to engage them in 'impure' conversation. It is curious to note that Ladies' Associations perceived married women, not just men, capable of deliberately corrupting the minds of single girls.[61] Working-class married women may have viewed this differently. On the contrary, married women's so-called loose talk might have served an educative function, inducting young women into sexual matters which they might have been reluctant to discuss with their mothers. Not surprisingly, Snowdrop members were exhorted to be pure in their relationship with the male sex and 'never allow him to be free or demonstrative with you. He will respect you all the more if a little quiet dignity and reserve are in your manner.'[62]

At the same time, other types of clubs, generally opened weekdays between 7:15 and 9:15p.m., were founded as a further weapon against the immorality which allegedly pervaded the working class. Once again, 'educated' (i.e. middle-class) women organised Evening Homes for the 'uneducated' (i.e. working-class) young women, to prevent them wandering the streets or visiting the pub.[63] 'It was felt that in Brampton there were many girls who were allowed to run wild in the street at night, and who, through no fault of their own, were placed in a position of great danger.'[64] The Ladies' Associations wanted to divert the youthful energies of working-class young women into safe channels and provide them with 'innocent' amusements and to persuade them to live 'better, purer lives'.[65] Leisure was therefore organised so that the educated could instil their own moral code onto the working class, persuading the latter to drop their 'coarse and rude' ways.[66] The rules of some of the clubs – 'no girl to loiter in the street on the way home or to be insubordinate or insolent; to come to the club with clean hands and not to eat sweets in the room'[67] – provide additional confirmation of the Ladies' Associations' mission to reinforce gentility and to modify the behaviour of their perceived social inferiors.

Not surprisingly, most clubs offered similar types of amusement which had the added advantage of preparing young women for their future lives as wives and mothers. Needlework, where members bought materials at cost price to make their own clothing, proved to be common. In Nottingham young women were taught rug making, toy making and crewel work; one London club offered wood carving, brass repoussé work, leather work and fancy basket making as well. At others, such as Pendleton, girls were taught how to cook and how to nurse the sick. However, not all leisure activities were so obviously utilitarian, possibly because few working-class young women would continue to follow such a narrow programme. The Nottingham branch offered pasting and painting scrap books, bagatelle and even Ping-Pong.[68] Many clubs had pianos, enabling the organisers to offer singing 'giving them something to sing at their work in place of street songs';[69] most popular of all was musical drill. The Norwich Ladies' Association Club even had its own musical Band.[70] Games were played but these tended to be the quieter sort. 'We used to allow romps such as "Blindman's Bluff", but we found it cost too much in furniture repairs and now we content ourselves with "Lotto", "Snap", "Dominoes", "Family Coach" and "Post".'[71] In Ancoats therefore younger girls were introduced to the 'quiet table games' of dominoes and table draughts and older ones provided with reading rooms and other tranquil areas.

According to the annual reports the majority of working-class girls seemed to take pleasure in this type of recreation. Indeed, the success of the Salford Club was considered to be due primarily to the indefatigable energy of a committee of six of the oldest girls who ran it.[72] Even so, clubs sometimes found it difficult to keep their members amused. Neither were young girls as obedient as the organisers desired. On one occasion in Bradford four club members climbed onto the roof and refused to get down, 'causing much nuisance and complaints from the neighbours';[73] in Folkestone, girls were so rude to the ladies and so quarrelsome among themselves that it was difficult to play any of the games provided for them; and in Nottingham police officers were called to evict riotous girls from the club.[74]

Petitioning branch: legal attempts to prevent prostitution

The second branch of the Ladies' Associations, known as the petitioning branch, pressurised Parliament to take a stronger interventionist stand against prostitution. Its decision to work with the same state that denied women the vote symbolised the determination of Ladies' Associations to sustain the pace of sexual moral reform at the expense of other rights. As Frank Mort points out, this signalled 'an important shift away from the traditional strategies of private philanthropy and rescue work' to utilising the state to champion sexual morality.[75] The Ladies' Associations of the late nineteenth century operated at what is sometimes perceived as a transitional moment in British politics when liberal individualism was being replaced by a more collectivist culture.[76] It viewed the criminal law as an agency of protection and saw the state as an agency of change in that governments could – as in the Poor Law of 1834 – legislate to alter the moral behaviour of its citizens.[77] The Ladies' Associations, in common with other organisations, demanded that young girls be given sexual protection against those who wished to seduce them. In so doing, it gave police greater powers of arrest over its young female citizens as well as those who mistreated them. Class power, in some respects, appeared to predominate over gender identity. However, as Frank Mort argues, the state was very much an unwilling partner in the move towards sexual regulation. The Liberal Party for instance generally believed that the state posed a danger to the freedom of individuals and was reluctant to interfere, not only in economic affairs, but also in matters of personal morality. The Ladies' Associations, along with others, therefore pushed a hesitant government to enact laws to regulate the sexuality of its citizens.

The Ladies' Associations were undoubtedly committed to challenging the legal status quo by making the law safeguard young women. Women were thought to suffer from a chain of legislative inequality in relation to sexuality. Laws, it was believed, encouraged prostitution but did not protect the prostitute. The English legal system was thought to support prostitution by the way in which it differentiated between the women, the customer and the market-place. The law acknowledged the existence of a market (i.e. men who wanted to purchase sexual favours) and acknowledged the existence of a commodity (i.e. the prostitute) but did not acknowledge the market-place (i.e. the right of women to solicit custom). Although prostitution in itself was not a criminal offence, soliciting by women was. In other principles of law it was the mutual responsibility of all concerned in the commission of a crime: those who knowingly purchased stolen goods were considered equally guilty as those who stole them. Indeed, Ladies'

Associations considered it unfair that soliciting by prostitutes remained an offence while solicitation by men was ignored and protested that 'one cannot but notice how very tender the law is in dealing with men, and how little care it takes for the protection of women".[78]

One of the first pieces of legislation, the Industrial Schools Act 1880, became known as the Ellice Hopkins Act in recognition of her campaign to get it passed. This Act gave local authorities the legal right to remove children from homes regarded as disorderly and immoral and place them in industrial schools.[79] Although the Act marked a radical attempt to safe-guard young children it removed them from their parents to less than perfect institutions and so was condemned by the Vigilance Association for the Defence of Personal Rights who claimed that 'Miss Hopkins . . . is at present . . . crying for the wholesale kidnapping of little girls who may not have perfect domestic surroundings and their consignment to large prison schools.'[80] The Vigilance Association was opposed to any form of protec-tive legislation because it feared that the general increase in state power which would result might deprive women of their freedoms.[81]

Ladies' Associations played a key role in the campaigns in support of the Criminal Law Amendment (CLA) Act 1885. Both Lucy Bland and Frank Mort have pointed out the contradictory nature of this Act.[82] On the one hand, it protected young girls by raising the age of female consent for sexual intercourse from 13 to 16.[83] On the other hand, it was repressive against prostitutes and homosexuals. The CLA Act gave the police greater powers to prosecute streetwalkers and brothel-keepers. Brothel-keepers and their agents could be fined up to £20 or sentenced to three months' impris-onment with hard labour for the first offence and £40 or four months for the second and subsequent convictions; and because of an amendment by the Liberal MP Labouchere the CLA Act criminalised homosexual acts between men, thus forming the basis of legal proceedings against homo-sexuals until the law was liberalised in the mid-twentieth century. These Acts, Frank Mort argues, signalled a new, 'more coercive system of state intervention into the realm of sexual politics';[84] like the CD Acts, they were part and parcel of the growing collectivisation and centralisation of the state. Indeed, as Lucy Bland points out, the pressure to legislate coin-cided with the moral panic over the urban working class at the end of the nineteenth century. Worsening economic conditions, the growth of socialism and trade unionism and the failure of philanthropy contributed to an alarm in official circles about the increasing immorality of the working class. Andrew Mearns' *The Bitter Cry of Outcast London* (written in 1883) exposed a vast mass of moral corruption whereas the Royal Commission on the Housing of the Working Classes in 1885 alleged that incest was rife among the working class. Moral laxity was equated with the decline of important virtues such as social and economic responsibility, law and order and family stability. It was imperative that something be done. However, as Frank Mort suggests, it is important not to fall into the conspiracy theory trap as it has been shown that official response was mixed. On the contrary, rather than give the demands of moral purists wholesale support, the state often opposed or delayed their suggestions. In reality the state was a 'relatively subordinate and passive partner'[85] in both the Industrial Schools Act and the Criminal Law Amendment Act and in both cases was reluctant to make the necessary legal changes.

It seems therefore as if philanthropic bodies were inherently more repressive than that of the formal state apparatus but this is too simple an explanation. In practice, Ladies' Associations focused on raising the age of sexual consent rather than the persecution of prostitutes and homosexuals. It alleged that thousands of young girls of 12 and 13 were driven to prostitution because they were too young to understand the moral implications and because the money was good in the early years. Fears were regularly expressed that such young girls were able to earn quite large sums of money – one earned £32 a day, another £20 in a week, yet another £100 in three months compared to earning 9s–12s in a shop or factory or as low as 2s per week working as a domestic servant in a small household.[86]

Moreover, Ladies' Associations were highly critical of a legal system which did not protect young girls from prostitution. Once a child had entered a 'disorderly house' (that is a brothel), it was thought impossible to prosecute any particular individual. 'The keeper of the lowest den of infamy in the neighbourhood can actually harbour that child, and sell her to the next comer, and he or she does not commit an indictable offence.'[87] Many examples were used to illustrate the inadequacy of the legal system as it stood. For instance, in Hull a man who kept what was locally nicknamed the 'Infants School' because young children – all under the age of 15 – were living there as prostitutes was charged with having sold unlicensed liquor in a disorderly house rather than violating children. They also referred to a 50-year-old male clerk who was prosecuted for seducing sixteen children but was not convicted because fourteen of the children had reached the age of limited consent – 13 – by the time the case had reached court. Magistrates too were criticised for taking a lenient view of sexual criminals. Ellice Hopkins expressed alarm that one child of 6, found in a brothel, had been through a Lock Hospital and was later committed to a penitentiary whereas one of her male abusers had been given only one month's imprisonment because the magistrate decided that he was not the only one to have violated the child.[88] This led Ladies' Associations not only to condemn England for liking its 'vice young and helpless' but also to campaign for the protection of young girls.

The Ladies' Associations, of course, did not campaign alone but were part of a larger movement which aimed to protect young girls from sexual exploitation. Key reformers like Alfred Dyer and Josephine Butler were equally convinced that young British girls were in great moral danger. Alfred Dyer even proved the existence of a white slave trade whereby young English girls were abducted to Belgium and elsewhere in continental Europe to be sold into prostitution. As a direct result of his and Josephine Butler's influence, the City of London formed the Association for the Suppression of Traffic in Women and Girls. Butler also presented a petition to the Foreign Secretary, signed by a thousand women, calling for changes in the law.

One can see evidence of the state's reluctance to intervene in the moral lives of its citizens by the way in which it reacted to protests of Ladies' Associations and other groups. At each stage in the moral reform process, the government was shown to be unenthusiastic. First of all it discounted the evidence of Dyer and Butler and only in the face of mounting pressure allowed Thomas William Snagge, a London barrister, to investigate the allegations put forward by them. Snagge reported that:

1   The exportation of English girls to Belgium, France and Holland for purposes of prostitution has been carried on systematically as a trade or traffic
2   English girls have been induced by misrepresentation and false pretences to leave England, and to become inmates of houses of prostitution in foreign towns
3   English girls have willingly or unwillingly become inmates, have been detained by duress or subjected to cruelty in such houses, and forced against their will to lead a life of prostitution.[89]

Eventually the government established a Select Committee of the House of Lords in 1881 to examine the extent of juvenile prostitution. Only after a desultory investigation, did the Select Committee publish its findings in 1882, reporting that juvenile prostitution was increasing

> to an appalling extent in England, and especially in London. The Committee are unable adequately to express their concerns of the magnitude, both in a moral and physical point of view, of the evil thus brought to light, and of the necessity for taking vigorous measures to cope with it.

It recommended that the age of sexual consent be raised from 13 to 16.[90]

The response by Ladies' Associations to the Select Committee's recommendations presents further evidence that pressure groups promoted stronger, and more restraining, measures than those put forward by the government. First, Ladies' Associations wanted the age of sexual consent to be raised to 21 so that the 'poor man's daughter was as efficiently protected by the English law as the rich man's heiress'.[91] Comparisons were drawn between young working-class women, heiresses and men: heiresses were protected from avaricious suitors by being unable to marry until the age of 21 whereas young men were protected from their own 'money follies' and the 'seductions of tradesmen' until they attained their majority because their debts were waived until that age. The Ladies' Associations advocated similar protection for working-class young women to preserve their virtue. Second, Ladies' Associations wanted young women who associated with known prostitutes to be prosecuted. Third, they demanded that magistrates be given extra powers to commit such women to a reformatory or home if they gained their living immorally. Finally, Ladies' Associations wanted magistrates to be empowered to issue search warrants for children suspected of being detained in a brothel and the keeper of the house fined or imprisoned.

In spite of these reservations, Ladies' Associations, along with organisations such as the Girls' Friendly Society and Church of England Purity Society, sent numerous petitions to Parliament to persuade it to implement the recommendations of the Select Committee. Ellice Hopkins mapped out the whole of England (and Scotland and Wales) with each town and its neighbourhood exhorted to petition Parliament. In 1883, over 300 provincial towns and cities sent in petitions; Exeter sent in a petition with 11,000 signatures and the total signatures amounted to 1,041,690.[92] In the same year, Ladies' Associations set up a Minor's Protection Joint Committee (formed out of delegates from many different London societies and a few sympathetic London barristers) to gain support for the Bill.

Several attempts were made to pass this Bill but it seemed doomed to fail, again because of the unwillingness of the government to legislate. The Bill was placed before the Commons at regular intervals in one form or another only to be suppressed, thrown out or shelved due to the pressure of parliamentary business. Gladstone, who was Prime Minister at this time, in spite of his hobby of rescuing prostitutes, had only a lukewarm commitment to the Bill. Despite the campaigns of groups like the Ladies' Associations and the support of Lord Shaftesbury, the CLA Bill ran into difficulties in the House of Commons. Even the Select Committee, who recommended the raising of the age of sexual consent, shared the belief that different rules applied to the working class:

> whether in the graver cases the age of protection should be higher is a difficult question, and certainly not one to be decided according to the habits and the notions of the upper classes. In the humbler ranks girls develop at an earlier age, morally if not physically. This precocity is the result of absence of restrictions, the crowded nature of their dwellings, the inability of parents to keep guard over them, and the frequent necessity for the children to be away from home earning wages.[93]

Without government support – which would be forthcoming only if there was vociferous pressure from outside Parliament in favour of the Bill – the CLA Bill would not be passed. It eventually became law because of a rather intriguing scandal that dominated newspaper headlines and swayed public opinion. The narrative of the plot has been well documented but it is worth exploring briefly here.

In the summer of 1885 Mrs Bramwell Booth, a leading figure in the Salvation Army, and her son-in-law, Bramwell Booth, joined forces with William Stead, editor of the *Pall Mall Gazette*, to publicise the allegedly widespread existence of white slavery. Their plan (which was based on abolitionists who bought slaves at auctions in order to set them free) revolved around the purchase of a young girl under the age of consent. To do this they persuaded a reformed brothel-keeper, Rebecca Jarrett, to purchase a girl, Elisa Armstrong, for £5 from her parents. Eliza Armstrong was then examined by a midwife to verify her virginity and removed to a brothel where she was given chloroform to keep her quiet. William Stead, pretending to be a potential customer, rented a room from the brothel-keeper to seduce her. Obviously he did not but on Monday, July 6th 1885, Stead published his experience in the *Pall Mall Gazette*, under the title of 'The Maiden Tribute of Modern Babylon' using emotive headings such as 'Why the Cries of Victims are not Heard', 'The Violation of Virgins' and 'Confessions of a Brothel Keeper'. Stead gave the white slave trade much needed publicity by describing it in kaleidoscopic – and salacious – prose: 'The screams of pain in the seduction chamber avail them nothing . . . To some men, the shriek of torture is the essence of their delight.' These articles not only invented a new genre of newspaper reporting but also caused a furore in Victorian England. *The Pall Mall Gazette* sold out and in less than three weeks the Salvation Army had gathered widespread support for their nation-wide campaign against white slavery.

On August 14th 1885 the CLA Act was carried in the House of Commons by 179 to 71 votes but the story did not end there. Paradoxically, a state which was unwilling to pass the CLA Act proved to be very active in prosecuting those who campaigned for it. Just after the CLA Act was passed Stead, Jarrett and Bramwell Booth were charged with abduction. The charge was that 'feloniously, by force and fraud' they had taken away Eliza Armstrong without parental permission. Rebecca Jarrett had given Eliza's mother, Mrs Armstrong, money but she vehemently denied this and, as permission had not been received from Eliza's father, the alleged abductors had technically broken the law. Booth was eventually found innocent but was subjected to a lot of venom; during the twelve days of the trial he was repeatedly dragged from his cab and physically attacked. Stead, who had suffered from torchlit crowds trampling through the garden of his house, received three months in prison but continued to campaign for social purity until his death on the *Titanic* in 1912. Jarrett received six months' imprisonment. She was met by Mrs Bramwell Booth after prison and lived for another forty years working (until 1929) for the army cause. The unfortunate brothel-keeper, Madame Mourez, received six months' hard labour and died in gaol. Eliza Armstrong was cared for by the Salvation Army, later married and had six children.

It has been argued, particularly by Lucy Bland and Frank Mort,[94] that organisations which promoted social purity were initially radical but were later co-opted by the right to become more repressive. In the case of the Ladies' Associations this shift did not seem to take place since, even at the very beginning, there was an emphasis on traditional and orthodox conduct. The Ladies' Associations may have sincerely believed in the development of a moral code which transcended class and gender but the ways in which this was enacted reinforced those same barriers they were at pains to break down. Adult women may have joined the same type of organisation, for example, the Mothers' Union, but they would have found themselves socially segregated at branch level. Younger women and girls, on the other hand, were kept firmly apart: Snowdrop Bands and Evening Clubs were only ever meant for the working classes.

The protective legislation envisaged by the Ladies' Associations was equally problematic. Any kind of protective legislation, of course, raises a number of key historical questions. It is argued, in relation to factory laws, that humanitarianism acted as a stimulus to protective legislation which (naturally) benefited women. Protective legislation is seen as 'a glorious step in the forward march of labour',[95] and as an 'unmitigated victory for the working class'.[96] Inspiration for sexual legal reform certainly appeared to originate from individuals and groups like the Ladies' Associations, who were shocked at what they perceived to be grave social injustices. On the other hand, some propose that protective legislation was not so clear cut. Protective legislation, they argue, was necessary to protect capitalism, not women and children.[97] This interpretation suggests that the family was an institution which maintained and perpetuated the capitalist system. By producing and reproducing labour power, by reproducing capitalist ideology, by constituting the major unit of consumption, by making men responsible for the family income, by providing an arena of psychology and emotional support the family was viewed as an essential component for the success of capitalism. It was therefore important for women to remain chaste and good because they were at the heart of the family life. Others regard protective legislation as a none too subtle patriarchal plot whereby the male state, the male government and the male worker colluded to protect their masculine interests against women. Recent research, however, favours a more nuanced approach by examining the ways in which gender is constructed within a particular socio-economic context.[98] Certainly, the Ladies' Associations seem to embody the characteristics of all these theories as their alleged humanitarianism was firmly located within the hierarchical and patriarchal world of Victorian and Edwardian England.

Notes

1 This chapter is based on my article, 'Preventing Prostitution: The Ladies' Association for the Care and Protection of Young Girls in Birmingham, 1887–1914', which was first published in *Women's History Review*, 7(1), 1998, pp. 37–60.

2 Ellice Hopkins, *How to Start Preventive Work* (London: Hatchards, 1884).

3 It was realised that preventive work encompassed all efforts at social improvement such as the campaigns for better housing, higher wages, temperance and increased religious observance but the focus of the Ladies' Associations was generally much narrower.

4 Edward Trenholme, *Rescue Work* (London: Society for the Promotion of Christian Knowledge, 1927), p. 7.

5 Barnsley, Barnstaple, Bath, Bedford, Belper, Birkdale, Birkenhead, Birmingham, Blackburn, Bournemouth, Bradford, Brighton, Bristol and Clifton, Burnley, Burton on Trent, Cambridge, Carlisle, Cheltenham, Chester, Chesterfield, Colchester, Coventry, Croydon, Derby, Devizes, Devon, Dorchester, Dorking, Dover, Durham, Eastbourne, Exeter, Folkestone, Gateshead, Gloucester, Godalming, Grantham, Great Grimsby, Great Yarmouth, Halifax, Hastings, Hitchin, Hove, Huddersfield, Hull, Hythe, Jersey, King's Lynn, Leeds, Lichfield, Liverpool, London (including Battersea, Brompton, East End, Kensington, Nottingdale, Paddington and Marylebone, Pimlico, St Martin and St Giles, Stratford, West Ham and Wimbledon), Macclesfield, Maidstone, Malvern, Manchester, Newcastle upon Tyne, North Staffordshire Potteries, Northumberland, Norwich, Nottingham, Oxford, Penzance, Plymouth, Poole, Portsmouth and Southsea, Preston, Ramsgate and St Lawrence, Redhill, Richmond, Rochester, Rotherham, Salisbury, Scarborough, Sheffield, Shrewsbury, Southampton, Southport, Sunderland, Surbiton, Torquay, Truro, Tunbridge Wells, Wakefield, Walsall, Wellington, Weston-super-Mare, Weymouth, Wigan, Winchester, Windsor, Wisbech, Worthing and York were among the many towns, cities and counties which formed a Ladies' Association (*Seeking and Saving,* 1880–1914). The only 'dead failure' was seen to be Hull because the 'state of Hull is so bad, that at present no association can be found to work in it, though children of twelve are perishing by scores'. By 1885, however, Hull had joined (*Seeking and Saving*, April 1883, p. 158).

6 Ellice Hopkins, *How to Start Preventive Work.*

7 In March 1889 there were twenty-eight branches of the society in London (*St George the Martyr Parish Magazine*, March 1889).

8 The Girls' Guild was founded by Mrs J.T. Rae of Hoxton Hall. By 1890 it had 1,207 members consisting of young women engaged in box making, button holing, envelope, jam, pickle, rope and soap making and other trades of the East End (*The Pioneer*, 1890).

9 Patricia Hollis, *Ladies Elect* (Oxford: Oxford University Press, 1987), p. 265.

10 Ellice Hopkins, *How to Start Preventive Work.*

11 *Seeking and Saving* (January 1883), p. 5.

12 *Seeking and Saving* (April 1882), p. 92.

13 *Leeds Ladies' Association for the Care and Protection of Friendless Girls Annual Report* 1884, p. 11. The Norwich branch had a much wider vision in that it wanted not merely to save young women but to reshape the morality of the entire city (*Norfolk Chronicle and Norwich Gazette*, August 24th 1895, p. 3).

14 See, for example, Philippa Levine, *Victorian Feminism, 1850–1900* (London: Hutchinson, 1987).

15 See Philippa Levine, *Feminist Lives in Victorian England* (Oxford: Basil Blackwell, 1990) for an analysis of a national women's network based upon familial and friendship groups. See also Jane Rendall (ed.), *Equal or Different* (Oxford: Basil Blackwell, 1987), pp. 112–138, for a discussion of the importance of women's friendships in political movements.

16 Philippa Levine, *Feminist Lives in Victorian England.*

17 For example, Mrs Cadbury, Mrs Impey, Mrs Osler and Mrs Rogers were among the many women in the Ladies' Association who supported votes for women.

18 For example, Mrs Ashford, Mrs Wilson, Mrs Kenway, Mrs C.D. Sturge and Mrs T. Bishop, all executive committee members, were well-known advocates for the repeal of the Contagious Diseases Acts. Josephine Butler had stayed at Mrs Kenway's home and was considered a personal friend.

19 Gerald Parsons (ed.), *Religion in Victorian Britain* (Manchester: Manchester University Press with the Open University, 1988), pp. 40–49.

20 *The Southwell Diocesan Magazine* (January 1889), p. 8.

21 Michael Mason, *The Making of Victorian Sexual Attitudes* (Oxford: Oxford University Press, 1994), p. 89.

22 For example, Lady Gifford was in charge of the Hampton Court branch and Lady Laura Ridding a leading member in Nottingham.

23 *Seeking and Saving* (January 1884), p. 13.

24 *Seeking and Saving* (January 1886), p. 78.

25 Ellice Hopkins, *How to Start Preventive Work*, pp. 42–43.

26 *Seeking and Saving* (January 1884), p. 14.

27 Mothers' Unions and the Woman's League were both regarded as preventive agencies (*NUWW Occasional Paper* June 1900, p. 12).

28 In fact the Ladies' Associations credited themselves with talking to mothers on the lines of the Mothers' Union before there was any formally organised work of this kind. Eventually, Mothers' Unions ceased to be part of Ladies' Associations and became a separate organisation under the auspices of the Church of England.

29 *Refuge and Reformatory Journal* (October 1904), p. 458.

30 *Mothers' Union Journal* (October 1895), p. 60.

31 Mothers' Meetings in Birmingham at least were the invention of the Ladies' Association. See Frank Prochaska, 'A Mother's Country: Mothers' Meetings and Family Welfare in Britain, 1850–1950', *History*, 74, 1989, p. 380.

32 Prochaska also claims that the Mothers' Meetings were ultimately unsuccessful in breaking down class barriers: ibid., pp. 389–399.

33 *Seeking and Saving* (January 1886), p. 78.

34 *NUWW Quarterly Magazine* (March 1892), p. 21.

35 *Mothers' Union Handbook and Central Report* 1903, p. 35.

36 *The Southwell Diocesan Magazine* (December 1888), p. 243.

37 *Mothers' Union Handbook and Central Report* 1903, p. 33.

38 Drawing Room meetings were regular events. In 1887 Miss Emily Janes spoke at thirty Drawing Room meetings in Edgbaston alone. Such meetings were probably regarded as recruitment meetings because several women joined the Moral Educational Branch after each one: *Birmingham Ladies' Association for the Care and Protection of Young Girls (BLACPYG) Annual Reports* 1887–1900.

39 *The Friend* (May 1st 1914).

40 The Nottingham Woman's League, which was the direct outcome of rescue work in the area, was also divided by class. It focused on 'mothers and women in positions of responsibility' to further preventive work among their children, employees and school pupils (*The Southwell Diocesan Magazine*, June 1888, p. 126).

41 Society of Friends Minute Books of Women's Monthly Meetings 1880–1914.

42 *Mothers' Union Handbook and Central Report* 1903, p. 29.

43 Prochaska has noted that dressmaking was a common activity at Mothers' Meetings. Dressmaking was popular with working-class mothers because materials were supplied at cost price: Frank Prochaska, 'A Mother's Country', p. 387.

44 Society of Friends Minute Books of Women's Monthly Meetings, April 7th 1903.

45 See Lucy Bland, 'The Married Woman, the New Woman and the Feminist: Sexual Politics of the 1890s', in Jane Rendall (ed.) *Equal or Different*, pp. 141–164.

46 *The Southwell Diocesan Magazine* (June 1888), p. 127.
47 Constitution and Rules for the Formation of Lodges and Branches of the Woman's League for Mothers and Women in Positions of Responsibility, Nottingham, *c.* early twentieth century.
48 *BLACPYG Annual Reports* 1887–1903.
49 *Seeking and Saving* (January 1886), p. 72.
50 See F.M.L. Thompson, 'Social Control in Victorian Britain', *Economic History Review*, 34(2), 1981, pp. 192–195, for a discussion of the role of parents in passing on societal values.
51 *The Pioneer* (September 1892), p. 7.
52 *Birmingham and Midland Counties' Vigilance Association (BMCVA) Occasional Papers* 1887–1893.
53 *The Vigilance Record* (February 1902), p. 3.
54 Two separate Bands, one for girls from 11 to 14, the second from 14 upwards, were formed in Birmingham. Members were divided into junior and senior sections under the leadership of an older woman. Bands were also formed in Batley, Beckenham, Bedford, Bolton, Bradford, Brighouse, Bushbury, Goole, Halifax, Harrogate, Hatton, Huddersfield, Irchester, Leeds, Leicester, Liverpool, London, Manchester, Marsden, Newton Abbot, Nottingham, Reading, Richmond, Sandwich, Sedbergh, Sheffield, Sutton Coldfield and other towns.
55 *The Snowdrop* (July 1912), p. 16. Not all the organisers, however, were well ordered. In Nottingham, 'unfortunately, a misunderstanding resulted in no bulbs being forthcoming' for the potting night (Hysom Green Home, Nottingham, Minute Book, November 17th 1904).
56 *The Snowdrop* (September 1912), p. 15.
57 *NUWW Quarterly Magazine* (June 1891).
58 Hysom Green Home, Nottingham, Minute Book, November 17th 1909.
59 Miss Nunneley, *NUWW Annual Conference* 1890, p. 23.
60 Of course, many working-class people would have subscribed to a similar moral code. See Carl Chinn, *They Worked All their Lives* (Manchester: Manchester University Press, 1988), pp. 144–146, for a fuller discussion of working-class morality in Birmingham.
61 This fear was widespread among some of the middle class. See Carl Chinn, *They Worked All their Lives*, p. 98, for some Birmingham examples. One of the explanations for the spread of the use of contraception among the factory workers was that women exchanged information on the shop floor. See Angus McLaren, *Birth Control in Nineteenth-Century England* (London: Croom Helm, 1978), pp. 215–231, for a discussion of birth control and the working class in England.
62 *The Snowdrop* (July 1912).
63 *Seeking and Saving* (1887), p. 121.
64 *The Southwell Diocesan Magazine* (December 1888), p. 237.
65 Ibid., p. 237.
66 Hysom Green Home, Nottingham, Minute Book, March 7th 1890.
67 *Seeking and Saving* (July 1887), p. 228.
68 *Hysom Green Club, Nottingham, Annual Report* 1906, p.12.
69 Hysom Green Home, Nottingham, Minute Book, March 7th 1890.
70 *St George's Club, Norfolk and Norwich Ladies' Association for the Care of Friendless Girls, Norwich, Annual Report* 1899, p. 4.
71 *The Southwell Diocesan Magazine* (December 1888), p. 238.
72 *Manchester and Salford Central Association of Societies for Girls and Women Annual Report* 1897.
73 *Seeking and Saving* (July 1883), p. 201.
74 Hysom Green Home, Nottingham, Minute Book, March 22nd 1890.

75 Frank Mort, 'Purity, Feminism and the State: Sexuality and Moral Politics, 1880–1914', in M. Langan and B. Schwarz (eds) *Crises in the British State, 1880–1930* (London: Hutchinson, 1985).
76 See M. Langan and B. Schwarz (eds), *Crises in the British State*, for an examination of this.
77 Frank Mort has suggested that the National Vigilance Association used the state apparatus as a weapon to fight against immorality: *Dangerous Sexualities* (London: Routledge and Kegan Paul, 1987), pp. 133–135.
78 *Seeking and Saving* (January 1883), p. 9.
79 See Michelle Cale, '"Saved from a Life of Vice and Crime": Reformatory and Industrial Schools for Girls, c.1854–c.1901' (DPhil thesis, University of Oxford, 1993).
80 Quoted in Frank Mort, *Dangerous Sexualities*, p. 125.
81 See Sonya Rose, *Limited Livelihoods* (London: Routledge, 1992), p. 67.
82 Lucy Bland, *Banishing the Beast* (London: Penguin, 1995); Frank Mort, *Dangerous Sexualities*; Frank Mort, 'Purity, Feminism and the State'.
83 It had been raised from 12 to 13 in 1875.
84 Frank Mort, 'Purity, Feminism and the State', p. 209.
85 Ibid., p. 209.
86 *Seeking and Saving* (January 1884), p. 36.
87 *Seeking and Saving* (1883), p. 159.
88 *Seeking and Saving* (January 1884), p. 37.
89 White Slave Traffic: Alleged Complicity between Belgian Police and Brussels Brothel Keepers (HO 45/9599/98018).
90 *Select Committee, House of Lords, State of Law Relating to the Protection of Young Girls* 1882.
91 *Seeking and Saving* (June 1883), p. 159.
92 Ibid., p. 159.
93 Confidential Report: The Law Relating to the Protection of Young Girls: Recommendations of the Select Committee of the House of Lords on This Subject (HO 45/9547/593431).
94 Lucy Bland, *Banishing the Beast*; Frank Mort, *Dangerous Sexualities*; Frank Mort, 'Purity, Feminism and the State'.
95 Mariana Valverde, '"Giving the Female a Domestic Turn": The Social, Legal and Moral Regulation of Women's Work in British Cotton Mills, 1827–1850', *Journal of Social History* 21, 1988, p. 626.
96 Wally Seccombe, 'Patriarchy Stabilized: The Construction of the Male Breadwinner Wage Norm in Nineteenth-Century Britain', *Social History*, 11, 1986, pp. 53–74.
97 Jane Humphries, 'Protective Legislation, the Capitalist State and Working Class Men: The Case of the 1842 Mines Regulation Act', *Feminist Review*, 7, 1981.
98 Sonya Rose, *Limited Livelihoods*.

4 'Wayward and troublesome girls'

Ladies' Associations offered practical assistance, as well as advice and legal protection, to those 'wayward and troublesome' working-class young women and single mothers perceived to be at moral risk. Such women were considered a potential danger to both themselves and the local community because prostitution was seen to be the next logical step. By offering systematic help, Ladies' Associations stopped the future supply of prostitutes and, perhaps more significantly, saved the nation from moral disgrace. This chapter examines the establishments set up to train 'wayward and troublesome girls' for domestic service and which provided them with suitable clothing and found them respectable jobs. It will show how single mothers were given financial assistance, moral guidance and help with their babies before being placed in employment. Once again, it will be argued, the motivations and practices of the Ladies' Association were complex. On the one hand, they undoubtedly helped numerous young women and single mothers without supportive families; on the other hand, they shared many of the values enshrined in the Poor Law about the deserving and undeserving poor.

Preventive branch: training homes, clothing clubs and registry offices

The third branch of the Ladies' Associations was the preventive branch, which set up training homes, registry offices and clothing clubs for domestic servants.[1] Training homes were founded to groom 'wayward and troublesome girls', seen to be at moral risk, for domestic service.[2] Once trained, registry offices found them work while clothing clubs provided the necessary uniform for their new position. In many ways, these training homes replicated the practice of institutions founded for the reform of prostitutes since they operated selection criteria, which excluded many potential applicants. In effect, the successful applicants stood in the middle of the rescue, reform and preventive charitable pecking order. Quite subtle distinctions were made between the different categories of girls and applicants were categorised into a hierarchy of respectability. They were not deemed worthy enough to join the Girls' Friendly Society or homes for 'respectable' girls but neither were they considered to be so morally deficient as to be sent to an institution for penitent prostitutes. Instead, they were deemed to constitute a special category. The homes targeted 'rough, untrained girls with serious faults of temper, veracity, cleanliness or modesty, under the age of eighteen and "unfallen" in the technical sense'.[3] The girls they rescued were allegedly taken from the 'very worst class' with the only recommendation being that they were absolutely friendless or in dangerous surroundings 'where those who should be friends are worse than none'.[4] The following quote is typical of the way in which the girls were perceived:

> Two of us ladies passing down Derby Place met a very pretty child of 13 or 14 paddling down the muddy flags with her bare feet, and roughly told to 'get along' by a policeman – an injunction which she greeted with a familiar laugh. Taking her kindly by the hand we led her back to what she called her home, – a common lodging-house and found that her mother, a drunken Irish woman, sold flowers, and left this pretty girl alone with a lot of low men in the lodging-house all day, and with absolutely no employment . . . she was fast going to ruin. The girl was almost naked, and the first step was evidently to clothe her for service; . . . She was literally alive from head to foot with vermin, her tender girlish body was scarred all over with blows, apparently inflicted with a poker, and one of her arms bore the marks of her mother's teeth, where in her drunken fury she had severely bitten her; and her voracious appetite showed she had been half starved.[5]

In fact, many of the girls were recommended to Ladies' Associations by Poor Law Guardians or School Board Officers who provided managers with the addresses of those leaving school known to be in destitute circumstances,[6] and thought uncontrollable. In Leeds, the girls were almost always brought to the home 'in rags so dirty that they have to be burnt, they are generally ill fed, stunted, neglected, often with tubercular tendencies'.[7] One girl was brought in nothing but a borrowed man's coat. Similarly, the Winchester Ladies' Association received youngsters like

> F who was little removed from a savage when first brought to Colebrooke House. The state of filth she was in was almost inconceivable. She snatched at food when it was placed on the dinner table, gnawed at it ferociously, and then dashed out into the garden, returning in a few minutes for another bite.[8]

Even so, the Rochester Diocesan Association, which did not run a permanent home of its own, found that many institutions refused to take Deptford girls on account of their language and conduct.[9] Police, who had been invited to take destitute and homeless girls to Ladies' Association's homes, also complained that some girls were refused entry.[10]

Accepting unsociable young women did not challenge contemporary middle-class wisdom about the deserving and the undeserving poor. On the contrary, it reinforced it. Like the single mothers who left their babies at the Foundling Hospital in London and penitent prostitutes who entered reform institutions, potential inmates to training homes were perceived as victims, which meant that they were not held responsible for their inadequate behaviour.[11] Instead, poor parenting was blamed as the following extract demonstrates:

> Parents and guardians seem unwilling or unable to exercise proper control over even young children, so that they grow up with thoroughly lawless ideas. Whatever they want to do, they do regardless of consequences. If they covet anything they take it, whether it be money, jewellery, clothes, or another person's character. If they do not want to work they are idle.[12]

Troublesome behaviour was directly attributed to problem, or single-parent, families where lack of discipline, intemperance, dishonesty and immorality were customary: 'Daisy and May, sisters of 15 and 16 having a drunken mother who has broken up the home and left them wandering from one lodging to another and in the greatest danger.'[13] Consequently, assertive and so-called 'wild' girls were accommodated and accepted because unsatisfactory behaviour was not considered their fault.

Once girls were admitted to the home, parents relinquished responsibility for their offspring by signing over all their authority to their respective association. There was some inconsistency here: on the one hand, Ladies' Associations espoused family values but, on the other hand, they severed ties with the girls' parents. This contradiction, of course, could be justified because the rejected parents had neglected their duties. In effect, the homes exerted as strong a measure of control as that enjoyed by reform institutions. Parents had visiting rights but these varied according to the wishes of the managers of each home. In Norwich friends and family were allowed to visit once a fortnight on any Thursday between 3 and 4p.m.[14] In Birmingham they were allowed to visit only at specified times every three months. If parents wished to take their daughter out at other times they had to have special permission. When a Leeds father wanted to take his daughter out on a Bank Holiday he not only had to have authorised approval but also had to agree to return her by 6p.m. or forfeit the right to take her out again.[15] Sometimes permission was refused. When a particularly 'immoral, troublesome and offensive' mother came to take her daughter away to live with her she was not only dissuaded from doing so but police were requested to keep an eye on her should she cause further trouble.[16] Once separated from their families – like the inmates of reform and other institutions – girls were encouraged to break with their working-class past to be recast in a conventionally safe image. The homes used this control to induce conformity and to instil the moral code of the Ladies' Associations.

The training homes founded by the Ladies' Associations became yet another mechanism whereby selected working-class girls were educated into the social mores of the middle-class community – but without accruing the economic benefits of such a shift. Education certainly reaffirmed their class position. The home managers did not seem to share the feminist belief that new educational opportunities provided the key to other forms of emancipation, at least for the working class. Whereas middle-class philanthropists had perhaps enjoyed a challenging academic education at prestigious schools or individual home tuition, the inmates of training homes were given no such choice. Instead, the educational aims of these homes reinforced the status quo as girls were given education that neither took them above their station in life nor forced them to challenge societal values. In essence, therefore, the philanthropists, unconsciously or otherwise, shared assumptions about what was deemed suitable education for working-class girls. Education in the training homes was little different from that of many board schools in England,[17] where the female section of the working class were offered a limited educational diet which emphasised basic literacy, numeracy and domesticity.[18]

Spiritual and moral guidance played a large part in the educative process: girls were supposed to remain pure, chaste and modest. Ellice Hopkins demanded that Ladies' Associations

> teach them plainly, that from the crown of their heads to the soles of their feet their bodies belong to Christ; that they must never defile them with dirty talk or dirty words; never allow rough lads to pull them about, or be rude to them, or write nasty letters to them; never to answer any strange man who speaks to them in the street; never to go with any man into public house; never to go a walk with him without knowing anything about him.[19]

White Ribbon Bands were formed to promote Temperance and Purity among the girls;[20] sometimes the more respectable girls were encouraged to join the Girls' Friendly Society.[21] Appropriate forms of womanly behaviour – namely behaviour that was subdued, submissive and assiduous – were rewarded at every opportunity. In 1908 the Birmingham Home awarded daily marks for conduct and neatness. Silver shield brooches engraved with the motto 'Forward' were awarded each month to those who had reached the highest standards. Once the medal had been won three times it became the property of the victor.[22] Such a scheme may well have strengthened the gender and class roles taught by rewarding – and thus holding up as an example – those who were successful. However, the social upshot of the decision to limit educational opportunity to reading, writing and religion was to limit job prospects.

Work not only contributed to the income of these homes but also was the medium whereby girls were checked in their moral attitudes, controlled in their behaviour and trained to be of useful service to the middle-class community. At no time did Ladies' Associations raise their sights beyond that of domestic service.[23] There was no wish by the committees which managed the homes to extend equal work opportunities to the inmates. Although some of these middle-class philanthropists were aware of current debates about female emancipation and knew about the achievements of Elizabeth Garrett Anderson and Sophia Jex-Blake in entering previously masculine professions, these ideas were not applied to the training homes. One can only assume that emancipation was perceived as a middle-class monopoly, which remained unavailable for working-class women to enjoy. According to the annual reports, the only jobs available were factory work, street selling or domestic service. Factory work and street selling were viewed as occupations which encouraged immoral behaviour and were thus not recommended. In contrast, domestic service was considered the most appropriate occupation for working-class girls, despite the fact that it was often a dangerously sexual environment. However, Ladies' Associations referred only to work, which contrasted, quite negatively, with domestic service. It is perhaps not surprising that inmates were not given training in masculine and/or middle-class occupations but no training was offered in clerical or shop work, both of which expanded in the late nineteenth century and recruited women from working-class backgrounds.

Nonetheless, domestic service was not a homogeneous occupation for it enjoyed its own hierarchy. Because the girls who were trained at these homes were perceived to be 'unfallen', the type of domestic service offered differed from that at reform institutions which tended to concentrate on laundry work. Ellice Hopkins considered that laundry work was inappropriate work for young girls,[24] but it may have been because parents or Poor Law Guardians were expected to pay towards their keep and wanted something other than laundry work for those over whom they had authority.[25] Consequently, no laundry training took place in the homes run by the Ladies' Associations.[26] Instead, inmates were taught 'how to clean floors, grates, plates, to boil potatoes, and prepare a simple meal, some instruction in washing and needlework',[27] in order to equip them as domestic servants in a respectable middle-class home and to prepare them for marriage later on. In Manchester the girls not only did all the housework of the home but also looked after the lodgers who rented rooms there.[28] The Birmingham Home offered child-care training by giving the young inmates experience of working in a full-time nursery.[29] Birmingham provided a day nursery, which was open from 7a.m. to 7p.m., where 'poor' mothers of the neighbourhood could leave their children for 4d a day inclusive of food.[30] Only ten to sixteen children were looked after in the home,[31] but the small income that this generated made it more or less financially self-sufficient. In addition, the crèche reinforced gender identity by providing job training in a traditional female role. It was work well suited to girls hoping to become either a children's nurse or in charge of children while in service.[32]

Crèche work acted as a mechanism for behaviour modification. Looking after children was intended to soften and humanise even truculent inmates and was a 'wonderful help in drawing out the best qualities of our girls, and it is pleasant to notice that however naughty and selfish they are the greater number at any rate have love to spare for these little ones'.[33] In addition, the crèche provided a model of middle-class child-care for the mothers of both the present and future generations. It was intended to be an educative experience for the mothers who left their children in the crèche, for it was believed that mothers benefited from seeing good middle-class child-care in practice. The Ladies' Associations were thus laying down desirable habits of child-rearing since they 'were training good mothers for a future generation'.[34]

In Torquay, girls were given cookery lessons at the home whereas in Nottingham they were sent to the Nottingham Cookery School to learn kitchen skills.[35] The Torquay Ladies' Association believed that, because the working class did not have access to gas cookers or the money to buy fancy food, only simple appliances and cheap substantial dishes – such as split lentil soup and poor man's grouse (which consisted of bacon, liver, cabbage and potatoes) – should be cooked. Of course, the virtue of prudence was thought to be inculcated by this method so classes were utilised as a good opportunity to teach 'the sinfulness of waste'. Moreover, it was believed that improvidence was intimately connected with vice (because it signalled a lack of self-control), so in insisting on the careful husbandry of food, the home allegedly protected their charges from potential sexual disgrace.[36]

Significantly, there is a great ambiguity in middle-class women's involvement in training domestic servants which raises interesting questions about the debate over the public and the private spheres. Domestic servants worked in what was considered to be the private world of the home, but because it was someone else's home and because it was paid work it became part of the public domain. However, instead of remaining in the private sphere, cleaning their own homes, cooking their own meals and bringing up their own children, middle-class women spent their time in another more public, albeit unpaid, domestic sphere. Thus the domestic world was both private and public. Running their own households may well be a private undertaking, but organising a home transferred it to the public domain. Significantly, middle-class women put forward a contradictory message, for they hoped to reinforce in working-class girls (i.e. domestic skills) that which they themselves had, if not rejected, then relegated to others.

Recreation for the most part was an exceptional treat, rarely indulged in and often with an educational purpose in mind. However, there was a certain paradox regarding these leisure activities. Training homes, like reform institutions, provided working-class girls with the opportunity to train for work that was distinctly working class and to learn a femininity that was definitely middle class. At the same time Ladies' Associations reinforced gendered class roles in limiting educational and job opportunities while

LIVERPOOL JOHN MOORES UNIVERSITY
LEARNING SERVICES

expanding horizons and offering alternative leisure activities. This may have been because if inmates were expected to work in middle-class homes, they needed to be a bit more sedate and dignified than the normal working class. Most leisure pursuits were sober, polite excursions to the country houses of benefactors where young women, because of their surroundings, undoubtedly behaved appropriately and may well have been intimidated by the conspicuous wealth they saw.[37] Excursions to outlying places of interest were organised.[38] These trips were carefully selected either because they were healthy or edifying. Certain important historical occasions, such as Queen Victoria's Jubilee Procession, were celebrated, thus reinforcing correct cultural values.[39] Some homes arranged longer holidays but these were the exceptions: in 1909 the Oxford Home organised a six-week holiday to the seaside while the Leeds Home sent their girls to a holiday home at Windermere for three weeks.[40]

Matrons, supported by volunteer visitors, called upon ex-inmates in their places of work, sometimes every month, to advise and encourage them and occasionally to report on their conduct to each committee. Visiting held a two-fold function, reflecting a similar blend of humanitarianism mixed with gender and class control. On the one hand, it kept a check on girls, but, on the other hand, it may well have made them feel a little less isolated in their new situation. Ellice Hopkins believed that the visitors

> can do much, not only in personally befriending girls, and making them feel that some one cares for them, and will have the heart-ache if they misconduct themselves, but also in inducing them to join Bible Classes, and other Christian agencies, which will help still further to strengthen their ambition to keep up a good character.[41]

Volunteers in particular were implored to take a real interest in those they visited, to ask about their daily lives, their hours of work, the children they looked after, all the while making sure that they said their prayers every night![42]

According to the literature the majority of girls not only acquiesced but also co-operated with the managers of the homes: certainly annual reports tended to stress the positive relationship between matrons and girls.

> It is very pleasing to find how these young girls . . . look upon the 'Home' as indeed a home. Sometimes this feeling is a source of perplexity to the House Committee as the tendency of many girls is to fly to its shelter, upon any pretext whatever. The Matrons often complain that the girls walk in and take off their hats and jackets and sit down with the others, as a matter of course.[43]

In Leeds, a number of former inmates contributed a tea service and ornaments to make the home bright and comfortable for the others who remained, one held a tea party for her twenty-first birthday in the home,[44] while many others were married from the home. On one occasion, when one of the matrons was ill, the older girls kept the home going and 'did all that the most experienced woman could have suggested or desired'.[45] Indeed, the Leeds Home found their girls reluctant to leave and each Sunday about thirty returned for tea.[46] The Leeds Home may have been blessed with a particularly good matron but the girls most likely had nowhere else to go in their spare time or no one else with whom to celebrate important events. Of course, just as in reform institutions, not all the matrons were so supportive. When the matron of the Norwich Ladies' Association Home tendered her resignation, it was a surprise but not 'altogether unwelcome as it had been found that Mrs O'Leary did not fall in with the wishes of the Committee and was more fitted for long training of girls as servants than to manage the short training and watching over girls in service'.[47] On another occasion a matron was condemned for not having 'the loving spiritual power or sufficient courtesy and gentleness to win girls from evil ways'.[48]

Training homes were not ineluctable institution, as the inmates, like those of reform institutions, did not always aspire to the values of the managers. Each year inmates absconded or else proved troublesome within the homes and sent back to their place of origin. For example, in 1898, Sarah Ann Carlington was sent back to Nottingham from a Chester training home on account of her bad behaviour and impertinence to the matron. So too was Emma Harris, who was said to be lazy, dirty and unsuitable for service.[49] The fact that there were constant problems in disciplining and controlling recalcitrant youngsters shows that control mechanisms and authority did not always work. When persuasion failed, subtle threats were used to bring them into line. Girls who complained about their work were given extra:

> If we grumble we have to do our work, and extra for grumbling. I have grumbled when I was in a temper. I said I was not going to do my work, and in the end I had to do it, and some more besides.[50]

Ellice Hopkins even advocated physical restraint although she stopped at deliberate violence. The committee reprimanded one notoriously poor matron in Leeds when she caned some girls: the committee not only expressed its great disapproval but also forbade the use of the cane thereafter.[51] This ambiguous incident was unusual and it seems as if there was little explicit cruelty and physical violence in the homes. However, this incident may be more representative of the abuse and indignity that may have been routinely suffered by helpless girls in residential training homes which were never officially inspected. Sometimes, inmates were excluded from the home if they had been very disobedient. Two girls, Mary Jane Milner from Torquay and Elizabeth Evans from Cardiff, after 'clamouring for admission and breaking in the panels of the door, and threatening to smash the windows', were refused readmittance to one London home because they had stayed out all night.[52] This type of treatment, of course, challenges – but perhaps does not destroy – the interpretation that the philanthropists were motivated by humanitarian principles, because it may well have been argued that the threats were for their own good.

Similarly, ex-inmates regularly absconded from their employers, sometimes stole their money and goods, and proved to be unreliable and ill disciplined. Girls were often written to concerning 'their naughty conduct, in leaving good situations and being insolent to their mistresses',[53] and were habitually reprimanded because they lost their tempers or stayed out late.[54] Some like Lolly Shelton from Huddersfield were sent back to the homes because they were unsuitable for service.[55] Others proved more refractory. For instance, in Leeds, one 13 year old stole 10s from the purse of a committee member, 2s from her mistress and a ring from a board school teacher,[56] while in Oxford a girl set fire to her master's house.[57] Particularly troublesome girls such as these – just like many women in similar institutions – were sent to the colonies to start a new life or perhaps more importantly to cease to be a burden to the mother country. In fact, Ellice Hopkins wanted the Ladies' Associations to be the centre of emigration work and that all girls who were willing should be sent to Canada, New Zealand or Australia. It was believed female emigration would serve two purposes. First, it would relieve England of the 'congestion of unmarried women, which makes women's labour so cheap',[58] second, it would remedy the 'evil' of a surplus population of men in the colonies. In addition, those who lived in the colonies were thought to be more tolerant towards the 'rough and ready' since servants were in such short supply and thus faults more readily overlooked.[59]

Clothing clubs and free registry offices were set up to ensure that girls leaving the homes were dressed appropriately and employed by respectable families. Most servants had to supply their own uniform, a financial outlay that would have been prohibitive for the inmates of a training institution. In her pamphlet on preventive work, Ellice Hopkins recommended that girls should be well equipped on leaving an institution. Ideally, they should be given a box to hold their clothes, two chemises, two pairs of drawers, two flannel petticoats, one top petticoat, one pair of stays, two night-dresses, two print dresses, one stuff dress, four coarse aprons, four white aprons, two pairs of stockings, one pair of boots, one hat, one jacket and one pair of slippers.[60] And so, in line with Ellice Hopkins' recommendations, clothing clubs provided servants with decent dresses and clothing at cost price. Members of Ladies' Associations either made the garments themselves or allowed their servants to make them up, which was seen as an indirect method of interesting their own servants in 'less fortunate girls' but may also have acted as a warning to them to remain chaste and respectable. The financial debt (outfits usually cost £2 15s in the 1880s) incurred by the girls linked them firmly to the institution until it was repaid and gave the Ladies' Committee a direct measure of power over those who had left their formal jurisdiction.

In the nineteenth and early twentieth centuries, young women obtained their posts as domestic servants through three main channels: word of mouth, advertisements in the press or employment agencies called registry offices. The respectability of some press advertisements and registry offices was called into question by the Ladies' Associations and other moral reform groups. For example, the National Vigilance Association worked with the Norwich Ladies' Association to monitor London agencies which regularly advertised for domestic servants in country papers, since they had reason to 'believe that such advertisements were the means of doing untold evil by decoying country girls to evil and ruin'.[61] It was believed that a large number of registry offices were run by unprincipled people who attracted young, usually country, girls by promising light and easy work for high wages. In reality these registry offices were recruitment agencies for brothels and persuaded young girls to become servants in brothels before they were 'irretrievably drawn into the net'.[62]

To avert this, the Ladies' Associations, along with others, established free registry offices where families could recruit trained servants and young women would know that the home in which they were to be employed was a decent one. These offices interviewed employers as well as employees to ensure that young girls were not overly exploited. Indeed Ladies' Associations were anxious that some employers provided no separate bedroom for their servants and condemned those who expected their servants to sleep in a damp kitchen where the only bed was the kitchen table.[63] In return registry offices provided mistresses with relatively well-trained and decently clothed young women. The scheme was well advertised: district visitors, relieving officers, charity organisations and Sunday school teachers were all contacted about the service. Teachers in board schools were visited at the end of the summer term, when most of the older pupils would be looking for work, to publicise registry offices and clothing clubs. In large towns 'a conspicuous board is put up at the Railway Stations, and the porters interested in it, and asked to point it out to any forlorn little servant girl arriving from the country'.[64] Letters were also sent to the local press and to the clergy asking them to send their young girls direct to the offices of the Ladies' Associations.[65]

The Workhouse Magdalen Branch

The fourth and final branch of the Ladies' Associations, the Workhouse Magdalen Branch, aimed to help young single women in their first 'illegitimate' confinement to find work and to care for their babies. Single women who were pregnant and without work or family to help them were generally forced to rely on Boards of Guardians to give them assistance. In some areas, such as Exeter and Norwich, the Board of Guardians granted outdoor relief to single mothers but most others expected them to enter the workhouse if they could not support themselves. Thus workhouses doubled as maternity hospitals where it was said that the annual number of births in England and Wales exceeded 11,000, of which 70 per cent were illegitimate births.[66] The Workhouse Magdalen Branch was founded as a particular response to this perceived problem. In some respects, it marked a shift away from the eighteenth-century foundling hospitals where girls were encouraged to give up their babies. This branch was part of a larger movement, which went beyond the Ladies' Associations: visiting single mothers in workhouses to help and reform them was common practice.[67] All over England, women guardians worked with philanthropic women to help single mothers confined in the workhouses.[68] In London, the Workhouse Girls Aid Society, which worked closely with local Ladies' Associations,[69] was founded in 1880 to help them. Other institutions, like Queen Charlotte's Lying-In Hospital, took in more single mothers, who had taken 'the one false step', than married ones.[70] Ladies' committees, supported by women guardians, were formed all over England to help single mothers find foster parents for their children and a job for themselves.[71] Such assistance seems, at first sight, to provide a fine example of the ways in which gender identity transcended that of class but it could simultaneously suggest the opposite as Poor Law Guardians were employed by the state and – like the philanthropists – were overwhelmingly middle class themselves. Undeniably, the Ladies' Associations viewed unmarried mothers at one and the same time as objects of feminine benevolence and a class burden on the rate system. In the process of helping single mothers, they would end a workhouse dependency that was seen to be destructive of both the individual and society.

The committees of Ladies' Associations subscribed to what has been termed the 'slippery slope theory' whereby single motherhood led inevitably to prostitution.

> The causes why young girls get entangled in this miserable degradation are these: first, a large number are the victims of seduction under a promise of marriage; a child comes; the mother has to support it; it is almost impossible for her to support her child, to pay 5s a week out of £16 wages annually; it leaves her only £3 to dress upon, and clothe her baby, and she is forced down into the outcast class, often by the highest feelings in her nature, her wish to support her own child.[72]

Time after time young girls were allegedly induced to 'take to the streets' from the necessity of supporting an infant which the father had abandoned.[73] It was believed – and feared – that single motherhood led directly to 'the ranks of the only trade that opens its arms to a helpless, ill-trained, homeless woman, burdened with a child, and with the stigma of the workhouse upon her character'.[74] The Ladies' Associations therefore wanted to stop women being forced into 'selling the sanctities of her womanhood' to support their children by giving them practical help.

It was commonly supposed that workhouses were promiscuous environments. There were no separate bedrooms, or even separate cubicles, in the workhouses, resulting in women of the most varied characters mixing with each other.[75] All too often, it was feared, older women led single mothers on to 'further ruin'. Pat Thane suggests that prostitutes peopled workhouse maternity wards.[76] Certainly, the Ladies' Associations felt that the workhouse was a corrupting influence on single mothers and wanted guardians to place them in the infirmary rather than the able-bodied ward 'among the vicious women, who make a dead set at her, and do their utmost to get her to join their ranks'.[77] Even the naming of the branch 'Magdalen' – like that of the reform institutions which bore the name of Magdalen Asylums – was resonant with ambivalent meaning. Single mothers, like Mary Magdalen herself, were to be 'saved' from moral obliquity.

Unmarried mothers – whether they became prostitutes or not – posed a threat to the social equilibrium. Marriage, home and family were seen as the bedrock of western civilisation and of order, stability and morality within England. Unmarried pregnant women, like prostitutes, were perhaps the living embodiment of immorality and an all too visible reminder of female sexual activity.[78] Moreover, since marriage was a major signifier in constructing middle-class female sexuality, single women presented a challenge.[79] Single mothers undermined the story-book image of female chastity and offered an alternative definition. If single mothers were helped, and discouraged from future immorality, the threat to the moral order might diminish.

The help given to working-class single mothers by workhouse visitors seemed to be more influenced by class prejudices than notions of female solidarity.[80] Although more than fifty years had elapsed since the passing of the notorious Poor Law Amendment Act in 1834, the Ladies' Associations shared some of the utilitarianism which that embodied about the poor, especially in relation to the bastardy clauses.[81] The Ladies' Associations' compassion towards single mothers was affected by their class convictions, categorising single mothers as either deserving or undeserving. Many members created moral hierarchies by differentiating between those they thought worthy of help and those they did not; and separated the 'hardened and depraved' from the younger and more innocent inmates.[82] As with countless other charity organisations such as Queen Charlotte's Lying-In Hospital in London and Poor Law Guardians all over England, Ladies' Associations accepted only those deemed deserving. Ladies' Associations distinguished between those who had led a life of 'professional vice' and those who had been led astray, but only once, by promises, ignorance or childish folly, believing that 'the first fall' was due to 'thoughtlessness, ignorance and inexperience and indicated not real depravity of character'.[83] The ordinary run of single mothers were not thought to be corrupt but had been betrayed by 'folly or by their strong undisciplined affections'.[84] Consequently, only mothers in their first illegitimate confinement who felt a desire to 'win their way back to an honest life' were visited and helped, a policy which was little different from that of Poor Law Unions which categorised women into innocent and depraved.[85] Indeed, Laura Ridding (a famous philanthropist) sent a young woman who had a second illegitimate child to the workhouse rather than to her home at Southwell House, Nottingham.[86] This, of course, undermines the image of the Ladies' Association as a particularly progressive force within moral reform politics, especially since not all Poor Law officials subscribed to the principle of selection. The notion of the deserving poor prompted Sophia Lonsdale, member of the Central Poor Law Commission, to comment:

> Will some one here kindly tell us once and for all the exact meaning of that blessed word 'deserving'; because 'deservingness' is so very vague. What do the people to whom it applied 'deserve' and why do they 'deserve' it? and can one human being ascertain exactly what another human being 'deserves'?[87]

Not surprisingly, given these definitions, many women were viewed as undeserving: unmarried mothers who produced more than one illegitimate child were refused help. At the same time, it was feared that some single mothers who lived with their parents were deliberately sent to the workhouse to avoid midwifery and other medical expenses, since they returned home after the ratepayers 'have borne the expense of their illness'.[88] Most single mothers had not been in receipt of Poor Law relief before their confinement and voluntarily discharged themselves within a few weeks of the birth of their babies. The Ladies' Associations had little desire to offer free maternity care to such women.[89] Compassion was therefore mixed with a heavy blend of class scepticism, for Ladies' Associations shared the Benthamite belief that the workhouse should not be regarded as a maternity home whose expenses were defrayed by ratepayers.

> Few ladies are aware of the light in which the Workhouse is regarded by thousands of girls who have fallen into sin. It is scarcely too much to say that the working of the Poor Law in this matter is a system of 'Sin made Easy'. They come to look upon the Workhouse as a home to which they have a perfect right to resort when they are in trouble. Into the house they are freely admitted, are lodged and fed, have the best medical aid and nursing at the expense of the ratepayers; and in the vast majority of cases not a penny can be recovered either from the girl herself, or from the man who is the author of such mischief.[90]

From the 1880s onwards, many women Guardians throughout England wanted women who had produced more than one illegitimate offspring to be compulsorily detained so they could not bear any more.[91] Several Boards of Guardians issued circular letters advocating legislation empowering Poor Law authorities to detain women with illegitimate children who entered the workhouse.[92] Quite significantly, a resolution (put forward by Agatha Stacey, Birmingham Poor Law Guardian and a leading member of the city's Ladies' Association) was passed in favour of the detention of single mothers at the Society for Promoting the Return of Women as Poor Law Guardians.[93] Of course, not all Poor Law Guardians or social reformers agreed. Beatrice Webb argued against compulsory detainment since they were

> unable to ascertain how far this compulsory detention is advocated for the purpose of educating the mothers; how far for that of deterring them from 'coming on the rates'; how far for that of punishing them for having caused expense; and how far for that of preventing them from further breeding.[94]

Others thought it unjust to detain unmarried mothers because it meant that only one parent (i.e. the mother) was penalised whereas the other (i.e. the father) was exempt.[95] Many women Guardians opposed compulsory detention because it resembled the anti-women clauses of the Contagious Diseases Acts but Ladies' Associations seemed to support Agatha Stacey.[96] Such attitudes, of course, would hardly be likely to break down class barriers and may well have caused resentment towards middle-class visitors.

Financial considerations were important when the Ladies' Associations eventually gave help. Single mothers were discouraged from being a burden on the rates so work was quickly found for them as domestic servants, while respectable and trustworthy foster homes were found for their babies.[97] In some places single mothers were expected to contribute about half their earnings towards the maintenance of their children.[98] Occasionally it was felt desirable to place the mothers in homes where they might be trained before being sent out to service.[99] In these cases, Ladies' Associations paid for the babies to be cared for[100] by the wives of clergymen or other Christians.[101]

Nevertheless, Ladies' Associations were all too aware of the inadequacies of the economic system. Domestic service wages in general were thought insufficient,[102] so young women like Bessie Limberly from Nottingham who 'only earns 8s a week at present is being helped until she can earn more'.[103] Low wages, of course, affected the health of children.

> If they go into service they must find persons who will keep the children for the smallest possible amount. Under these circumstances, without any intention of ill-treatment, it is next to impossible that the children should be properly fed and cared for.[104]

Babies taken out of the lying-in wards of workhouses rarely survived: many were dead within a few weeks.[105] Ladies' Associations feared that unless single mothers were helped financially, there were only two courses open to them: either to kill their babies or support them by sin.[106] Consequently, Ladies' Associations supplemented the income of single mothers and provided their children with clothing and footwear.[107] The Oxford branch generally contributed over one-fifth and sometimes as much as half of the expenditure, especially when the single mother was not in robust health and could at intervals earn little or nothing.[108] Nottingham combined charitable help with state assistance: Poor Law Guardians were encouraged to pay for the children while the home helped mothers financially survive.[109]

The seemingly benevolent gestures of the Ladies' Associations were hedged with class assumptions. First, it was cheaper to donate a small amount of money towards the upkeep of children than to support both in the workhouse. Even when mothers were placed in rescue homes (many of which charged 5s a week for young women and from 6s 6d to 7s 6d a week for mothers and children in 1911) it was thought to cost less than the workhouse.[110] Such help prevented single mothers from claiming on the rates and was seen to be considerably cheaper than consigning them to a reform house or lock ward later on.

> Were it not for the reformatories, penitentiaries, . . . and other voluntary and benevolent associations, the rates would be frightfully increased, merely by the children cast out of the Workhouses, and returning as girls and women . . . Individual charity certainly lessens the burden of ratepayers.[111]

Second, this type of help tended to reinforce the middle-class work ethic. In the process Ladies' Associations thought to end a workhouse dependency that was seen to be destructive of both the individual and of society. Third, it is not inconceivable that having financial responsibility for babies may, by deepening their sense of responsibility, have had a steadying effect on young unmarried mothers.[112] Certainly, the Nottingham branch tried to cultivate the mother's maternal love as fully as possible by sending them frequent reports and photographs of their children in order 'that mother love which has driven many an unwedded mother into lower depths of shame to earn money for her child, is thus used as a blessed lever to help her to rise into a purer life'.[113] And of course, Ladies' Associations threatened benefit withdrawal if single mothers reneged on their responsibilities. Some, perhaps not surprisingly given the ideological climate of the day, criticised even this limited financial aid to single mothers because it was thought to encourage vice.[114]

Ladies' Associations encouraged mothers to apply for affiliation summonses to force fathers to pay towards the cost of their illegitimate offspring. Money was often advanced to mothers to start legal proceedings (which was later repaid from affiliation orders) or else special officers were paid a guinea for each successful case brought to the magistrates.[115] To some extent this provides an example of how the sexual double standard was challenged in practice as Ladies' Associations were concerned that men, not just women, should be held responsible for children.[116] However, the reason that fathers were held responsible for illegitimate babies was as much to do with fiscal prudence as with moral equality: once again Ladies' Associations were conscious of the cost to the ratepayers. As Ellice Hopkins rather sarcastically remarked:

> You may ruin this poor girl: we as rate-payers will pay the expenses of the confinement of the mother of your child; we will see after her and your little one; and we will set you perfectly free to go and do the like to another respectable girl, and then we will undertake her too.[117]

However, there were great difficulties in collecting maintenance from fathers and so the practice was discontinued in many towns and cities.[118]

By the late 1880s Ladies' Associations and Poor Law Guardians advocated a new solution to the problem of workhouse single mothers. In line with other contemporary moves towards the specialisation of social problems, homes for single mothers were set up by Ladies' Associations, often with the help of female Poor Law Guardians, in Liverpool in 1889, London in the 1880s, Portsmouth in the 1890s, Oxford in 1899 and Birmingham and Nottingham in the early part of the twentieth century.[119] Of course, homes for single mothers were not new: the Homes of Hope established in the 1860s (and managed by all-male committees who appointed paid workers) for the 'less degraded class of Penitent Young Women', targeted single mothers. However, these homes were regarded as inadequate. In fact the Charity Organisation Society criticised the Homes of Hope because no women were employed at committee level, for poor financial management, and for ill-equipped, small, dreary and dirty institutions.[120] By the 1880s experienced rescue workers apparently made little use of them. The Salvation Army also set up a series of homes for unmarried mothers which were thought to be more successful than the former. Quite often homes for single mothers took over institutions for the reform of prostitutes exhibiting once again the perceived relationship between single mothers and prostitution.

There were a number of reasons why Ladies' Associations founded homes for single mothers. First, it was feared that infanticide was on the increase.[121] Flora Villas, a home for single mothers and their babies at Carshalton, required prospective inmates to stay at the home for at least six months because of a fear of infant death and illness.

> They are mostly considerably under weight, and are often in a deplorably neglected condition. They have had a bad start in life even before their birth. The mothers are too frequently in a debilitated state . . . Of the fifteen babies taken into the Home during the past year only one was up to normal weight.[122]

LIVERPOOL
JOHN MOORES UNIVERSITY
AVRIL ROBARTS LRC
TEL. 0151 231 4022

Second, the workhouse was thought to be an inadequate place for young single mothers and their babies. Both Ladies' Associations and Poor Law Guardians wanted to ensure that single mothers did not fall totally from moral grace and believed that first offenders needed to be protected from the immorality of those who were considered to be hardened and irredeemable cases:

> the committee have felt that for some long time their work has been very sadly handicapped for the want of a home to which these young girls might be sent, instead of mixing for long periods of time – as many often have to do – with the degraded and vicious women who haunt our workhouses all over the country . . . The moral atmosphere of a workhouse is such that no young girl should be introduced into it if we have any hope or wish to reclaim her.[123]

Third, the system of baby fostering was thought defective because it undermined the ideal of natural motherhood. The law of nature, it was believed, dictated that their mothers should look after babies. It was not only considered unnatural for babies to be separated from their mothers but also was thought to weaken the mothers' sense of responsibility.[124] Single mothers who paid for the keep of their babies, but who rarely saw them, came to view their babies as a 'hindrance and obstacle' rather than objects of love and affection.[125] Fourth, Ladies' Associations were able to influence single mothers more effectively in a home than a workhouse because they remained there longer. In Portsmouth, mothers were able to stay in the home for two years;[126] from 1909 the babies of Oxford single mothers remained in the home while their mothers worked elsewhere. Finally, the usual economic considerations played a significant part in the setting up of the homes as it was argued that a home for single mothers would effect a saving to the ratepayers.[127] In the long term it was thought to be cheaper. Of course, this argument may have been used to convince Poor Law Guardians who were less sympathetic to specialist homes for single mothers.

Once again, many single mothers failed to live up to expectations: in Oxford young women seemed to 'fall in to sin' and reports that 'she is now living an immoral life, she is going on in her own wilful way, in the midst of danger and temptation' were quite common.[128] In 1913, as a result of the National Insurance Act 1911, all working mothers, whatever their marital status, received free medical treatment, the services of a midwife, a grant of 30s which helped them defray the cost of maternity care and possibly sickness benefit of 10s a week for thirteen weeks, all of which may have helped a number of working-class single mothers to avoid the workhouse infirmary, and with it charitable 'do-gooders', completely.

As a consequence of their educational, legislative and organisational actions, one is led to believe that the Ladies' Associations were neither prudish nor exceptionally radical but that they contained a complex mixture of humanitarianism, feminism and class prejudice. On the one hand, the committees of the various Ladies' Associations formed part of a circle which regarded themselves as a progressive force in local politics. They aimed to break down class barriers by promoting female solidarity and one cannot assume that the stated policies were insincere. In questioning the double standard, in attempting to block prostitution at what it considered to be the source, by offering practical solutions to the problems of single mothers, by training potentially troublesome young women for a job, by removing children at moral risk and by campaigning to raise the age of sexual consent the Ladies' Associations challenged orthodox opinion and provided useful assistance to a number of young women. On the other hand, the managers of the Ladies' Associations were inhibited by a powerful class ideology which undermined their attempts at creating a united womanhood. Time after time, working-class women were categorised into the deserving and the undeserving, a division consonant with the class ideology of the time. Expectations of appropriate working-class female behaviour also informed the policies and practice of the Ladies' Associations. As a consequence young working-class women were recast into an appropriate domesticated feminine mode – based, of course, upon middle-class expectations. Moreover, the women who managed the Ladies' Associations may have promoted an idealised picture of female solidarity but their wishes remained unfulfilled. Despite the energies of these women, each of the branches enjoyed only a limited success, largely because the working class had little desire to imbibe the cultural and moral values put forward by their middle-class 'superiors'. More importantly, despite the efforts of the Ladies' Associations, prostitution continued.

Notes

1 Ellice Hopkins provided the inspiration for training homes, registry offices and clothing clubs, but others were responsible for putting her theory into practice (*NUWW Occasional Paper* February 1910).
2 *Birmingham Ladies' Association for the Care and Protection of Young Girls Annual Reports* 1887–1914.
3 'Unfallen' was probably a euphemism for virginal (*NUWW Quarterly Magazine*, December 1892, p. 6).
4 Leeds Ladies' Association for the Care and Protection of Friendless Girls, Minute Book, March 1888.
5 Ellice Hopkins, *How to Start Preventive Work* (London: Hatchards, 1884), p. 15.
6 *Leeds Ladies' Association for the Care and Protection of Friendless Girls Annual Report* 1884, p. 13.
7 Copy of a letter from Florence Kitson, Honorary Secretary of Leeds Ladies' Association for the Care and Protection of Friendless Girls, sent to unknown person/s *c.* 1910.
8 *Seeking and Saving* (September 1885), p. 14.
9 *Rochester Diocesan Association for Friendless Girls Annual Report* 1895, p. 5.
10 Police Orders, Birmingham City Police, October 31st 1910.

11 See Michelle Cale, '"Saved from a Life of Vice and Crime": Reformatory and Industrial Schools for Girls, *c.* 1854–*c.* 1901' (DPhil thesis, University of Oxford, 1993), for a discussion of this in relation to industrial schools for girls.

12 *BLACPYG Annual Report* 1905.

13 Rochester Diocesan Association for Friendless Girls, Minutes, January 3rd 1900.

14 Norfolk and Norwich Ladies' Association for the Care of Friendless Girls, Minute Book, May 1884.

15 Leeds Ladies' Association for the Care and Protection of Friendless Girls, Minute Book, February 1913

16 Ibid., October 4th 1900.

17 See Pamela Horn, 'The Education and Employment of Working-Class Girls, 1870–1914', *History of Education*, 17, 1988, pp. 71–82, for a discussion on working-class education for girls.

18 In Birmingham, weekly lessons were held to help the young women learn to read and write – but they were rarely taught more than basic literacy. Sometimes, as at Oxford, the Ladies' Association sent younger girls to a National School or, as at Leeds, to the local board school (*Leeds Ladies' Association for the Care and Protection of Friendless Girls Annual Report* 1893, p. 7).

19 Ellice Hopkins, *How to Start Preventive Work*, p. 28.

20 *BLACPYG Annual Report* 1912.

21 *Manchester and Salford Central Association of Societies for Girls and Women Annual Report* 1891, p. 27.

22 *BLACPYG Annual Reports* 1908–1914.

23 *BLACPYG Annual Reports* 1887–1914.

24 Ellice Hopkins, *How to Start Preventive Work*, p. 23.

25 Payment was required by the girls' family or the Poor Law Union towards the cost of upkeep and training. For example, Norwich Ladies' Association charged 2s 6d for Norwich girls, 3s 4d for workhouse cases and 3s 6d for those outside of Norwich, whereas Nottingham charged 4s 6d weekly.

26 Apparently there was great discussion about the advisability of taking in family washing and at first the Norfolk Committee decided against it because of the constant change of the girls in the home, and it would be inefficient as the girls were to be trained as domestic servants not laundry maids (Norfolk and Norwich Ladies' Association for the Care of Friendless Girls, Minute Book, October 1885). However, the Norfolk and Norwich branch did introduce laundry work in 1897, but in fact the home, which had been open for fourteen years, closed soon after so the introduction of laundry work may well have been a last desperate attempt to make it financially viable (*Norfolk and Norwich Ladies' Association for the Care of Friendless Girls Annual Report* 1898).

27 Ellice Hopkins, *How to Start Preventive Work*, p. 9.

28 *Manchester and Salford Central Association of Societies for Girls and Women Annual Report* 1891, p. 28.

29 This nursery developed over the years; initially it had been the young women's evening dining room which was not deemed satisfactory. In 1887 a new nursery was built. As a result the larger, brighter nursery became increasingly popular among local parents (*BLACPYG Annual Reports* 1887–1914).

30 *BLACPYG Annual Report* 1887.

31 Ibid., 1888.

32 Pamela Horn's *The Rise and Fall of the Victorian Servant* (Dublin: Gill and Macmillan, 1975), p. 76, has shown that lower-middle-class families would often employ a nursemaid to look after their children. The job of the maid would be to dress the children, play with them and take them for walks. Nannies were employed only in richer establishments.

33 *BLACPYG Annual Report* 1906, p. 8.

34 *Birmingham Daily Post* (March 10th 1909), p. 3.
35 Southwell House, Nottingham, Minute Book, January 1893.
36 *Seeking and Saving* (July 1884).
37 Organising recreation for the working class was quite common. For instance, Lady Charlotte, in Wales, took her male workforce to the Great Exhibition of 1851. See Angela V. John (ed.), *Our Mothers' Land* (Cardiff: University of Wales Press, 1991).
38 *BLACPYG Annual Reports* 1887–1914.
39 Ibid., 1887–1914.
40 *Leeds Ladies' Association for the Care and Protection of Friendless Girls Annual Report* 1902, p. 5.
41 Ellice Hopkins, *How to Start Preventive Work*, p. 16.
42 In Nottingham a silver thimble was given after three years' service (*The Southwell Diocesan Magazine*, May 1888, p. 73).
43 *Leeds Ladies' Association for the Care and Protection of Friendless Girls Annual Report* 1885, p. 3.
44 Ibid., 1903, p. 6.
45 Ibid., 1902, p. 8.
46 Leeds Ladies' Association for the Care and Protection of Friendless Girls, Minute Book, April 1892.
47 Norfolk and Norwich Ladies' Association for the Care of Friendless Girls, Minute Book, September 1885.
48 Ibid., September 1885.
49 Case Books, Southwell House, Nottingham, 1897–1901.
50 Letter sent by ex-inmate of Southwell House to the Ladies' Committee, 1885.
51 Leeds Ladies' Association for the Care and Protection of Friendless Girls, Minute Book, February 1911.
52 *Daily Telegraph* (October 14th 1878), p. 6.
53 Leeds Ladies' Association for the Care and Protection of Friendless Girls, Minute Book, June 1892.
54 Ibid., June 1892.
55 Case Books, Southwell House, Nottingham, 1885–1914.
56 Leeds Ladies' Association for the Care and Protection of Friendless Girls, Minute Book, March 1893.
57 *Oxford Ladies' Association for the Care of Friendless Girls Annual Report* 1897, p. 6.
58 Ellice Hopkins, *How to Start Preventive Work*, p. 33.
59 *Leeds Ladies' Association for the Care and Protection of Friendless Girls Annual Report* 1885, p. 7.
60 Ellice Hopkins, *How to Start Preventive Work*, p. 12.
61 Norfolk and Norwich Ladies' Association for the Care of Friendless Girls, Minute Book, April 1886.
62 Mrs Percy Bunting, *NUWW Conference* 1890, p. 58.
63 Ibid., 1890, p. 59.
64 *Seeking and Saving* (October 1883), p. 280.
65 *Rescue Society Annual Report* 1881, p. 76.
66 *Minority Report of the Poor Law Commission* 1907, p. 93.
67 For example, the Homes of Hope were established for the 'less degraded class of Penitent Young Women', mostly single mothers (draft report of COS Visit 1888 in Correspondence between COS and Homes of Hope, A/FWA/C/D23/2).
68 See Patricia Hollis, *Ladies Elect: Women in English Local Government, 1865–1914* (Oxford: Clarendon Press, 1987), pp. 267–271, for a discussion of the role of women Guardians in the rescue of unmarried mothers, nationally.
69 For example, a member of the committee of the Rochester Diocesan Association for the Care of Friendless Girls was responsible for superintending the placing

out of babies for the Workhouse Girls' Aid Committee (*Rochester Diocesan Association for the Care of Friendless Girls Annual Report* 1895, p. 7).

70 *Queen Charlotte's Lying-In Hospital Annual Report* 1874, p. 8.
71 See Patricia Hollis, *Ladies Elect*, p. 268. See *Southwell House Annual Report* 1885, p. 6, for a Nottingham example of this.
72 Ellice Hopkins, Minutes of Evidence Taken Before Select Committee on Law Relating to the Protection of Young Girls, June 16th 1882, p. 8.
73 *Seeking and Saving* (July 1883), p. 180.
74 *NUWW Quarterly Magazine* (December 1892), p. 10.
75 *Minority Report of the Poor Law Commission* 1907, p. 7.
76 Pat Thane, 'Women and the Poor Law in Victorian and Edwardian England', *History Workshop Journal*, autumn, 1978, p. 39.
77 Ellice Hopkins, *Seeking and Saving* (October 1883), p. 256.
78 See Regina G. Kunzel, *Fallen Women, Problem Girls* (New Haven, CT: Yale University Press, 1993), who draws attention to the need by the American authorities to contain the sexuality of single mothers.
79 See Carol Smart, *Regulating Womanhood* (London: Routledge, 1992), for a discussion of marriage as a form of control over women.
80 The Birmingham workhouse was certainly not full of prostitutes. In 1891 the majority of inmates were over 60 years of age and many were in their seventies (Census Returns 1891).
81 Pat Thane, 'Women and the Poor Law in Victorian and Edwardian England', pp. 39–44, has demonstrated that the values and attitudes of the Poor Law Amendment Act 1834 were still held in later Victorian and Edwardian England.
82 *NUWW Quarterly Magazine* (December 1892), pp. 10–11.
83 Ibid., p. 10.
84 *Seeking and Saving* (October 1883), p. 255.
85 See Pat Thane, 'Women and the Poor Law in Victorian and Edwardian England', pp. 28–51, and Patricia Hollis, *Ladies Elect*, pp. 267–271, for a discussion of the treatment of single mothers in workhouses.
86 Southwell House Committee Minutes, February 1897.
87 *NUWW Conference* 1910.
88 *BLACPYG Annual Report* 1892, p. 14.
89 *Minority Report of the Poor Law Commission* 1907, p. 94.
90 *NUWW Quarterly Magazine* (March 1892), p. 14.
91 Helen Bosanquet, *The Poor Law Report of 1909* (London: Macmillan, 1909), p. 246, believed that it was highly desirable to have powers of detention for a certain section of unmarried mothers. See also Patricia Hollis, *Ladies Elect*, p. 269.
92 Helen Newill, *West Midland District Poor Law Conference*, p. 9.
93 *Englishwoman's Review* (July 14th 1888), p. 324.
94 *Minority Report of the Poor Law Commission* 1907, p. 98.
95 Miss Clifford, 'Unmarried Mothers and their Children', *NUWW Conference* 1911, p. 24.
96 Patricia Hollis, *Ladies Elect*, p. 269.
97 *Greenwich and Deptford Workhouse Girls' Aid Committee Annual Report* 1895, p. 2.
98 *Oxford Ladies' Association for the Care of Friendless Girls Annual Report* 1895, p. 7.
99 Ibid., 1893, p. 7.
100 For example, in Nottingham there was a Children's Fund which provided payment for the boarded out babies of mothers who were being trained in homes (*Southwell House Annual Report* 1905).

101 *Seeking and Saving* (October 1883), p. 256.
102 *The Southwell Diocesan Magazine* (September 1889), p. 179.
103 Southwell House, Nottingham, Committee Minutes, February 24th 1897.
104 *Oxford Ladies' Association for the Care of Friendless Girls Annual Report* 1895, p. 7.
105 *Minority Report of the Poor Law Commission* 1907, p. 98. If mothers remained in the workhouse they fared no better. In 1907, 1,050 out of 8,483 babies were born in the workhouse. Ann Higginbotham has suggested that 'nineteenth century medical men estimated that 60% or more of nursed-out infants died in the first year' (Ann Higginbotham, 'Respectable Sinners: Salvation Army Rescue Work with Unmarried Mothers, 1884–1914', in Gail Malmgreen (ed.) *Religion in the Lives of English Women, 1760–1930* (London: Croom Helm, 1986), p. 224).
106 *Seeking and Saving* (April 1882), p. 73.
107 *BLACPYG Annual Report* 1888.
108 *Oxford Ladies' Association for the Care of Friendless Girls Annual Report* 1893, p. 8.
109 Case Books, Southwell House, Nottingham, 1897–1901.
110 Mrs Nott-Bower, *South Eastern District Poor Law Conference*, 1911–1912, p. 175.
111 Anonymous letter printed in *Report of the Workhouse Visiting Committee* (London: Longman, Brown, Green, Longman and Roberts, 1860), p. 15.
112 *Greenwich and Deptford Workhouse Girls' Aid Committee Annual Report* 1896, p. 2.
113 *The Southwell Diocesan Magazine* (September 1889), p. 179.
114 *Seeking and Saving* (April 1882), p. 73.
115 Southwark Association for Girls, Minute Book, February 14th 1906.
116 *Seeking and Saving* (October 1883), p. 255.
117 Ibid., p. 255.
118 There are records of forty-one men being charged with 'bastardy' between 1899 and 1900 in Birmingham and asked to pay maintenance fees of about 1s–3s a week. It is not known whether these prosecutions were as a result of the Workhouse Magdalen Branch's influence (Register of the Court of Summary Jurisdiction, 1899–1900).
119 The Salvation Army also set up a series of homes for unmarried mothers. See Ann Higginbotham, 'Respectable Sinners'.
120 Draft report of COS Visit 1888 in correspondence between COS and Homes of Hope (A/FWA/C/D23/2).
121 Anon, *Betrayers and Betrayed*, c. 1896.
122 *Rochester Diocesan Association for the Care of Friendless Girls Annual Report* 1906, p. 19.
123 Helen Newill, Minutes of Evidence, *Royal Commission on the Poor Laws* 1909, p. 402.
124 Mrs Herbert Phillips, *NUWW Conference* 1890, p. 67.
125 *Seeking and Saving* (April 1890), p. 490.
126 Miss Clifford, *NUWW Conference* 1911, p. 30.
127 Helen Newill, *West Midlands District Poor Law Conference*, p. 29.
128 *Oxford Ladies' Association for the Care of Friendless Girls Annual Report* 1892, p. 8.

Part III

The making of the mentally deficient

Prostitution and the 'feeble-minded'

5 The background

(By the late nineteenth century prostitution became more and more associated with the 'feeble-minded', a fact which, in turn, prompted new initiatives to prevent prostitution.) Homes for 'feeble-minded' young women, who were either perceived to be at moral risk or who had 'fallen', were founded throughout England by a number of influential (mostly female) social reformers concerned that working-class 'feeble-minded' young women could not cope alone. On the one hand, this part of the book will argue, the homes were a benevolent gesture on the part of a group of committed philanthropists who sought to ameliorate the lives of those perceived to be in moral danger. Their attempts to help the 'feeble-minded' can be seen to demonstrate a nurturing philosophy since middle-class women wanted to protect a vulnerable section of the female population who had been rejected by society. On the other hand, this caring approach was undermined by a powerful class ideology. The women who founded and managed the homes, like women involved in other preventive organisations, were middle class, and clearly driven by middle-class values and prejudices. This chapter argues that the reasons why homes were built must also be considered within the context of a number of significant social changes: in mental health provision; in attitudes towards female madness; in the development of eugenics; and in the economic ideology of the late nineteenth century. Chapter 6 examines how these ideas were put into practice.

Changing perceptions of the 'feeble-minded'

Developments in mental health theories

The relationship between prostitution and the 'feeble-minded' can be understood only within the context of the 'psychiatric revolution' of the nineteenth century which helped modify the categorisation, perception and treatment of the 'feeble-minded'. Before the nineteenth century, those who were deemed 'mad' were either thought to be possessed by the devil (needing to have the demons beaten out of them) or believed to be wild beasts (needing to be tamed). Viewed as animals, the 'mad' were thought to be insensible to cold, hunger and human emotion so were put in locked cells, chained up, constrained in strait-jackets, frequently whipped and often kept naked. In the Bethnal Green asylum

> a woman subject to violent seizures was placed in a pigsty, feet and fists bound; when the crisis had passed she was tied to her bed, covered only by a blanket; when she was allowed to take a few steps, an iron bar was placed between her legs, attached by rings to her ankles and by a short chain to handcuffs.[2]

Visitors to the eighteenth-century Bethlehem asylum in London, commonly referred to as Bedlam, 'paid their pennies to see howling maniacs, naked and chained, alien creatures in whom irrationality and filth had reached the extremes of the recognisably human'.[3] Willoughby Hyatt Dickenson, chairman of the National Association for Promoting the Welfare of the Feeble-Minded (NAPWFM), noted in 1903:

> It is hardly a hundred years since the spirit of the Revolution came to the rescue of the insane in Paris and struck off the iron manacles with which the patients in the Bicetre Hospital were tortured. Within living memory the cure of lunatics was by lashes, surprise baths and rotating chairs.[4]

Historians have viewed such madhouses as these more as menageries than as institutions for the care of mentally ill people.[5]

Historians tend to believe that the 'Enlightenment' heralded a softening of attitudes towards the mad with the result that madness came to be defined as an illness rather than a state of evil or a bestial condition. Doctors began to assert that madness had a somatic, that is a bodily, base, which could therefore be treated physically.[6] Andrew Scull has observed that 'madness was increasingly seen as something which could be authoritatively diagnosed, certified, and treated only by a group of legally recognised experts'.[7] As a consequence of new psychological theories those perceived to be mad or mentally deficient came to be viewed as sympathetic objects of pity to be cared for rather than demons and animals to be restrained. Instead of brutal captivity, patients were encouraged to develop self-respect and self-control within a therapeutic rather than a physically disciplinary context.[8] As the definitions of mental patients changed so did the architecture of the buildings in which they were housed. Before the Lunatics Act 1845, those considered mad were sent to public hospitals such as Bethlehem, to the workhouse or to private 'madhouses'.[9] The construction of a number of new lunatic asylums (between 1845 and 1847 approximately thirty-six new public asylums were built) as a result of this Act marked a physical as well as a psychological break with the past. Indeed, the nineteenth century can be considered to be as much an 'institutional' age as an industrial one,[10] with specialist buildings, prisons, workhouses, constructed for the care of the criminal and the poor, schools built for working-class children and newly built mental hospitals, such as Colney Hatch in London, replacing what was commonly considered the brutal incarceration of the madhouse.

The nineteenth century marked another turning point in the classification of those deemed mentally ill. It became clear that the insane had been inaccurately grouped together into a homogeneous body whereas at least two main categories could be identified: those who were clearly insane and who displayed abnormal and deranged mental characteristics; and those who suffered from a lack of intellectual power.[11] Moreover, a distinction was made between treatable illnesses such as temporary insanity and those that were permanent due to congenital defect. By the end of the nineteenth century, the medical profession felt able to identify different categories of congenital mental defect and to differentiate between those deemed to be mentally deficient. Those with learning difficulties were thus classified as idiots, imbeciles and feeble-minded. It is difficult to determine the origin of the term 'feeble-minded'. It has been suggested that it was first coined by Charles Trevelyan in 1876,[12] but the classification was used at least ten years before in 1866 by Peter Martin Duncan, who set out terms for the classification, training and education of the 'feeble-minded', imbecile and idiotic.[13] It was certainly used by the Charity Organisation Society in its evidence to the Royal Commission on the Blind and Deaf Idiots Act 1886, the International Congress of Hygiene's Special Committee in 1891, and above all the Royal Commission in 1908; it was in widespread medical use by the early twentieth century. Nonetheless, there is no doubt that those concerned with the 'feeble-minded' constructed their own rather wide and (perhaps to modern eyes) unscientific and spurious definitions:

> This title has been applied by experts to those young people who are too mentally deficient to be properly educated or trained in an ordinary school or training home, who are not only below the average, but below the normal child, yet are neither 'idiots' nor 'imbeciles'.[14]

The Royal College of Physicians' definition, which was later adopted by the Royal Commission, alleged that the 'feeble-minded' were

> persons who may be capable of earning a living under favourable circumstances, but are incapable from mental defect, existing from birth or from an early age: (1) of competing on equal terms with their normal fellows, or (2) of managing themselves and their affairs with ordinary prudence.[15]

It was believed to be a congenital defect which like blindness or deafness was incurable.[16] However, even the Royal Commission of 1908 recognised that it had no precise medical definition as it had not been 'the subject of

Table 5.1 Percentage of 'feeble-minded' people in selected towns, 1901

	Population	*F-M*	*% per pop*
Stoke-on-Trent	154,889	328	0.21
Birmingham	245,216	421	0.17
Manchester	712,420	818	0.11
Hull and Sculcoates	254,884	141	0.05
Durham	132,738	73	0.05
Somerset	153,725	328	0.21
Wilts	151,871	340	0.22
Notts	145,339	232	0.16
Lincoln	150,351	224	0.15

any scientific or uniform investigation',[17] and its exact meaning was the subject of much debate until the Mental Deficiency Act 1913.[18] Table 5.1, taken from the *Eugenics Review*,[19] indicates that the category 'feeble-minded' was most definitely an unstable one: why Durham should have so significantly fewer 'feeble-minded' (F-M) people than Stoke-on-Trent remains a mystery, making it important to remain critical of this medical paradigm.[20]

The influence of eugenics

Eugenist theories may well have determined the perception and treatment of the 'feeble-minded'.[21] Many leaders of the 'feeble-minded' movement – people such as Mary Dendy, Ellen Pinsent, William Potts and A.F. Tredgold – were members of the Eugenic Society and there was close co-operation between the two main 'feeble-minded' organisations (the National Association for Promoting the Welfare of the Feeble-Minded and the National Association for the Care of the Feeble-Minded) and the Eugenic Society in general. Eugenists were committed to the 'science of race culture, the improvement of the human stock, the encouragement of worthy parenthood, and the prevention of the unfit'.[22] Nature, it was argued, was stronger than nurture. There were two branches of eugenics: 'positive' eugenists wanted to increase the numbers of those who would be a credit and advantage to the race; 'negative' eugenists wanted to reduce the number of 'undesirables', among them the 'feeble-minded'. Negative eugenists wanted to prevent the 'insane, the alcoholic, the deaf-mute, the tuberculous, and often the criminal (e.g. the prostitute) from marrying',[23] since they believed that the world was overpopulated with inadequates who had to be taken care of. *The Malthusian* even declared that

> those who say that we are not over-peopled will surely agree that we in 1889 would have been better off without 84,340 lunatics . . . Think of the numbers besides whose intelligence has to be devoted to the care of these and those other miserable products of human folly, whose

incurable diseases are due for the most part to the fatal inheritance of a degenerate constitution.[24]

Eugenists alleged, without much scientific evidence, that 70 per cent of 'feeble-mindedness' was inherited. They believed not only that there was 'ample evidence to show that the offspring of feeble-minded persons usually inherited their defectiveness in some degree',[25] but also that the child of 'feeble-minded' parents might be at least one degree worse.[26] The doctrine that physical and mental limitations were handed on to a second generation and the desire to arrest the transmission of these defects to unborn generations,[27] therefore, lay at the heart of the desire to guard and protect 'feeble-minded' women.[28] In addition, the 'feeble-minded' were viewed as sharing an inability to appreciate the differences between right and wrong,[29] especially concerning issues of sexual morality. They were judged to be lacking in will-power and defined as being incapable of existing 'normally' in society since they were clearly unable to sustain themselves economically: 'feeble-minded' women were always the last to be taken on when work was to be had and yet the soonest to be dismissed when it ran out, and certainly always the least well paid.[30]

It was natural for eugenists to equate a weak intellect with the working class and poverty; they considered the 'feeble-minded' to constitute a source of pauperism, crime and immorality.[31] The East End of London, for example, was seen to be composed almost entirely of the 'feeble-minded' for 'if we could take out of it all the feeble-minded, the inebriates, the early mental cases, who would recognise the East End?'[32] Indeed, the National Association for Promoting the Welfare of the Feeble-Minded argued that there were at least 42,000 children of the 'poorer', that is working class, who if left to themselves 'infallibly add to the vice, the misery, the degradation of our race, and pass on to another generation the ills they have brought on their own'.[33]

'Feeble-mindedness' was certainly perceived to be intimately connected with crime. A.F. Tredgold, the 'medical expert' to the Royal Commission on the Feeble-Minded, was convinced that 10 per cent of 'feeble-minded' had criminal tendencies sufficient to be a menace to society. He associated 'feeble-mindedness' with

> insanity, epilepsy, alcoholism, consumption and many other conditions of diminished mental and bodily vigour . . . which give rise to such a large proportion of our criminals, paupers and unemployables . . . In investigating the family history of the feeble minded, again and again I have found that their brothers and sisters, if not actually defective, were criminals, prostitutes, paupers or ne'er-do-wells.[34]

In fact, it was believed that 'feeble-mindedness' led inevitably to criminality: 'Unfit for ordinary school education, turned adrift from home, these feeble-minded individuals wander about living as best they can. Their history is made out of vagabondage, larceny, incendiaryism and criminal assaults.'[35] Negative eugenists offered a biological explanation for this type of social failure,[36] with some demanding the 'replacement of social reform based on the control of the environment by reform based on the control of heredity'.[37] To their minds, poverty, crime and prostitution could be eliminated once it was recognised that these were inherited characteristics rather than environmentally determined.

Dysfunctional families not only were feared for themselves but, also, because they reproduced at an alarming rate, threatening to overwhelm the better endowed. It was assumed by eugenists that the 'feeble-minded' produced more children than 'normal' parents.[38] A.F. Tredgold claimed that the average number of births to 'feeble-minded' women was 7.3, which contrasted with 4.63 for those considered normal.[39] The differential birth rate between the normal and the 'feeble-minded' would inevitably increase the number of 'feeble-minded' children who, in turn, would give birth to 'feeble-minded' children of their own.

> I know one feeble-minded woman who has given birth to nine children, and I once saw a feeble-minded girl whose defective mother had had eleven illegitimate children, three of whom were known to have inherited the mother's mental weakness . . . The method of dealing with this large and important group is obvious: such children should never have been born.[40]

By the 1880s, middle and upper classes were using birth control measures to restrict the size of their families;[41] eugenists were particularly concerned that those of an inferior breed would swamp the higher social classes.[42] A 'feeble, helpless and half-witted population', it was alleged, might overrun Britain,[43] because the feeblest, the least moral, and the most worthless classes of the community multiplied the most rapidly.

> It is the pauper and the criminal class which supplies the human rabbits who multiply in the warrens of our great city. The educated and the well to do increase much less rapidly. Hence, the annual increase in the population proceeds mainly from the classes which add no strength to the nation . . . with low cerebral development, renewing the race more rapidly than those of higher attainments.[44]

These ideas were rooted in the fear that an unimpeded increase in the 'feeble-minded' population would lead to Britain losing its place among the world's leading nations. Eugenic theories must be placed within the context of the British defeat in the Boer War, with its shocking revelations of the general unfitness of the recruits, and an agricultural and industrial depression. From the 1870s onwards the British economy also faced serious competition from overseas trade. These anxieties reinforced fears that a demographic deterioration would result in further national decline.[45] Arnold White, a leading eugenist, believed that if the British nation, 'with its command of the sea and a premier place among the empires of the earth', was to survive, it needed to 'check the multiplication of the unfit'.[46] His views were shared by other eugenists. A.F. Tredgold stated:

> National Degeneracy is no myth but a very serious reality. In the past, more nations have sunk to a position of utter insignificance or have been entirely blotted out of existence, as the result of the moral, intellectual, and physical degeneracy of their citizens, than of wars, famine or any other conditions. Today the contest is perhaps rather more one of intellect than of muscle, but competition between nations is still as keen as ever it was in the past, and it is impossible for any nation to progress or even to hold its own, which contains a preponderance of individuals who are deficient in moral, intellectual and physical vigour.[47]

It was thought impossible for Britain to progress if it contained too many individuals who were deficient. Indeed, the 'feeble-minded' were considered to impede the advance of Britain because they diverted the resources and energies of the country.[48] In addition, because the 'feeble-minded' mixed – and mated – with the so-called healthy members of the community, they were seen to 'drag fresh blood into the vortex of disease and lower the general vigour of the nation'.[49] The British, it was supposed, were committing race suicide.[50] As a consequence, reformers thought they were 'rescuing posterity from the ever growing army of defective and helpless creatures which now impairs our national virility and poisons our national life' by providing special institutions for the 'feeble-minded'.[51]

Perceptions of women

Victorian and Edwardian ideas concerning appropriate female behaviour helped to shape attitudes about the 'feeble-minded'. 'Feeble-minded' men were alleged to be drunkards and thieves whereas women's crimes tended to be of a sexual nature; both were thought to be inherited.[52] In the case of women, 'feeble-mindedness' was associated with the crimes of immorality and prostitution. In turn immorality and prostitution were associated with 'feeble-mindedness', making it difficult to separate cause and effect. Nevertheless, not all prostitutes were thought to be 'feeble-minded'; the successful, those who serviced the middle and upper classes, and those, like the notorious Mrs Jeffreys, who operated in a higher social milieu, were considered in full control of their wits. Dr W. Potts assumed that 'the woman who is a "professional prostitute" is seldom 'feeble-minded'; casual prostitutes, however, – women who are prostitutes only when other means of livelihood fail – and the paramours of feeble-minded and criminal men, are frequently feeble-minded'.[53] The single mother forced into prostitution fell into this category. Elaine Showalter has even suggested that unmarried mothers were often classified as 'feeble-minded' in order to undermine the challenge to the concept of the unmarried virgin.[54]

'Feeble-minded' girls allegedly populated the prisons, workhouses and of course reform institutions.[55] However, the statistics used as evidence for this vary, demonstrating the instability of the category of 'feeble-minded': the National Association for the Care of the Feeble-Minded (NACF) maintained that 2,521 out of 14,725 females in Magdalen asylums were 'feeble-minded', of whom 1,000 had produced illegitimate children;[56] the Royal Commission stated that 16 per cent of women in rescue homes were considered 'feeble-minded';[57] and a medical investigator reckoned that one in three inmates in reform institutions were 'feeble-minded'.[58]

Links between female sexual activity and mental instability have a long history in the annals of mental health. Anatomy was considered destiny, long before Freud coined the phrase, so madness in women was attributed to the (specifically female) womb rather than the (more masculine) brain.[59] Andrew Scull has observed that women were the products of their reproductive systems;[60] the menarche, that is the start of the menses or period, pregnancy and the menopause were said to directly affect women's psychological make-up. Indeed, menstruation was held to be a pathological condition,[61] which made women especially vulnerable to mental instability. Women, defined by their menstrual cycle, were particularly biologically prone to hysteria; indeed the word 'hysteria' originates from the Greek word for womb. As Elaine Showalter points out, the

> female life cycle, linked to reproduction, was seen to be fraught with biological crises . . . Having survived puberty, women still faced mental shipwreck in pregnancy and childbirth . . . The end of women's reproductive life was as profound a mental upheaval as the beginning.[62]

Just being a woman meant that madness was never far away.

Not surprisingly, given these beliefs, women's sexuality was seen to be dangerous.[63] The middle-class conventional image of the perfect married woman was as an asexual entity who suffered the indignities of the marriage bed to please her husband and to produce children. The ideal unmarried female was chaste, modest and at all times virtuous. Any female sexual activity outside the confines of marriage was associated with psychological disorder, so women who were considered promiscuous were often sent to asylums in order to control and subdue their so-called deviant behaviour. If they were unlucky enough to be the patient of Isaac Baker Brown, who believed that onanism (masturbation) was the primary cause of madness, they might even have had to suffer a clitoridectomy. As a consequence, according to Andrew Scull, the 'opening of state-run asylums for the poor was matched by an upsurge in the number of female patients'.[64] There was apparently a dramatic increase in the number of women admitted to asylums from 1850, and by the end of the century females accounted for more than half those incarcerated in various mental institutions.[65] Moreover, in defining women who were sexually active as mad, rather than normal, it allowed the conventional image of the sexually passive female to remain unchallenged.

By the end of the nineteenth century 'feeble-mindedness' was added to the list of reasons why women were sexually active. Those defined as 'feeble-minded' were believed to be more sexually precocious than the rest of the population since their limited intellect made their powers of inhibition and moral constraint correspondingly low. This led to a 'loss of control over the lower propensities'.[66] Indeed it was common for this sort of sexual behaviour to be used as 'evidence for, rather than the consequence of, mental defect'.[67] 'Feeble-mindedness' in women, therefore, attracted a moral as well as a mental stigma: prostitution, illegitimacy and sexual promiscuity were taken to be the expected outcomes – the natural consequences – of 'feeble-mindedness'. These beliefs encouraged the distinguished eugenist Francis Galton to proclaim with confidence that 'feeble-minded' women commonly became prostitutes.[68]

Unmarried mothers were singled out as being of special concern: as regular inmates of workhouse maternity wards they were an increasing burden on the rates.[69] 'Poor Law Guardians know from experience how in their maternity wards "feeble-minded" mothers return to give birth to "feeble-minded" children again and again and again.'[70] Moreover, the perceived hereditary nature of 'feeble-mindedness' meant that illegitimacy too was passed on from generation to generation. One workhouse medical officer testified to the existence of four generations of women who were all 'feeble-minded' and of illegitimate birth.[71] 'Year after year they return to the workhouse to bear children, ... some of whom live to repeat their mothers' experience. Year after year they become more degraded, wretched and restless.'[72] For example, Elizabeth P., aged 19, who was admitted into the Bristol Salvation Army Rescue Home in 1902, was

> the fourth generation of illegitimacy. Her uncle is her father. Her mother is a very low woman, and has had several illegitimate children by different fathers. I understand that the mother and grandmother have, at different times, been the keeper of brothels.[73]

It was considered iniquitous, by eugenists in particular, for parents to bring children into the world if they could not financially support them and 'must in time be seen in its true light, as one of the most unsocial and selfish proceedings'.[74]

While reformers presented an ambivalent and somewhat incoherent attitude to 'feeble-minded' women, regarding them variously as moral victim, moral imbecile and moral criminal, there was some unifying agreement about the development of their condition. 'Feeble-minded' women, it was agreed, were totally at the mercy of their female, womb-generated passions;

these passions undermined not only their mental powers, but also their moral discernment and integrity since women's ensuing 'fall from virtue' was an entirely predictable outcome of the condition's virulent disorder.[75] 'Feeble-minded' women were thought to be particularly open to the seductions of unscrupulous men: 'prey to the first emotion that assails them, and are absolutely incapable of resisting any impulse. They are open to any suggestion, vicious or otherwise . . . and have easy opportunities of immoral conduct.'[76] Such women were seen to be of a clinging and affectionate disposition and thus would follow any man who chose to speak kindly to them.[77] It was believed that 'feeble-minded' young women, particularly those who lived in cities, were subject to overwhelming temptations and pressure towards sexual immorality. Indeed, many of them were 'sexually tampered with',[78] as with the case of

> S G: She has an extremely immoral home. When her mother was away hop-picking in the summer it is said that her father behaved in such an immoral manner with the girl that the neighbours interfered, and took S G out of the house until her mother's return. The girl herself has immoral tendencies, and will be a great danger to the community.[79]

In cases like this and the one of A.D. below, it is evident that the community was felt to need protection from the 'moral imbecile' rather than the 'imbecile' protected from the community.

> A D – Age 11. A moral imbecile. Her parents are fairly respectable people, but have no control over her. She is very deficient mentally, and can never be made very useful, but will be a great danger and expense to the community if left at liberty. She is violent and obstinate, and kicks and bites when interfered with. She uses very bad language, and has very immoral tendencies. Has lately almost killed a small child in the street. Cruel to animals.[80]

It is therefore safe to assume that attitudes towards the 'feeble-minded' were composed of a mixture of benevolence and hostility. On the one hand, those involved with the 'feeble-minded' were informed by the newer humane theories of the nineteenth-century 'psychiatric revolution'. On the other hand, their class and gender assumptions meant that they believed 'feeble-minded' women posed a potential danger not only to the moral fabric of society but also to the advancement of the British nation.

Inadequacies in the treatment of the 'feeble-minded'

Once women had been diagnosed as 'feeble-minded' there were only two institutions which would accept them: the lunatic asylum or the workhouse, neither of which was thought appropriate. By the late nineteenth century it was believed that there were enough 'feeble-minded' in England alone to constitute a separate category of care;[81] while specialist accommodation had been created for the 'feeble-minded' at places such as Earlswood Asylum, Surrey and the Eastern Counties, this was still inadequate since 'feeble-minded' women were treated alongside idiots and other imbeciles. Similarly, workhouse arrangements were thought deficient. Specialist provision had been established in some London authorities,[82] but in general, and especially in small country workhouses where there was no special classification care or training, the 'feeble-minded' were placed in the main wards which were thought 'insufficient, unsatisfactory and unsuitable'.[83]

By the early twentieth century the Education Department and the school boards had made provision for the special treatment of 'feeble-minded' children.[84] Roy Lowe has pointed out that several local authorities, along with the NAPWFM, pressed for legislation to deal with 'feeble-minded' children. As a result of their combined efforts, a committee was appointed by the Education Department in 1897 to research the subject of Defective Children that led, in 1899, to the Elementary Education Act. This Act gave school authorities the power to make special arrangements for the education of 'feeble-minded' children, to place them in separate classes and to enforce compulsory attendance to the age of 16. However, this was only a permissive Act and was put into force by only a quarter of the country.[85] Moreover, even when school boards in London, Birmingham and elsewhere established special classes for children, they were discharged into the 'community' after the age of 16.[86] Campaigners pointed to the large numbers of 'feeble-minded' teenagers leaving school who were expected to earn their own living. It was feared that, because 'feeble-minded' young women had been brought up in the seclusion of a separate class in school, they were unable to face 'a world which contains not a few of those who will send the weakest to the wall, without a tinge of compunction'.[87] Moreover, it was feared that most 'feeble-minded' young women could perform only unskilled work, and that 'slowly and badly, and for the most part they need constant supervision. They can rarely earn enough to maintain themselves and their mental and moral weakness exposes them to many temptations.'[88] Of course, this was a strong argument as the wages of 'normal' women was generally half or two-thirds of men's. Prostitution, therefore, seemed an attractive possibility.

Those designated as 'feeble-minded' fell between two psychiatric stools: they were not considered strong enough to care for themselves yet not weak enough to be incarcerated in a lunatic asylum.[89] There was thus a residuum of girls who had nowhere else to go but to the workhouse. Poor Law authorities dealt with the greater number of 'feeble-minded' because such persons were, by reason of their infirmity, in a state of destitution and unable to take proper care of themselves.[90] Figure 5.1[91] shows how most of the 'feeble-minded' placed in the workhouse remained in the main wards.[92]

Campaigners for 'feeble-minded' young women put forward various objections to workhouse provision. At the same time the 'feeble-minded' were

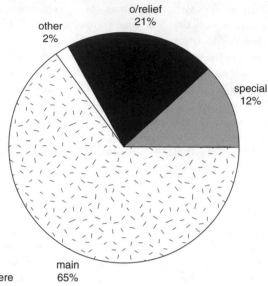

Key:
o/relief: those on outdoor relief
special: those in special wards
main: those in main wards
other: those looked after elsewhere

Figure 5.1 'Feeble-minded' in workhouses in 1907

Source: compiled from *Royal Commission on the Care and Control of the Feeble Minded* 1908

regarded as objects of pity, moral contaminators and financial burdens. Reformers were usually anxious about the effects of the workhouse on young women. It was considered unjust and cruel to imprison the 'feeble-minded' for actions for which they were not responsible and yet, because they were classified as able-bodied inmates, they were treated in the same way as those of sound minds.[93]

> The officers are very kind to these poor unfortunates, but they have no time to give special attention to them; even if they had, very few of them have any kind of qualification to train them in any way, without the result that they are allowed to go their own way, and to live their own lives, which is very little superior to that of a well-cared-for dog or other animal.[94]

The meagre diet, the rule-bound regimes and general surroundings of most workhouses were considered unsuitable for the 'feeble-minded', who were thought to need plenty of fresh air, nutritious food and a certain amount of liberty and diversity in their lives. More importantly, they should not be treated as able-bodied paupers when their condition was not their own fault.[95] They were, in fact, the 'deserving' poor. Moreover the stressful atmosphere of large institutions or to be in any way 'hurried or excited, confuses and irritates them and considerably diminishes their powers of usefulness'.[96] It was maintained that the 'feeble-minded' learned nothing of value in workhouses since they required special management and more patience and supervision than the workhouse authorities were likely to be able to afford.[97] Fears were expressed that the 'feeble-minded' might, like first-time single mothers, learn undesirable behaviour and inevitably become corrupted because they mixed with women of an 'inferior moral character'.[98]

> In the London workhouse with which I have long been acquainted there are constantly in the able-bodied female ward some 12 or 15 (about half the inmates) cases of women too weak minded to earn their living out . . . They share the treatment of the rest of the inmates over 60. As the large majority of these are brought there by immorality, intemperance, or laziness, it is manifestly impossible to make it a pleasant resort, and their lives are a dreary round of monotonous work, scarcely better in fact than prison life, with no brightness and none of the indulgence accorded to the old . . . it is a fact that these poor weak girls, often by childishness and wilfulness, draw upon themselves more constant and severe punishment than any other inmates . . . But punishment does to these girls more harm than good. They have not the sense to be deterred by it, and it only calls out the worst part of their nature.[99]

Reformers were equally concerned about the effect of the 'feeble-minded' on other inmates.[100] The 'feeble-minded' were generally housed with aged and infirm people, who required a calm atmosphere. This they were unable to get since the more physically and energetically inclined young 'feeble-minded' disturbed their tranquillity,[101] and were not only a serious annoyance to them but also a danger.[102] One workhouse 'feeble-minded' inmate whose mother had recently died 'startled one of the workhouse quiet old "ladies" by thus addressing her: "Mother, I thought it was you: you can't leave me alone – you've come back from Hell to plague me".'[103] More importantly, workhouses had no powers of detention and 'feeble-minded' women could leave the workhouse at will. Moreover, because the workhouse failed to treat them as a separate category, the 'feeble-minded' tended to be among the 'ins and outs' of the workhouse who tended to go and come as they pleased.[104]

There were strong economic motives for criticising workhouse provision for the 'feeble-minded'.[105] Complaints were often voiced that ratepayers had to bear the cost since 'huge families of the incompetent, incorrigible and irresponsible, absorb a large amount of public and private money, and also the time and attention of whole armies of officials and volunteer workers in ministering to their various needs'.[106] Both Ellen Pinsent and A.F. Tredgold believed that the 'feeble-minded' were a huge financial burden on the nation as two-thirds were supported by the British public. Ellen Pinsent argued that 'we who pay the rates and taxes will have to support these girls in the end. Would it not be wiser to do so at once, instead of waiting until they have produced others for us and our children to support?'[107] Furthermore, the 'feeble-minded' woman was seen to 'do the rounds' of the maternity ward of the workhouse, the lock hospital and the lunatic asylum, all of which cost the ratepayer double the ordinary workhouse fees. 'In some cases the mothers have pronounced erotic tendencies, and many of them seem to be utterly lacking in any sense of shame, modesty or even ordinary decency.'[108] Poor Law Guardians were financially responsible for the illegitimate children produced by such women so not surprisingly both the Majority and Minority Poor Law Report advocated specialist treatment. It was considered cheaper to segregate twenty 'degenerates in moderate comfort than it would be for posterity to deal with their descendants a generation or two hence',[109] which would be a heavy indirect charge to the community. To some extent the following quote reflects the symbiotic relationship between economics and morality:

> is it fair to the community, for a weak-minded girl to be able to go in and out of the Workhouse at pleasure, all her life, even after she has brought another feeble being into the world to be a burden upon our rates? She can go out at any time at 24 hours notice, and come back the next week to repeat the process ad lib. This system works nothing but harm to the girl herself, for she is sure to get into further trouble after the first fall, drifting from the maternity ward to the Lock ward, from the Lock ward to the Imbecile ward, from thence very quickly to the Lunatic Asylum, where, and this again is a notable fact, she costs the rate payer exactly double what she costs in the Workhouse, added to which we probably have to bring up two, three and often more of her illegitimate children.[110]

Undoubtedly, the prevention of prostitution movement was affected by transformations in medical and genetic theory. Philanthropists, who had failed to curb prostitution by other measures, sought explanations for its continuation within a more 'scientific' and 'rational' discourse. The 'psychiatric revolution', by classifying mental disorder, rejected the mad-and-bad approach to mental health and promoted humane treatment for those so designated. These new theories complemented the belief that prostitutes were victims since those with impaired mental powers could not be blamed for any moral lapse. However, this compassionate approach was undermined by eugenist ideas and gender expectations, both of which influenced the debate about 'feeble-minded' women. Such women, thought to be devoid of moral consciousness, would become prostitutes and produce huge numbers of illegitimate babies. This, it was argued, would inevitably threaten the stability of the British nation.

Medical opinion may have helped shift attitudes towards 'feeble-minded' women but endeavours to improve their treatment proved to be misconceived. All institutions which had custodial care of the 'feeble-minded' were thought to be inadequate. Evidence of the need to provide specialist accommodation for those diagnosed as 'feeble-minded' grew to over-whelming proportions.

Notes

1 Until the work of David Wright and Anne Digby, *From Idiocy to Mental Deficiency* (London: Routledge, 1996) and Mathew Thomson, *The Problem of Mental Deficiency* (Oxford: Clarendon Press, 1998), the history of mental deficiency, a term now seen not only as politically incorrect but also socially and medically unacceptable, was largely neglected by historians of social policy as well as by those of psychiatry. Similarly, historians of prostitution have largely ignored the effects of the psychiatric revolution on attitudes towards prostitutes.
2 Michel Foucault, *Madness and Civilization* (London: Tavistock, 1961), p. 72.
3 Elaine Showalter, 'Victorian Women and Insanity', in Andrew Scull (ed.) *Madhouses, Mad Doctors, and Madmen* (London: Athlone Press, 1987), p. 313.
4 Willoughby Hyatt Dickenson, *The Treatment of the Feeble-Minded* (London: Westminster, 1903), p. 3.
5 Michel Foucault, *Madness and Civilization*, p. 72.
6 Andrew Scull, 'The Social History of Psychiatry in the Victorian Era', in Scull (ed.) *Madhouses, Mad Doctors, and Madmen*, p. 7.
7 Ibid., p. 6.
8 Elaine Showalter, 'Victorian Women and Insanity', p. 314.
9 Ibid., p. 315.
10 See Michel Foucault, *Discipline and Punish* (London: Penguin, 1975), for a fuller exploration of these ideas.
11 Reginald Bray, 'The Guardians and the Feeble-Minded', *South Eastern District Poor Law Conference* 1904–1905, p. 562.
12 Lucia Zedner, *Women, Crime, and Custody in Victorian England* (Oxford: Clarendon Press, 1991), p. 271.
13 Peter Martin Duncan, *A Manual for the Classification, Training and Education of the Feeble-Minded, Imbecile and Idiotic* (London: Longmans, Green, 1866).
14 *NUWW Conference* 1898.
15 Miss A. Kirby, *Eugenics Review* (1909–1910), p. 85.
16 Reginald Bray, *South Eastern District Poor Law Conference* 1904–1905, p. 568.
17 *Royal Commission on the Care and Control of the Feeble Minded* 1908, p. 223.
18 Lucia Zedner, *Women, Crime, and Custody in Victorian England*, p. 271.
19 *Eugenics Review* (1892).
20 Roy Lowe has suggested that the influence of eugenics was linked to local elite patronage and the placement of supporters in key health roles (see R. Lowe, 'Eugenicists, Doctors and the Quest for National Efficiency: An Educational Crusade, 1900–1939', *History of Education*, 8, 1979, pp. 293–306). I am indebted to Ian Grosvenor for this reference.
21 By 1914 the Eugenic Society had only 624 members but its membership was nonetheless an influential one: Lyndsay Farrall, *The Origins and Growth of the English Eugenics Movement, 1865–1915* (London: Garland, 1985), p. 211.
22 *Woman's Medical Book* 4(42): 5,086.
23 Lyndsay Farrall, *The Origins and Growth of the English Eugenics Movement*, p. 28.
24 *The Malthusian* (May 1894), p. 37.
25 *The Lancet* (May 26th 1902), p. 1,477.
26 Mary Dendy, *NUWW Conference* 1902.
27 F. May Dickenson Berry, Assistant Medical Officer to the School Board of London, Letter to *The Lancet* (June 7th 1902), p. 1,644.

28 Ellen Pinsent, Presidential Address, Birmingham Ladies' Literary and Debating Society 1905, p. 6.
29 *NUWW Quarterly Magazine* (1896), p. 7.
30 *National Association for Promoting the Welfare of the Feeble-Minded Annual Conference on After-Care* 1911, p. 18.
31 *The Lancet* (June 18th 1898), p. 1,703.
32 *National Association for Promoting the Welfare of the Feeble-Minded Annual Conference on After-Care* 1911, p. 19.
33 *National Association for Promoting the Welfare of the Feeble-Minded Annual Report* 1901, p. 6.
34 A.F. Tredgold, *Eugenics Review* (1909–1910).
35 *The Lancet* (February 11th 1905), p. 371.
36 Mathew Thomson, *The Problem of Mental Deficiency*, p. 22.
37 Lyndsay Farrall, *The Origins and Growth of the English Eugenics Movement*, p. 262.
38 'The Eugenic Principle and the Treatment of the Feeble-Minded', *Eugenics Review* (1910–1911), p. 189.
39 A.F. Tredgold, *Eugenics Review* (1909–1910), p. 101.
40 Dr Potts, *Royal Commission on the Care and Control of the Feeble-Minded* 1908, p. 472.
41 Angus McLaren, *Birth Control in Nineteenth-Century England* (London: Croom Helm, 1978), p. 141.
42 A letter from Louisa Twining and others to *The Lancet* (June 1912), p. 1,784, argued: 'Thus one family, where the weakness first showed itself as moral defect, increased in two generations to 27 descendants, only four of whom were normal individuals, the others being either thieves, prostitutes, paupers, inebriates, lunatics or feeble-minded.'
43 Mary Dendy, *NUWW Conference* 1902.
44 Arnold White, 'The Problems of a Great City', quoted in *The Malthusian* (July 1887), p. 49.
45 See Richard Soloway, 'Counting the Degenerates: The Statistics of Race Deterioration in Edwardian England', *Journal of Contemporary History*, 17, 1982, p.137, for a fuller discussion of these issues.
46 *The Malthusian* (June 1896), p. 43.
47 Lyndsay Farrall, *The Origins and Growth of the English Eugenics Movement*, p. 100.
48 A.F. Tredgold, *Eugenics Review* (1909–1910), p. 100.
49 Ibid., p. 102.
50 See Richard Soloway, 'Counting the Degenerates', p. 154.
51 *St Mary's Home for Working Women Annual Report c.*1910, p. 9.
52 E.B. Sherlock and H.B. Donkin, *The Feeble-Minded* (London: Macmillan, 1911), p. 197.
53 Dr Potts, *Royal Commission* 1908, p. 470.
54 Elaine Showalter, *The Female Malady: Women, Madness and English Culture, 1830–1980* (London: Virago, 1987).
55 Ellen Pinsent in a speech to the Birmingham Ladies' Literary and Debating Society 1904–1905 spoke of her concern that England's prisons were full of the 'feeble minded'.
56 Miss A. Kirby, 'The Feeble Minded and Voluntary Effort', *Eugenics Review* (1909–1910), p. 91.
57 *Seeking and Saving* (formerly *Refuge and Reformatory Journal*) (September 1913), p. 413.
58 *Seeking and Saving* (January 1912), p. 4.
59 I am indebted to Robert Pearce for this idea.
60 Andrew Scull, 'The Social History of Psychiatry in the Victorian Era', p. 23.

61 Vieda Skultans, *English Madness: Ideas on Insanity, 1580–1890* (London: Routledge and Kegan Paul, 1979), p. 93.
62 Elaine Showalter, 'Victorian Women and Insanity', p. 322.
63 Vieda Skultans, *English Madness: Ideas on Insanity*, p. 96.
64 Andrew Scull, 'The Social History of Psychiatry in the Victorian Era', p. 23.
65 Elaine Showalter, 'Victorian Women and Insanity'.
66 N. Kerlin, 'Moral Imbecility', in M. Rosen, G. Clark and M. Kivitz (eds) *The History of Mental Retardation* (Baltimore, MD: University Park Press, 1976), p. 306, originally published 1889.
67 Mathew Thomson, *The Problem of Mental Deficiency*, p. 22.
68 F. Galton, 'Segregation', in *Abstract of Royal Commission on the Feeble-Minded* 1908, p. 82.
69 F. May Dickenson Berry, Assistant Medical Officer to the School Board of London, Letter to *The Lancet* (June 7th 1902), p. 1,644.
70 Willoughby Hyatt Dickenson, *The Treatment of the Feeble-Minded*, p. 7.
71 *NAPWFM Annual Report* 1897, p. 6.
72 Mary Dendy, 'The Feeble-Minded and Crime', *The Lancet* (May 24th 1902), p. 1,462.
73 Mrs Bramwell Booth, *Royal Commission* 1908, p. 174.
74 Arnold White, 'The Problems of a Great City', *The Malthusian* (July 1897), p. 50.
75 Miss Maria Poole, *Royal Commission* 1908, p. 147.
76 Ellen Pinsent, Presidential Address, Birmingham Ladies' Literary and Debating Society 1905, p. 6.
77 Ellen Pinsent, 'The Permanent Care of the Feeble-Minded', *The Lancet* (February 21st 1903), p. 514.
78 *The Lancet* (September 26th 1908), p. 959.
79 Dr O'Connor and Ellen Pinsent, *Royal Commission* 1908, p. 464.
80 Ibid., p. 463.
81 Havelock Ellis, 'The Eugenic Principle and the Treatment of the Feeble-Minded', *Eugenics Review* (1910–1911), p. 184.
82 David Wright and Anne Digby, *From Idiocy to Mental Deficiency*, p. 7.
83 *Royal Commission* 1908, Part 1, p. 33.
84 Roy Lowe, 'Eugenics and Education: A Note on the Origins of the Intelligence Testing Movement in England', *Educational Studies*, 6(1), 1980, p. 2.
85 Anon, *How to Help the Feeble-Minded* (London: NAPWFM, 1899), p. 5.
86 *NUWW Quarterly Magazine* (1896).
87 *NUWW Quarterly Magazine* (1892).
88 *The Lancet* (June 18th 1898), p. 1,704.
89 Willoughby Hyatt Dickenson, *The Treatment of the Feeble-Minded*, p. 5.
90 *Abstract of Royal Commission* 1908, p. 31.
91 Figure 5.1 is compiled from *Royal Commission* 1908.
92 Special wards might sometimes include other people, apart from the 'feeble-minded', suffering from some form of mental illness.
93 Miss Clifford, *Royal Commission* 1908, p. 29; Miss Ellen Gregory, ibid., p. 217.
94 Mr T. Jones, *Royal Commission* 1908, p. 32.
95 Miss Harriet Wemyss, Hon. Sec. for St Mary's Home, Painswick, *Royal Commission* 1908, p. 430.
96 Ibid., p. 430.
97 Dr O'Connor and Mrs Ellen Pinsent, *Royal Commission* 1908, p. 463.
98 Miss Emily Bartholomew, *Royal Commission* 1908, p. 307.
99 Family Welfare Association, *The Feeble-Minded Child and Adult* (1893), p. 114.
100 Miss Joseph, *Royal Commission* 1908, p. 31.
101 Mr T. Jones, *Royal Commission* 1908, p. 31.

102 Miss Townsend and Miss Jeffries, *Royal Commission* 1908, p. 225.
103 Miss Ellen Gregory, *Royal Commission* 1908, p. 217.
104 *NAPWFM Annual Report* 1897, p. 5.
105 Agatha Stacey had little desire for Poor Law Guardians to establish homes because of the tendency for them to be institutions.
106 'The Eugenic Principle and the Treatment of the Feeble-Minded', *Eugenics Review* (1910–1911), p. 183.
107 Ellen Pinsent, 'The Permanent Care of the Feeble Minded', p. 514.
108 A.F. Tredgold, *Mental Deficiency* (London: Baillière, Tindall and Cox, 1908), p. 292.
109 *Woman's Medical Book*, 4(42), no date but *c*.1900, p. 5,086.
110 *NUWW Quarterly Magazine* (1894).

6 Care rather than cure

The move to improve conditions for the 'feeble-minded'

It is safe to assume that little or nothing would have been achieved for 'feeble-minded' women without the commitment of voluntary groups since the state, despite a decided increase in intervention in other areas, was reluctant to commit itself to further expenditure. Various groups, from across the philanthropic spectrum, tried to promote better care for 'feeble-minded' women perceived to be in moral danger. As Mathew Thomson and others have noted, women pioneered these services.[1] This chapter charts the developments in providing 'suitable' care for those diagnosed as 'feeble-minded' and will examine how campaigners put their theory into practice.

Until the age of 16 orphaned girls were brought up in a workhouse school, an orphanage or a certified industrial school, but after this age there was nowhere else for them to go. Women Guardians, along with workhouse matrons, were worried about the number of 'feeble-minded' young women who – incarcerated in workhouse orphanages for the first sixteen years of their life – were forced to look after themselves when they left their respective institutions.[2] In order to assess the scale of the problem, eight women Guardians sent out a circular to all workhouse matrons in England and Wales, and received 141 replies, of which 136 stated that their workhouse held women who were 'feeble-minded'.[3] At the same time, various other groups and organisations, again composed predominantly of women, became concerned about the lack of provision for the 'feeble-minded'. These groups attracted the attention of the British Medical Association in 1888 and formed the subject of a Royal Commission Inquiry in 1889. In 1890 representatives from a diverse range of organisations such as the British Medical Association, the London School Board, Boards of Guardians, the Ladies' Associations, the Metropolitan Association for Befriending Young Servants, the National Vigilance Association, the Girls' Friendly Society and the Charity Organisation Society met together to discuss the appropriateness of leaving 'feeble-minded' women in the workhouses, refuges, rescue homes and reformatories of Britain. Of course, many of these organisations were equally concerned about the potential immorality of uncontrolled 'feeble-minded' women let loose within their communities.

In 1895 many of these same women, under the auspices of the Charity Organisation Society, helped to found the National Association for Promoting the Welfare of the Feeble-Minded to publicise the question of the 'feeble-minded'.[4] Their aims certainly reflect the prejudices and fears of the middle-class philanthropists as much as their humanitarian concern:

1   To offer such provision for the feeble-minded as may improve them mentally, morally and physically; to fortify and lift them up in order that, so far as possible, they may be rendered self-supporting, and saved from becoming vagrant, pauper and criminal;
2   To collect and diffuse information on the subject of practical aid and of investigation on scientific lines;
3   To initiate the formation of Homes and branches of the association, and of after-care circles for the study and practical assistance of the mentally defective who are over school age;
4   To assist by information and advice, matrons, teachers, parents and others who have the charge of individuals of this class;
5   To promote legislation on behalf of the feeble-minded.[5]

Three years later, in 1898, the Unitarian Mary Dendy, a member of Manchester's School Board, founded the Lancashire and Cheshire Society for the Permanent Care of the Feeble-Minded not only to campaign for greater rights but also to fight for their permanent care.[6]

All of these organisations worked hard to improve the position of the 'feeble-minded'. Petitions were signed, papers read and published to try to amend the Act of Parliament which enabled Boards of Guardians to send blind, deaf and dumb people to institutions, to include the 'feeble-minded'. They also put pressure on the government.[7] As a result, the Royal Commission on the Care and Control of the Feeble Minded was appointed in September 1904, studied the subject for four years and eventually published its findings in the autumn of 1908. The Commission recommended that the 'feeble-minded' should be wholly removed from workhouses, that they should be taken out of Poor Law control and that the Destitution Authorities should have nothing to do with their maintenance or treatment.[8] Instead, the Commission advocated that the 'feeble-minded' be placed under the care of specially qualified authorities.

In the mean time, because the government appeared reluctant to implement the findings of the Royal Commission, private philanthropy stepped in.[9] Women worked hard to establish homes within their local communities. For instance, the impetus within the West Midlands was led by women and in particular by Agatha Stacey, a former Quaker who had converted to Anglicanism, a Birmingham Poor Law Guardian and committed campaigner for women's charities.[10] She was helped by a committee consisting of women workhouse visitors, other women Poor Law Guardians and women workers from the Prison Gate Mission, the Girls' Night Shelter and the

Ladies' Association for the Care and Protection of Young Girls, once again demonstrating not only the links forged between middle-class women philanthropists and those employed in an official capacity but also the links between 'feeble-mindedness' and immorality.

Homes for the 'feeble-minded'

The homes built for the 'feeble-minded' shared many of the characteristics of reform and preventive institutions, possibly because the women who entered them were considered to be of the same social group. Life in the homes was a blend of humanitarianism mixed with middle-class perceptions of what was beneficial for working-class young women. Reformers may have genuinely believed they were providing humane shelter for those incapable of living independently but a cost-conscious philosophy underpinned their practice. As with those involved with establishing reform and other types of preventive institutions, those concerned with the 'feeble-minded' spoke much of the language of social justice while at the same time rejecting the radical policies needed to ensure that the 'feeble-minded' were treated well.

The Victorian age witnessed a transformation in the care of the 'feeble-minded' from workhouse and lunatic asylum to smaller specialist homes, many of which were located in rural areas. The renting of rather fine houses set in country districts suggests that social reformers were influenced by the newer humanitarianism prevailing within nineteenth-century mental health care,[11] but it could equally suggest that they were concerned about the corruption of city life upon their charges. Certainly, it was thought that the 'feeble-minded' could be allowed greater liberty in the country than in towns because there was less opportunity to get up to immoral mischief. In addition, the healthy rustic air was thought to strengthen them mentally and morally, as well as the physically weak. The first of the homes, St Mary's Home for Working Women, was opened in Painswick, a small town in Gloucestershire, on the slope of a Cotswold valley. Three cottages, which had previously been a convalescent home for children, two villas with a small front garden, a kitchen garden and a field were rented.[12] Similarly, a home at Hitchin was established in an old country house with a big garden in the middle of what was considered a pretty village.[13]

The homes built for the 'feeble-minded' tended to be smaller than reform or other preventive institutions because reformers wanted to bestow individual care and to secure as near an approach as possible to family life.[14] As Figure 6.1 demonstrates, all of these homes sheltered, on average, approximately twenty young women over the age of 14.[15]

It was stressed that homes for the 'feeble-minded' must be made into homes in the truest sense of the word so that inmates could be treated as individuals rather than as an assemblage of inadequates.[16] Indeed, personal treatment within a family-type atmosphere – the idea was to make the

Figure 6.1 Numbers of young women in homes for the 'feeble-minded' in 1900
Source: National Association for Promoting the Welfare of the Feeble-Minded Annual Report 1901, p. 16

'feeble-minded' happy and comfortable[17] – was deemed to be necessary in order to bring out the best in them.[18] 'The first aim is to make the new comer happy, to impress upon her that someone really cares for her.'[19] At Painswick, all the inmates, including matrons, were expected to live together as one family.[20] At a home in Shepherd's Bush matrons had breakfast and dinner with the inmates, ate the same food and allegedly shared a similar lifestyle.[21] As the following aims and objectives indicate, reformers aimed to provide a shelter rather than a prison. Theirs was felt to be a sympathetic hand that promoted self-respect and independence:

Aims

To make the Homes abodes of love and Christian influence, free from the cramping restraints of an Institution;

To teach the inmates some branch of industry suited to their limited capacities, enabling them to earn part of their maintenance, thus fostering a spirit of self-help;

To develop the feeling that they are all members of one family, and that they must work loyally for the common good, and for the welfare of the Home which shelters them.[22]

Not all female munificence, however, stemmed from altruistic motives as economic considerations sometimes overruled humanitarian concerns. Each home aimed to be financially self-supporting rather than rely on the rates or charitable donations.[23] Maria Poole of the Metropolitan Association for

Befriending Young Servants argued that homes should not be too luxurious as 'feeble-minded' women must not live in more comfort than the rest of the working class.[24] In fact, she advocated that they should live as simply – and therefore as cheaply – as possible. Many homes depended on a triple economic arrangement: charitable support; the earnings of inmates; and the money[25] paid by either the Board of Guardians or relatives towards their keep.[26] The home at Shepherd's Bush charged 10s a week for each inmate, 7s of which was supplied by the Board of Guardians and 3s by the charitable public.[27] Furthermore, if the relative or Board of Guardians proved reluctant to pay then inmates were discharged. Homes were encouraged to 'deliver up the girl to her friends or to the Board of Guardians when the payment ceases, whether she is fit or not to enter into ordinary domestic service'.[28] This was no idle threat to persuade reluctant contributors to pay in advance as young women were returned to their Board of Guardians if payment was discontinued. Humanitarian support was provided on the condition that it could be afforded.

Life in the homes

The 'feeble-minded' may have lived in a home but, unlike most real households in England, daily life revolved around unpaid work, guided leisure and formalised religion, just as it did in other institutions. Ideally, the 'feeble-minded' required different training from that of normal adults and were to be given varied tasks because of their limited attention span and because they were easily mentally fatigued.[29] It was recommended that there should be constant change of work interspersed with occasional intervals of songs and music. For example, it was expected that inmates would look after bees and poultry and help with the gardening as well as participating in traditional industrial occupations such as sewing, rug and basket making, weaving and chair caning. Mrs Dickenson, one of the leaders of NACF, favoured light industries – needlework, glove making, artificial flowers and matchbox making. Moreover, she thought that jobs should be individually tailored so that each girl – depending on strength, capability and taste – was given work best suited to them.[30] At Handford House, Ipswich, inmates were taught housework, sewing, rug making and basket making; at Hampton Poyle, inmates were taught to sew and help with the poultry and garden.[31] At Gloucestershire, they were kept busy refurbishing mattresses (by taking them to pieces, cleaning them and remaking them) as well as caning chairs, making lace and dressing dolls;[32] at Hitchin and in the West Midlands, they were employed in basket making;[33] at Aubert Park, they were taught reading, writing, singing and drilling and played with the local children two or three days a week.[34] Other occupations, such as knitting dishcloths, were organised for those considered physically weak even though many of the inmates found knitting difficult.

Here we saw one girl who has been two years at the home and has only just learnt to knit. The girls are never forced to continue any work which seems too hard for them, over and over again the knitting pins (which this poor girl could not hold properly when she came) were laid down and the work given up as hopeless, but the healthy emulation of the place stimulated her to fresh attempts, and the day she succeeded in knitting a floor cloth, which could be sold for the good of the home, was a proud one in her calendar.[35]

The social reformer and Poor Law Guardian, Agatha Stacey, introduced rug making to occupy the inmates in the institutions she founded.[36] Even so, volunteers, not the inmates, cut and hemmed the mats and cut the ragged ends of the wool to the required size.

Work aimed to promote self-respect and self-help but in practice this was not always the case. Certainly, much of the work on offer could not have engendered the self-esteem envisaged by the aims and objectives of their founding members. Several of the homes – Aubert Park, North London; Scott House at Hitchin, Hertfordshire; Shepherd's Bush, London; Chasefield, Bristol; Arrowfield Top and Enniskery, Knowle, West Midlands; Cumnor Rise, Oxford – expected their 'feeble-minded' inmates to work in the laundry.[37] In so doing, these homes sent out a message that 'feeble-minded' women were no better than reforming prostitutes. Laundry work was favoured because it afforded constant movement and inmates were said to enjoy it. Emily Bartholomew, secretary of the Clapton Home, maintained it kept girls healthy and happy, took them into the open air and 'fetching and returning the work brings them into contact with many other people'.[38] However, as with those who justified laundry work in reform institutions, these views must be treated with certain scepticism. More importantly, perhaps, laundry work enabled the inmates to contribute something towards their own maintenance.[39] At the Clapton Home inmates contributed £3 10s towards an average annual cost of £20 6s.[40] Material concerns therefore underpinned moral issues.

'Feeble-minded' young women were not considered responsible enough to do simple domestic work:

after the feeble minded child has been shown how to dust a room perhaps, or to do other domestic work, she must be watched and followed up day by day, or she will contrive to do it wrong, or leave it half done. It is no uncommon thing to find the dusters and aprons needed for the work lying on the floor; the children seize the first thing, whether suitable or not, for their work, and never think of putting things back in their regular place.[41]

If 'feeble-minded' young women were perceived to be incapable of simple housework then laundry work – which involved washing in hot water, mangling clothes through rollers and ironing with hot irons – with its associated dangers, must have been highly inappropriate.

Nevertheless, the laundry did not dominate as much as it did in reform institutions. One of the leaders of NACF, Mrs Dickenson, believed that it was unlikely to be remunerative. It was, she argued, too difficult for the 'feeble-minded' to accomplish a really good day's labour as it took about three of them to match that of one competent laundress. Some homes refused to provide laundry employment altogether. The managers of the Shepherd's Bush Home, which took in single mothers, rejected it, first, because it required too much toil and drudgery. They argued that when inmates were confined to the wash tub and ironing board from Monday morning to Sunday night they were not being prepared to be moral and upright citizens. Second, laundry work was vetoed because of its association with the punishing regime of penitentiaries rather than the forgiving one of a home. 'Feeble-minded' single mothers might well be considered potential prostitutes but, because they had not yet become so, they should not be penalised in the same way. Moreover, it was argued, some were much too physically delicate to stand up all day washing and ironing. Finally, it was believed that, even if the inmates were 'feeble-minded', they were still 'sharp and cunning' enough to know when they were being exploited and this made them disobedient. Instead, the management at Shepherd's Bush placed their faith in developing the mothering skills of inmates so that they would know how to take proper care of their babies and perhaps prevent a future vicious circle of maternal deprivation.[42]

Even institutions which took in washing to help with the finances did not always use inmates for this function: St Mary's Home, Painswick, engaged a superintendent and six experienced maids to do the laundry, leaving the 'feeble-minded' to help with the cooking and other tasks.[43] Inmates were also employed in a nearby safety-pin factory or as domestic servants in local private houses.[44] All work, whatever its nature, was geared to encourage financial responsibility, obedience and modest behaviour. In several homes, inmates were given a small wage to buy (with the matron's help!) their own clothes and other personal belongings:

> Each girl at Hitchin is provided with an account book, with a debit and credit side; on the one side is entered weekly a sum, which stands for wages, or rather the value of work done, on the debit is the cost of food, lodging and clothing . . . Wasted time is charged against the girls, because in this case they are not entitled to any payment, and destruction of clothing or any other article is also entered.[45]

Gender and class defined recreational activities. Physical exercise was favoured because it allegedly kept discipline, ensured good health and got rid of excess energy. Every day, rug makers in homes were expected to take a long walk in order to keep fit – an expectation that was denied to laundry workers on the grounds that they had sufficient exercise. Other physical activities included the ubiquitous musical drill and dancing;[46] in Oxford inmates were allocated small gardens of their own which they were encouraged to cultivate;[47] and at Hitchin inmates kept pets such as fowls, rabbits and pigeons, no doubt to encourage a sense of responsibility.[48]

Apparently, it was difficult to provide simple recreational facilities because of the short attention span of the inmates but it may be that most of the leisure activities organised for the inmates were unknown to them or simply disagreeable. As in other institutions, inmates were not offered a familiar menu of working-class leisure activities such as skittles and other street games. Religious education was provided: Bible lessons and attending the local church were standard practices. 'Skipping ropes are generally popular. In winter evenings, such games as "Snap" and "Tiddly-Winks" amuse some of them.'[49] Occasional outings and social evenings – such as parties and the usual, though infrequent, Coronation festivities – supplemented these leisure pursuits.

Inmates enjoyed a little more freedom than at reform institutions but less than they enjoyed at preventive homes. At one of the Midland homes inmates were sometimes allowed to go shopping at Redditch (which was four miles away from the home) to spend their hard-earned pence. At Painswick they apparently entered into the village life as much as possible, taking tea with servants at neighbouring houses, going on walks, attending church and taking part in school meetings or festivities.[50] For the most part inmates were allowed out only on errands or to deliver laundry to customers. In all homes, discipline remained strict. Obedience was enforced through a system of financial rewards: a penny a week pocket money – with the potential treat of spending it in the shops – was given for good behaviour but withdrawn if inmates 'wilfully' misbehaved. Compassion therefore merged with authority to produce a caring yet rigidly disciplined regime.

The responses of the inmates

Public statistics from the homes – between 1892 and 1914 only four inmates absconded from the Midland homes, only two from Painswick, and none from Aubert Park, Highbury – reinforce the impression that, on the whole, institutions looked after their charges well.

> It has surprised some gentlemen to hear that none of the girls have attempted to run away; we should indeed have been disappointed if they had done so. When annoyed or vexed, they do sometimes talk of going back to their friends, but this is only a passing desire.[51]

This extract suggests that homes for the 'feeble-minded' were a little more humanitarian than some other institutions but it may equally have been the treatment of an individual matron which led to this. 'Our experience is that the girls never wish to leave the Home where there is a kind matron: they are anxious to stay and to keep in touch with her.'[52] Moreover, the fact that many inmates may have found it much too difficult to take control over their lives may also have been a contributory factor. More importantly perhaps, these homes were situated in country areas that made it difficult even for determined inmates to run away successfully:

> Restlessness frequently seems to attack them in the spring, and this year was no exception to the rule, the result being that we had to ask the lady interested in the case, to remove one of the girls, who had only been with us for about a year. This girl was most systematic in her efforts, carried a road map about with her, tried to induce other girls to join in an attempt to run away, and was always doing her best to pack her belongings.[53]

Dissatisfaction was expressed in other ways and evidence suggests that inmates were less acquiescent than managers desired. Annual reports frequently refer to cases of restiveness, fits of frenzy, temper or insubordination. The home at Shepherd's Bush sometimes found the inmates ungovernable and prone to outbreaks of violence.[54] 'The restless, uncontrollable girls are usually physically strong and they have no hesitation in throwing about knives, pails or bricks when the restlessness has produced a violent fit of temper.'[55] Home managers constantly complained of the difficulties in teaching decent manners and suitable (i.e. bourgeois) attitudes because of the women's short attention span and lack of ability to comprehend abstract ideas.

> The Lady who takes the Sunday Bible Class says that she finds they are only able to receive a very little instruction at a time, and that she does not attempt to set them hymns or texts to learn by heart, as she finds that if they succeed in committing them to memory they appear to miss the sense of the words they learn.

However, poor behaviour may have as much to do with resistance as incapability.

Those in charge of homes offered a unique combination of threats and treats to persuade recalcitrant young women to behave. 'A threatened outbreak of insubordination or temper can often be averted by tactful treatment, or perhaps by musical drill ... which is an excellent outlet for the misdirected energy which would otherwise vent itself in passion.'[56] In the case of one young woman who 'was extremely troublesome at first; she had an evil temper and was very insolent to the people over her – often refusing to do the work',[57] the managers of the home used a subtle combination of coercion and kindness. Carrying the threat of immediate expulsion for any disobedience, she was taken on excursions to places like Windsor Castle

LIVERPOOL
JOHN MOORES UNIVERSITY
AVRIL ROBARTS LRC
TITHEBARN STREET
LIVERPOOL L2 2ER

and sent to the seaside for four weeks in an effort to improve her conduct. Nevertheless, young women were usually sent to bed if they misbehaved;[58] in severe cases refractory inmates were discharged because they were seen to exert a negative influence on other inmates.

The statistics in Figure 6.2, unlike the written reports, imply that homes for the 'feeble-minded' did not have the high success rate claimed for them by their managers, since as many women were returned to the workhouse as were consigned to domestic service.[59] More were 'sent to friends', which may have been a euphemism for the civilian equivalent of a dishonourable discharge.

Furthermore, homes took only the most manageable cases, refusing in the main to accept those who were violent, dangerous or too troublesome. 'We cannot deal with those who . . . are dangerous. Sometimes a girl has sudden fits of passion before you know what it is, and nearly kills a child.'[60] Several girls from the Shepherd's Bush Home in London, who were considered to have the characteristics of 'obstinacy, sullenness, untruthfulness, want of self control and laziness',[61] were expelled to make room for more suitable cases. Some were discharged from London homes because they were thought dangerous or because their habits were so pernicious that it was undesirable to keep them.[62]

Nevertheless, these homes were extremely oversubscribed. In six years the NAPWFM received 2,686 applications but could accommodate only 217 in

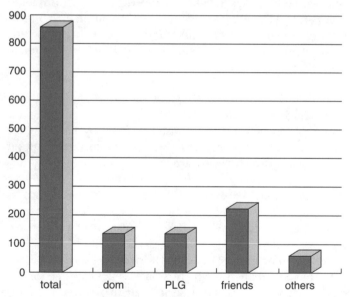

Key: Total – number of 'feeble-minded' incarcerated in institutions
      Dom: number of 'feeble-minded' sent to domestic service
      PLG: number of 'feeble-minded' returned to Poor Law Guardians
      Friends: number of 'feeble-minded' returned to friends
      Others: number of 'feeble-minded' sent elsewhere

Figure 6.2 Statistics showing the destination of 'feeble-minded' women discharged from their institutions 1890–1914

its own homes and place 238 elsewhere.[63] In general, there were at least 10 applicants for each place, not necessarily because what was on offer was so attractive but because the alternative – the workhouse, the lunatic asylum, being looked after at home or in expensive private care – was considered to be far worse. By 1908, despite the efforts of campaigners, there were still only eighteen homes available for those designated 'feeble-minded'.[64]

The move towards permanent care

Some homes encouraged inmates to find work outside whereas others kept them within bounds for quite a considerable length of time. It was thought that, as long as there was reasonable supervision and decent conditions, a certain proportion of young women could be self-sufficient, and become servants or factory workers. A number of 'less severe' cases were 'employed' by local philanthropists.[65] Nevertheless, fears remained that inmates would leave their homes prematurely and cause potential moral havoc within their communities if they did so. Because 'feeble-mindedness' was also perceived to be irreversible by either education or environment,[66] Mary Dendy and others believed it essential to have powers of detention. Medical opinion,[67] the Eugenic Society and the Lancashire and Cheshire Society as well as those in charge of homes, all supported permanent care. Not all agreed with permanent care: Willoughby Hyatt Dickenson (chairman of the National Association for Promoting the Welfare of the Feeble-Minded) disagreed with compulsory powers of detention and believed not only that it would evoke a public protest but also that relatives would be deterred from sending patients to homes if they were designated as permanent.

Those who advocated permanent care did so for controlling, rather than compassionate, reasons. First, it was believed that permanent care would lead to an improvement in behaviour:

> Many of the girls we have been forced to dismiss as uncontrollable would probably have remained in the Homes, fairly well behaved and peaceable, if they had known that insubordination would inevitably result in their forcible detention under less pleasant circumstances.[68]

Second, it was alleged that Guardians and relatives wanted to release the 'feeble-minded' as soon as they had been trained in domestic service to avoid continuing fees. The law would give the home powers to withstand such pressure.[69] Third, a large proportion of the 'feeble-minded' were not considered ever to be fit to leave the homes because they were unable to distinguish between right and wrong.[70] These women were thought to be potential prostitutes and criminals and would thus be a danger to society. 'There seems to be no just reason why feeble-minded persons who have no visible means of subsistence should be permitted uncontrolled liberty which they are unable to use except for the injury of themselves and the community.'[71] Indeed, the most 'dangerous' class of the 'feeble-minded' were thought to be those who would not stay in a home unless forced to do so. Certainly, Miss McKee (president of the St Marylebone Workhouse Girls' Aid Committee and chairman of the Coningham Road Home for Feeble-Minded Girls and their Babies) advocated permanent detention because she believed that 'feeble-minded' young women could hardly expect to prevail against the temptations of the outside world.[72]

Similarly, both Mary Dendy and Ellen Pinsent wanted the 'feeble-minded' to be detained and

> never be allowed the liberty which they can only misuse to their own
> degradation and to the degradation of the society in which they live
> . . . Ultimately such people do have some restriction or other put upon
> their personal liberty; too often in gaol, too often in penitentiaries . . .
> We are only asking for restriction a few years sooner.[73]

Finally, those such as Dr Potts believed that permanent care would relieve the various charitable homes, prisons and the casual wards of the work-houses of at least 10 per cent of their inmates. He referred to 'MC', aged 20 from Stoke-on-Trent, as a typical example in that she had been in prison four times, was in and out of the workhouse, twice in the Girls' Refuge and also once in a Girls' Home.[74]

A few eugenists advocated much sterner methods to control the 'feeble-minded'. Measures, it was argued, should be taken to ensure that the births of those unfit were restricted,[75] so that undesirable characteristics were not handed on to later generations. The eugenic solution to this problem was to detain and segregate 'feeble-minded' people to ensure that their fertility was controlled.[76] If young women were contained within one of the homes then their capacity to breed would be greatly diminished: 'the result of the establishment of such Homes must be the diminution of the number of the half-idiotic children that are born into the world, and a consequent reduction of the poor rate'.[77]

It was also suggested by a small number of eugenists that the mentally weak should be 'eliminated either by allowing disease to run rampant or by the ancient custom of exposure of unhealthy babies',[78] but this was never taken up as a serious issue. Some also suggested sterilisation – by 1914, eight American states enforced sterilisation as a remedy for the control of the feeble-minded population[79] – but this was, again, never seriously consid-ered in England, even though Churchill once said: 'I am drawn to this . . . Of course it is bound to come some day'.[80]

Instead, Mary Dendy, Agatha Stacey, Ellen Pinsent and others campaigned to change the law to make detention of the 'feeble-minded' compulsory. Roy Lowe shows how leading eugenists such as these used the press and their friendship with Members of Parliament (MPs) not only to keep the issue in the public domain but to make their views acceptable.[81] In 1913, they succeeded. The Mental Deficiency Act 1913 made it possible for those considered to be feeble-minded to be detained permanently in suitable institutions upon the certificate in writing of a qualified medical practitioner. However, although the 1913 Act was theoretically operational in early 1914, the outbreak of war that year suspended its practical application until 1918.

By associating prostitution with 'feeble-mindedness', those who worked hard to prevent prostitution were able to maintain their belief that prostitutes were not to blame for prostitution. Women with impaired mental facilities could not possibly be held responsible for any immoral action they committed since they were unable to distinguish between right and wrong. This perspective, although an enlightened response towards those who were in danger of falling into prostitution, was influenced by the eugenic movement. Agatha Stacey, for example, very much involved with the reform of prostitutes, was a leading member of the 'feeble-minded' movement and a eugenist. Such women, however sensitive to the needs of the 'feeble-minded', shared the assumptions of the Eugenic Society: 'feeble-minded' women, deemed to be without moral discernment and who bred widely and unwisely, were likely to become part of a criminal under-class who would ultimately undermine the national stock.

Hidden, not just from history, but from their own contemporaries, the care of 'feeble-minded' women provides a valuable example of the tensions between humanitarianism and subjugation. Compassion was assimilated with economics, eugenics and class control to create a particularly repressive ideology and practice. Well-intentioned middle-class women, with their own political agenda, sought to provide suitable 'homes' for largely working-class 'feeble-minded' women (perceived to be at moral risk) but failed to transcend their own particular class and nationalistic ideologies. In fairness, it must be remembered that the alternative was even less appealing, as those termed 'feeble-minded' were ignored, incarcerated in lunatic asylums, confined in a workhouse, restricted in a reform or preventive institution or left to survive as best they could. The effects of the 1913 Act are still working themselves out as very elderly women, once categorised as 'feeble-minded', and who were often single mothers, remain locked up in the state institutions later established for them. Incarcerated, hidden away and forgotten, such women paid a heavy penalty for challenging the gendered norms of a certain section of the middle class.

Notes

1 Mathew Thomson, *The Problem of Mental Deficiency* (Oxford: Clarendon Press, 1998), p. 229.
2 Homes for the 'feeble-minded' were said to originate from the personal efforts of a few women Guardians who had independently, yet simultaneously, started homes for 'feeble-minded' young women (*NUWW Quarterly Magazine*, 1896).
3 *NUWW Quarterly Magazine* (1896).

4　Willoughby Hyatt Dickenson, *The Treatment of the Feeble Minded* (London: Westminster, 1903), p. 7; Anon, *How to Help the Feeble-Minded* (London: NAPWFM, 1899), p. 7.

5　*How to Help the Feeble-Minded*, p. 7.

6　Patricia Hollis, *Ladies Elect* (Oxford: Clarendon Press, 1987).

7　Ibid.

8　*The Break Up of the Poor Law, Being Part of the Minority Report of the Poor Law Commission* 1909, p. 305.

9　Patricia Hollis has shown that most 'feeble-minded' women remained in workhouses until they were turned into hostels for the mentally handicapped in the 1930s: Patricia Hollis, *Ladies Elect*.

10　Agatha Stacey and Ellen Pinsent, both from Birmingham, joined with Mary Dendy from Manchester in publicising the plight of mentally handicapped people at Poor Law conferences.

11　This may have been because cities were associated with degeneracy. It may have been because Agatha Stacey Homes had a wide catchment area, making geographical location less important for visitors. Some young women came from Birmingham and the surrounding areas like Cannock and Walsall. Others were drawn from Bath, Cheltenham, Halifax, Lancaster, Liverpool and London, mostly paid for by Boards of Guardians (*Agatha Stacey Homes Annual Reports* 1893–1914).

12　In the first few years only between sixteen and seventeen young women lived in each of the homes. Over the years, largely as a result of extensions or moves, numbers gradually increased, by 1907, to twenty-one at Arrowfield and thirty at Enniskerry. Applications outnumbered places, though these in later years were in decline. In the first few years there were about two hundred applications annually but by 1907 this declined to eighty-nine. By 1913 only seventy applied.

13　Mrs Hazeldine, 'Permanent Homes for the Feeble-Minded' (*NUWW Quarterly Magazine*, 1894), p. 20.

14　Miss Grayson, 'Care and Training of the Feeble-Minded', *NUWW Conference* 1898, p. 89.

15　*NAPWFM Annual Report* 1901, p. 16.

16　Willoughby Hyatt Dickenson, *The Treatment of the Feeble Minded*, p. 11.

17　*The Lancet* (June 18th 1898), p. 1,704.

18　Miss Grayson, 'Care and Training of the Feeble-Minded', *NUWW Conference* 1898, p. 86.

19　*NUWW Quarterly Magazine* (1895).

20　*St Mary's Home for Working Women Annual Report* 1913, p. 7.

21　Miss McKee, *Royal Commission on the Care and Control of the Feeble Minded* 1908, p. 294.

22　*Agatha Stacey Homes for the Feeble-Minded Annual Reports* 1892–1914.

23　*Royal Commission* 1908, p. 162.

24　Miss Maria Poole, *Royal Commission* 1908, p. 148.

25　Miss Grayson, *NUWW Conference* 1898, p. 85.

26　The money received from the Board of Guardians would not have been sufficient to keep the young women in the home. Charitable donations were equally crucial. There was a high staff–inmate ratio which increased salary bills. Consequently young women proved more costly to look after than in the workhouse. Nevertheless, because of charitable donations, they were not a burden on the rates.

27　*The Lancet* (June 18th 1898), p. 1,704.

28　*Agatha Stacey Homes for the Feeble-Minded Annual Report* 1896.

29　Miss Kirby, 'How Best to Utilise Existing Homes and Refuges for the Care of the Feeble-Minded', *NUWW Conference* 1907, p. 7.

30　Family Welfare Association, *The Feeble-Minded Child and Adult*, 1893, p. 121.

31 *Oxford Branch NAPWFM Annual Report* 1910, p. 3.
32 Mrs Walker, 'Dull Children and How to Deal with Them', *NUWW Conference* 1891, p. 44.
33 *Agatha Stacey Homes for the Feeble-Minded Annual Report* 1909.
34 *Seeking and Saving* (formerly *Refuge and Reformatory Journal*), (1894–1896), p. 58.
35 *NUWW Quarterly Magazine* (1895).
36 These rugs, when complete, were shown at the annual Home Arts and Industries Association at the Royal Albert Hall and the Church Congress at Bristol (*Agatha Stacey Homes for the Feeble-Minded Annual Reports* 1893–1914).
37 Elaine Showalter has indicated that laundry work was recommended as therapy for female lunatics because it was an outlet for excess physical energy: Elaine Showalter, *The Female Malady* (London: Virago, 1987).
38 Miss Emily Bartholomew, *Royal Commission* 1908, p. 308.
39 *The Lancet* (May 24th 1902), p. 1,477.
40 *Royal Commission* 1908, p. 163.
41 *Seeking and Saving* (formerly *Refuge and Reformatory Journal*) (1894–1896), p. 58.
42 Miss Townsend and Miss Jeffries, *Royal Commission* 1908, p. 232.
43 *Royal Commission* 1908, p. 170.
44 Family Welfare Association, *The Feeble-Minded Child and Adult*, p. 126.
45 *Seeking and Saving* (formerly *Refuge and Reformatory Journal*) (1894–1896), p. 57.
46 *St Mary's Home for Working Women, Painswick, Annual Report* 1913, p. 7.
47 *Cumnor Rise, Oxford, Annual Report* 1910, p. 7.
48 Mrs Hazeldine, 'Permanent Homes for the Feeble-Minded' (*NUWW Quarterly Magazine*, 1894), p. 20.
49 *Agatha Stacey Homes for the Feeble-Minded Annual Report* 1899, p. 6.
50 Family Welfare Association, *The Feeble-Minded Child and Adult*, p. 127.
51 *Agatha Stacey Homes for the Feeble-Minded Annual Report* 1893.
52 Miss Maria Poole, *Royal Commission* 1908, p. 148.
53 *Agatha Stacey Homes for the Feeble-Minded Annual Report* 1894.
54 Miss Townsend and Miss Jeffries, *Royal Commission* 1908, p. 232.
55 Miss Emily Bartholomew, *Royal Commission* 1908, p. 307.
56 *Seeking and Saving* (formerly *Refuge and Reformatory Journal*) (1894–1896), p. 56.
57 Hon. Maude Stanley, *Royal Commission* 1908, p. 393.
58 *St Mary's Home for Working Women, Painswick, Annual Report* 1913, p. 7.
59 Statistics taken from annual reports.
60 Hon. Maude Stanley, *Royal Commission* 1908, p. 394.
61 Miss McKee, *Royal Commission* 1908, p. 292.
62 Hon. Maude Stanley, *Royal Commission* 1908, p. 393.
63 *Abstract of Royal Commission on the Care of the Feeble Minded* 1908, p. 57.
64 By 1908, despite the efforts of campaigners, there were only eighteen homes. The Royal Commission listed the following homes: Alexander House, Hammersmith (1887); St Mary's Home of Industry, Painswick (1890); Adcote, Liverpool (1892); Girls' Training Home, Clapton (1892); Laundry and Homes of Industry, Birmingham (1892); Scott House, Hitchin (1892); Chasefield, Bristol (1893); Laundry and Homes of Industry, Morpeth (1896); Mary Carpenter Home, Bristol (1897); Ashton Home, Chester (1898); Elizabeth Barclay Home, Bodmin (1898); Handford Home, Ipswich (1898); Field Heath Home, Hillingdon (1901); The Croft, Suffolk (1901); Coningham Road Home, Shepherd's Bush (1902); St Ann's Home, Yiewsley (1902); Romanhurst, Oxford (1903); Convent of Mercy, Midhurst (u/d) (*Royal Commission* 1908, pp. 226–227).
65 This philanthropy continued even after the foundation of the National Health Service. In the 1950s female philanthropists, like the grandmother of Sarah Bowler, 'employed' young women with learning difficulties to help in the home (oral interview, September 1998).

66 Lucia Zedner, *Women, Crime, and Custody in Victorian England* (Oxford: Clarendon Press, 1991), p. 264.
67 *The Lancet* supported permanent care.
68 Miss Emily Bartholomew, *Royal Commission* 1908, p. 307.
69 *The Lancet* (October 21st 1911), p. 1,159.
70 Miss Maria Poole, *Royal Commission* 1908, p. 148.
71 Miss Emily Bartholomew, *Royal Commission* 1908, p. 307.
72 *Royal Commission* 1908.
73 Ellen Pinsent, 'The Permanent Care of the Feeble Minded', *The Lancet* (February 21st 1903), p. 515.
74 Dr Potts, *Royal Commission* 1908, p. 471.
75 Galton believed that the inmates of prisons, hospitals and asylums were unfit to breed.
76 *Eugenics Review* (1910–1911), p. 178.
77 Agatha Stacey, talk to the council of the London Charity Organisation Society (May 25th 1891), reprinted in *NUWW Quarterly Magazine* (1891).
78 *The Lancet* (December 9th 1905).
79 *The Lancet* (February 11th 1905), p. 370. The first sterilisation law was passed in Indiana in 1907 followed by Washington State, California, Connecticut, New Jersey, Iowa, New York and Nevada over the next seven years: Margaret Adams, *Mental Retardation and its Social Dimensions* (New York: Columbia University Press, 1971), p. 31.
80 I am indebted to Robert Pearce for this quote.
81 Roy Lowe, 'Eugenicists, Doctors and the Quest for National Efficiency: An Educational Crusade, 1900–1939', *History of Education*, 8 (4), 1979, pp. 293–306.

Part IV
Purifying the nation

7   Suppressing prostitution

By the 1880s it was clear that penitentiaries, reformatories and other curative and preventive agencies were ineffective in stemming prostitution. A fourth, and broader solution, was advocated by social purity groups to tackle immorality and its underlying causes: social purists attempted to curb prostitutes and prostitution, eliminate child sexual abuse, make men chaste and improve common morality. Overall, it will be argued, social purists endorsed a more or less consistent policy of repression, even though their stated intentions were protective. This chapter outlines the miscellaneous social purity groups and examines the ways in which they sought to restrict prostitution. While it is commonly accepted that social purity groups enjoyed a measure of success in restricting prostitution and eliminating brothels, this chapter examines the scale of their achievements.

Social purity groups

From 1885 social purity groups became increasingly active and numerous. Various societies were formed, ranging from the London Council, the Moral Reform Union, the Social Purity Alliance, the White Cross Army and the Church of England Purity Society, the Friends' Association for the Promotion of Social Purity through to the historically notorious National Vigilance Association. Some groups, like the Social Purity Alliance, focused on educational work, aiming to raise the general standard of social and personal morality. It hoped to make a sustained attack on the causes that led to prostitution, one of which was the demand for it by men. Founded in 1873 by Josephine Butler and others, the Social Purity Alliance remained numerically small.[1] The London Council, although equally modest in size, was more interventionist in spirit with the objective to 'fight against disorderly houses and strive to banish them altogether'.[2] Ellice Hopkins also tried to promote a Union of Fathers and Mothers for the Abolition of Prostitution, but it never quite got off the ground.[3] The two major groups, and probably the two most well known, were the White Cross Army and the NVA, both of which have been the subject of some historical debate.

In 1883, in order to strike at the perceived root of immorality and to help create a higher form of public morality, Ellice Hopkins and the Bishop of Durham founded the White Cross Army 'for the protection of women and children from prostitution and degradation'.[4] This became the chief work of the last twenty-one years of the indomitable Hopkins. Its name was chosen carefully: 'White' stood for purity, the 'Cross' demonstrated that the fight was for Christ, and 'Army' implied a disciplined strength.[5] The White Cross Army was undenominational, contained Nonconformists as well as Church of England members, and was targeted at working-class men. At about the same time the Church of England Purity Society was formed under the presidency of the Archbishop of Canterbury, Dr Benson,[6] with support from the Archbishop of York and thirty other bishops in England for the upper class.[7] In spite of the different target audience, there were great similarities between the two groups: both worked at a diocesan level and were based on the doctrines of the Christian faith; both relied on the 'pulpit power' of the parish priest, Sunday school teachers and others who had spiritual charge over their congregations; and both targeted men rather than women on the basis of their belief that men should take responsibility for sexual virtue.[8] These two organisations, conscious that their work was being duplicated, joined together in 1891 to become the Church of England Purity Society of the White Cross League, commonly known as CEPS. Much of the success of CEPS can be attributed to Ellice Hopkins, who spent a significant part of her life working for the organisation. During her time of activity, she addressed hundreds of meetings and wrote most of the pamphlets, which sold over 2 million copies in the USA and Britain. Branches of the White Cross were formed in the army, the navy and in local dioceses in Britain and the rest of the world. Africa, Australia, Canada, China, Jamaica, Japan, New Zealand, Trinidad and the USA all had thriving branches.

In 1885 the National Vigilance Association, the second of the most influential social purity organisations, was founded to help enforce the Criminal Law Amendment Act passed in the same year.[9] The CLA Act, it will be remembered, raised the age of sexual consent to 16, gave police greater powers to close down brothels and made male homosexuality illegal.[10] Some of the leading figures in the NVA were well known in radical circles: Millicent Fawcett, Lord Lytton (Constance Lytton's brother), Catherine Booth, Josephine Butler and Ellice Hopkins were among them. Various local organisations affiliated to the NVA – for example, in the Midlands, the Birmingham and Midland Counties' Vigilance Association (which emerged from the Midland Counties' Electoral Union for the Repeal of the Contagious Diseases Acts Relating to Women) – were formed.[11] Until 1894, when it amalgamated with the NVA, the Midland branch acted as an autonomous and independent body that was only loosely affiliated to its parent organisation.[12] This branch, in common with the NVA, sought to question, challenge, curtail and change men's sexual behaviour as well as women's:

Objects of the Association

1 The Society has been established to form a Central Union of Vigilance Associations Midland Counties, for the purpose of creating and sustaining a healthy public opinion on questions of social morals between the sexes, of promoting social purity, and of co-operating with similar institutions throughout the country.

2 The Society will render such assistance as may be practicable to aid in bringing into operation and giving effect to, the provisions of the Criminal Law Amendment Act 1885; to protect women and children; to discover and check the causes of criminal vice; to watch legislation, and obtain needful amendments of the law; to prosecute offences against the law, and to expose offenders to public censure; to advocate pure morality through the press, and by public meetings and lectures, and to take such measures as may, from time to time, appear desirable to repress morality.[13]

As with the reform and other preventive organisations, the social purity movement overall was a complex mixture of repression, protection and liberation.[14] To a great extent, it mirrored the philosophy of the Ladies' Associations and it is evident that those involved with social purity did not break with the past but merely built on the foundation of reform and preventive work.

Curbing prostitution

Unquestionably, the attitude and practice of social purists towards *impenitent* prostitutes was oppressive. In contrast to the assistance offered to the repentant 'fallen woman', the abandoned mother and the abused child, unremorseful prostitutes were treated harshly. Such prostitutes were excluded from the category of the deserving and fell outside the moral boundaries set up by social purists. In engaging in prostitution women defied the concept of 'femininity',[15] violated their gender role and relinquished their rights to the care and protection usually extended to the 'weaker sex'.

> We are clear that vice ought not to be made safe, we should be equally clear that it ought not to be made easy ... The fallen woman who lives on her miserable trade is a pest to society. Pity her, reform her by all means, but do not feel bound to give her liberty to ply her harmful trade any more than you give liberty to any other corrupters of society.[16]

On the whole, working-class women remained the targets of social purity workers: certainly there were no charges for male soliciting in London in the early years of the twentieth century. Social purists used the newly passed CLA Act to try to prevent soliciting and to close down brothels.[17] Letters and petitions, orchestrated by social purists, were constantly forwarded to the police to ensure that this happened. The language used by the authors of these complaints did not suggest even a modicum of sympathy and compassion towards prostitutes. In fact, they viewed prostitutes as an infected group who would contaminate society rather than as victims in need of rescue.

Social purists certainly took exception to the public nature of prostitution. Prostitutes, by working on the streets and other places used by the local community, made life intolerable for respectable inhabitants and so were treated as public nuisances.[18] The chemist of Euston Square, London, who wrote to his local authority was only one of many protestors. He complained about the

> great nuisance caused by the prostitutes infecting this district, and shall feel obliged by your using your authority in removing the same. It is of very common occurrence, for my doorstep to be used by these women, for disgusting purposes, and the language used by them is simply disgraceful.[19]

In December 1886, the Clapham Vigilance Association objected that not only was 'solicitation openly and offensively practised, but actual fornication is shamelessly committed on the numerous benches and in other places upon the Common even in close proximity to the public roadway'.[20] The North Kensington Ratepayers' Association were equally alarmed about 'the immorality, the obscene and blasphemous language' in their area.[21]

Whereas repentant prostitutes were deemed innocent victims and were looked after, unrepentant ones needed to be restrained, as the criticism implicit in this quote demonstrates, because they threatened the status quo:

> They are a serious injury to the respectable neighbours. The constant sight of vicious manners, and of the ease, independence, and finery obtained by vicious means, is a perpetual danger to the virtue of the sons and daughters of respectable inhabitants . . . For the evil indicated, they feel that there is only one remedy – repression. By the joint action of policeman and citizen, it can be repressed.[22]

There was unanimity that prostitutes annoyed the general public and made the streets unsuitable places for young respectable men and women. Time after time, residents demanded the right to live in districts free from the soliciting of prostitutes. One resident of Endsleigh Gardens, London, called attention to

> the fearful prevalence . . . of a gross state of street prostitution attended by features of a very disgusting character, particularly between the hours of 10 and 12 at which it is not fit for any respectable female to walk about and young men cannot do so without molestation.[23]

Similarly, a group of residents in Euston Road complained of the 'annoyance caused to the respectable inhabitants of the district, by women of loose character who frequent this road night after night ... and who ply their unlawful calling in the most persistent manner possible',[24] and of the number of brothels masquerading as hotels on Euston Road and King's Cross.[25] Petitions were delivered to the Home Secretary: in 1901 8,500 people in Westminster signed a petition to

> bring under your notice the existing disgraceful condition of the streets of the parish and its vicinity resulting mainly in the opinion of your petitioners from the unsatisfactory state of the law as regards brothels and common prostitutes. The way in which the latter (dressed and conducting themselves in such a manner as to leave no doubt as to their vocation) infest the streets at the south part of the Parish is disgraceful.

Westminster residents claimed that the presence of young prostitutes had a most pernicious effect on 'young persons of both sexes and especially on young girls in the lower ranks of life'.[26] Objections were not always directly linked to issues of sexual morality since this petition also maintained that prostitution had lowered property values in the area and had driven away respectable families.

Historians have generally claimed that social purity groups were successful in suppressing, if not eliminating, prostitution. Lucy Bland suggests that the 'years 1901–6 saw the most intense repression of prostitutes in London'.[27] Social purists were able to do this because, Frank Mort alleges, they moved away from using philanthropy to prevent prostitution to utilising the criminal law.[28] However, one cannot accept these judgements unreservedly as it is difficult to determine exactly how successful the complaints of social purists were.

Evidence about the decline of prostitution is certainly contradictory. At the same time, social purity groups claimed success in closing brothels and curbing prostitution and yet continued to express alarm about their growth. On the one hand, social purists alleged that prostitution had diminished. In 1893 London social purists pronounced a victory when prostitutes working in Euston Road and Endsleigh Gardens found themselves facing charges:

> During the last six months thirty known prostitutes have been charged with drunkenness, disorderly conduct and soliciting prostitution ... in addition to which there have been two charges of men and women violating public decency by having sexual intercourse in Endsleigh Gardens.[29]

The London Council for the Promotion of Public Morality even managed to boast that the moral condition of the streets had improved due to the energetic work of themselves and the Metropolitan Police Force.[30] On the other hand, *The Social Gazette*, the official newspaper of the Salvation Army, insisted that there were more streets 'given over to the open bartering of virtue' and more 'houses of shame' than ever before.[31] In Clapham, the Sub Committee of the Vigilance Association frequently visited the Common at night to complain about the 'disgusting and demoralising traffic openly and unblushingly carried on'.[32] Similarly at St Martin's Field, prostitutes continued to 'ply their trade . . . until the streets, which belong equally to all classes of the community, have become the market in which this most hideous traffic is openly carried on'.[33] Certainly, in the first few years of the twentieth century, St Pancras Borough Council constantly protested to the Metropolitan Police Authority about the prevalence of prostitution in its district.[34]

In provincial towns the NVA claimed success but, once again, this is not indisputable. The Oxford Vigilance Association maintained that, because it had always received effective help from the police, prostitution was curbed. In Oxford 'a brothel of some years existence was closed early in the year' and several brothels were closed as a result of a very active vigilance association. In general, a combination of compassion and threats was used to curtail prostitution: whenever the NVA received information about brothels, members first visited them to try to reform the prostitutes working there. If this failed then landlords or agents were cautioned and told of their liability under the CLA Act. In Southampton the police and the magistrates worked as one and in all cases of prostitutes behaving indecently the men were also arrested for aiding and abetting.[35] In Sheffield the 'magistrates supported the police by imposing heavy penalties, in many cases imprisonment, and the effect has been that prostitution in this city has almost been abolished'.[36] In Aldershot twenty-two houses were suppressed (interestingly only one out of approximately four hundred prostitutes residing there chose to be rescued).[37] In at least two large towns patrols of 'respectable citizens' were established who cautioned brothel-keepers and detected – and seemingly shamed – the men who frequented them.[38] However, there is no record as to whether or not social purists achieved anything of long-lasting effect since many of the achievements claimed by them were temporary or even illusory: by 1891, despite the raids, the closure of brothels and the curtailment of prostitution in Aldershot there were in fact as many prostitutes working as ever before.[39] Similarly, prostitution continued in Sheffield and it is clear that the chief of police there, as mentioned in the introduction, was naive in his assertion that prostitution had been virtually eliminated in the city.

Pressure was also brought to bear on landlords to refuse to rent rooms to women thought to be prostitutes.[40] In Manchester property-owners were warned that they would be liable to heavy fines and imprisonment if they continued to rent their houses to known brothel-keepers.[41] In Royal Leamington Spa, as a result of local vigilance pressure, several landlords dismissed tenants who used their homes for prostitution.[42] Nevertheless, vigilance societies were not always in a position of unchallenged authority. In Royal Leamington Spa both the town council and the police were criticised because they systematically ignored offences against morality:[43]

> a few months ago there was a period of intense dismay. Every reasonable effort had been used to wake the police authorities to the fact that a disgraceful amount of public immorality was going on in the town unchecked and even professing to shelter itself under the sanction or indulgence of the police. The Watch Committee was memorialised in vain.[44]

Police and social purists

Social purists depended on the police to enforce the law but, unlike the Scottish police in Linda Mahood's research,[45] the English police force was not always willing to do so. Overall, the response of the police towards prostitution was ambivalent and depended on the sympathies of the local police commissioner and the opinions of a more widespread public rather than the minority voices of vigilance groups. As with much legislation, the CLA Act was interpreted subjectively. For instance, London Parish Vestries, pressurised by social purists, instructed the police force to keep surveillance on certain brothels in order to collect the necessary evidence with which to prosecute their owners. At first, the London police were willing to do this, observed alleged brothels and furnished reports of them to the Vestries who in turn prosecuted or warned them. In 1887 the relationship between the police and the Vestries broke down,[46] when the newly appointed Metropolitan Police Commissioner, Sir Charles Warren, gave directions that the police were no longer to watch known brothels for the parish authorities as it was not strictly part of their duty.[47] This change in policy occurred for a number of reasons. First, Warren believed that brothel surveillance was a waste of police time because it removed police officers away from the prevention and detection of more serious crime. Second, he complained that when Vestries received information from the police they cautioned rather than prosecuted brothel-owners, which led to them simply moving elsewhere. Third, Warren favoured a policy of containment rather than a policy of repression, as the vigilance societies

> are in the habit of routing out the brothels from the back slums and driving them into respectable places . . . and as long as there is a demand for prostitutes on the part of the public there is no doubt they will exist in spite of the Vestries and the Vigilance Societies, and the more they are driven out of their brothels back slums, the worse it becomes for law and order and decency.[48]

Generally, Warren seemed less concerned about the morality of prostitution than its associated crimes of drunkenness, riotous behaviour and disturbance of the peace.

Moreover, the Metropolitan Police claimed that vigilance societies' assertions that certain areas were 'literally infested' with drunken and disorderly prostitutes were somewhat exaggerated.[49] In fact, social purists were criticised for their obsessive behaviour in rooting out immorality:

> A number of seats are placed on the Common, some of them in very secluded spots, and although I have never seen it, I cannot doubt that if gentlemen conceal themselves, and watch, they could detect persons committing fornication.[50]

The Metropolitan Police therefore tended to disregard prostitution especially since the behaviour of prostitutes seldom justified arrest.[51]

> I found that prostitutes . . . conduct themselves much better, and are more orderly than I should have expected . . . during the whole time I did not see either them worse for drink, neither did I witness any act of indecency; they generally accost men who are by themselves and . . . if they get a reply in the negative, they walk away . . . they are not accompanied by the usual tout or what is commonly called a 'bully' . . . I also noticed that several men made overtures to these unfortunate women.[52]

The Metropolitan Police preferred a policy of containment rather than one of attempted elimination because it kept the problem within the confines of a well-policed area. It was recognised that when police and vigilance societies suppressed prostitution in one district, it simply broke out with renewed vigour elsewhere, leading to criticisms that vigilance groups were simply moving vice from one part of London to another.[53] The Westminster City Council believed that the police were reluctant to prosecute since 'even if drastic measures were adopted in any particular district I suspect the main result would be, not to get rid of the evil, but to drive it elsewhere'.[54] Although the London police were opposed to a crusade against brothels, they suppressed the most glaring cases when public opinion so demanded.[55] In addition, the police took action when brothels were a special nuisance or were conducted in 'such a manner as to be an annoyance to passengers or neighbours by reason of lewd and indecent conduct or solicitation or nightly disturbance'.[56]

Social purists accused London police not only of tolerating prostitution but also of complicity with prostitutes. In a pamphlet that allegedly contained evidence from an official shorthand report from the Royal Commission on the London Police 1907, police officers were accused of taking money and drink from prostitutes who worked in flats opposite a police station. According to the pamphlet, constables 'made the Acquaintance' of many of the prostitutes living there and visited them regularly in their flats.

> 'Am I to understand that you often saw policemen going up and down the staircase?'
> 'Oh, yes; I did, always – many times.'
> 'Going into various rooms or sets of rooms or flats?'
> 'Yes, that I saw. I had my birthday there, and they all came up to a singing party at my flat.'[57]

Police officers were accused of taking bribes, receiving free drinks and cigarettes, and using the flats of prostitutes for personal entertainment. One witness claimed that a police officer had advised her husband to rent flats to prostitutes because of the large profit to be made – the said police officer to receive cash for advice and general help.[58]

More importantly, perhaps, the police felt themselves constrained by the law in relation to prostitution and soliciting. Prostitution, in itself, was not a crime and soliciting was a matter of the greatest difficulty to prove, so much so that Metropolitan Police magistrates became wary of convicting on the unsupported evidence of a constable, making the law 'practically a dead letter'.[59] Arresting a prostitute for soliciting and seeing the charge through to conviction was thought to be fraught with difficulties:

> Action is attended by much trouble, by very likely a scuffle, by cross-examination by the Station Inspector, by the necessity of making out a written report, by the loss of at least four hours' rest next day at the police court, by risk of blame by the magistrate and of other consequences . . . excessive zeal in this direction would at once arouse the suspicion of his superiors that he was paying too much attention to this class of case to the neglect of other duties.[60]

Understandably, the police felt themselves to be at serious risk of making a mistake, which might involve damage to a rising career in the police service, so that constables would not arrest a prostitute unless absolutely compelled.[61] This was confirmed by the bad publicity received in a number of cases of wrongful arrest. For example, in July 1887 a police officer, Constable Endacott, had arrested and charged a Miss Cass, aged 23, for solicitation and although the magistrate discharged her, he had written down her occupation as prostitute and cautioned her as to her future conduct. Miss Cass indignantly denied the allegation. Her case

> led to much excited comment in the Press, a debate in Parliament leading up to an adjournment of the House of Commons, an enquiry by the Lord Chancellor into the conduct of the magistrate and by the Commissioner into that of the Constable. This case brought matters to

LIVERPOOL JOHN MOORES UNIVERSITY
LEARNING SERVICES

a crisis and there was a general outcry as to the undue amount of power in the hands of the Police.[62]

Indeed, much was made in Parliament and the press about the respectability of Miss Cass, who had recently arrived from Stockton, County Durham, was engaged in honest employment as a dressmaker to an equally respectable householder and had been a member of the eminently respectable Girls' Friendly Society. The portrayal of the innocent victim (Cass) contrasted with that of the police officer (Endacott) who had perjured himself by testifying that he had seen Miss Cass on the streets a number of times previously. As a consequence, the Chief Commissioner, Sir Charles Warren, issued instructions to police officers directing that under no circumstances were they to prosecute any women without corroborative evidence.[63] Not surprisingly, the number of prostitutes arrested in London declined for some time (see Figure 7.1).[64]

Similarly, in 1891, when Miss Millard was charged by Aldershot police with being a disorderly prostitute she was found, on medical examination, to be a virgin, with the result that magistrates urged police to be more cautious in their arrests.[65] In 1900 the Metropolitan Police were again criticised in the press and in Parliament as 'uniformed ruffians' and condemned for wrongfully arresting and charging Madame Eva D'Angely with soliciting.[66] Madame D'Angely had been arrested by Constable Page at the corner of Conduit Street and Regent Street at 11:30p.m. on April 24th 1906 and taken to Great Marlborough Police Station, where she was charged as a 'common prostitute behaving in a riotous and indecent manner'.[67] Her husband protested her innocence, newspapers published her story and the Home Secretary was questioned in the House of Commons. In the same

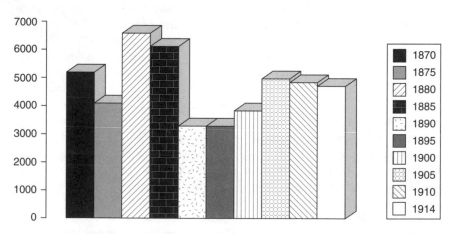

Figure 7.1 Numbers of arrests of prostitutes in London 1870–1914
Source: compiled from Metropolitan Police Statistics 1870–1914

ycar Mrs X, reputed to be married to a respectable professional, was wrongfully charged with soliciting in Regent Street. It was alleged that she had
been arrested by a revengeful police officer who was upset by Mrs X's refusal
to join him in a glass of wine. As a result of such cases a Royal Commission
was set up to deal with police corruption and other criminal matters.[68]
    According to police,

> the main difficulty in enforcing the law is caused by the over-sensitiveness
> and impatience of the public whenever there seems ground, however
> slight, for alleging that there has been a mistake in arresting a woman on
> a charge of solicitation. The proceedings of the Metropolitan Police are
> widely reported in the newspapers, and if a Magistrate refuses to convict
> . . . a wave of indignation passes throughout the community.[69]

Not surprisingly, therefore, police thought it was the safest policy to ignore
prostitution. These incidents led, according to the Metropolitan Police, to
women becoming bolder in soliciting.[70] Certainly, as indicated in a debate
in the House of Commons in 1900, the police (mindful that Constable
Endacott had been suspended from duty in 1887) remained wary of arresting
prostitutes so much so that it was allegedly 'impossible to walk down
Piccadilly at that time without molestation'.[71] A number of magistrates in
London would not even listen to charges of soliciting unless the person
solicited was present. This meant that fewer charges were made.[72] Even the
National Vigilance Association admitted defeat in London, complaining
that because Scotland Yard withheld its assistance it made it practically
impossible to curb prostitution.[73] Moreover, it was felt that the Metropolitan
Police did little to suppress prostitution because they were directly responsible to the government rather than to a more accountable local authority.[74]
Magistrates too were regularly blamed for giving light sentences or small
fines. In 1886 social purists had prosecuted a notorious and very wealthy
brothel-keeper, Mrs Jeffries, who maintained four houses in Chelsea, a
brothel devoted to flagellation in Hampstead, a brothel in Euston which
offered other perversions and a 'white slave' house at Kew. She pleaded
guilty and was fined an easily affordable £200 because she allegedly had
protection from the higher echelons of society. Nearly thirty years later, in
1913, magistrates were equally lenient: Queenie Gerald, charged with
keeping a disorderly house, was given only a three months' prison sentence
(the maximum sentence was two years) because she enjoyed the support of
influential men.[75] Similarly, in many provincial districts the CLA Act was
seen as a 'dead letter owing to the supineness of some of our magistrates'.[76]
    Certainly, the police were more wary of criticism – and condemnation
– from the general public, than from the vigilance societies. The Metropolitan Police believed that dealing with street prostitution was a delicate
issue because of the 'uncertainty of public feeling on the matter'.[77] Public
opinion was thought to be 'strangely indifferent' to immorality and at such

a low ebb that it was judged impossible to make much headway.[78] Several of the most active members of the St Jude's Vigilance Association were

> insulted in the streets, have had their windows broken, their bell-pulls wrenched off, knocking at the door and the bells rung between twelve midnight and 2am and have had nuisances committed on the doorsteps it is believed by the friends of those prosecuted by members of the Association.[79]

Frank Mort has suggested that there was greater co-operation between the police and social purity workers in cities with a high Nonconformist influence – such as Birmingham, Bristol, Manchester and Liverpool – than in Anglican ones and that this resulted in a higher success rate of prosecutions.[80] He argues that 'the police and the NVA worked in close contact, closing brothels'.[81] On the surface, the vigilance associations of these cities enjoyed good relationships with the magistrates and the police, which reinforces Frank Mort's claim. For example, the Midland group asserted that

> we should not have accomplished many of the things that we have, had it not been for assistance . . . of Mr Farndale, the Chief of Police. The records of the police are always open to the Secretary of this Association, and the assistance of the police, when asked for, has always been readily given.[82]

The chief of police was not the only official sympathetic to social purity. The chair of the Watch Committee and at least one stipendiary magistrate were members of the NVA and many others were sympathetic to its aims, according to reports in the social purity press.[83] Indeed, in 1891 there were forty-one complaints about brothels in Birmingham by the NVA. Every one of the forty-one complaints was investigated and when there was sufficient evidence to obtain a conviction they were referred to the superintendent of the police for prosecution.[84] Once again, in 1899, fifteen 'disorderly' houses were prosecuted and ultimately closed.[85] In Bristol too the Vigilance Committee was responsible for closing five brothels and prosecuting their brothel-owners, who were eventually sentenced to between six and eight weeks' hard labour.[86] The keepers of other houses were said to be 'thoroughly frightened, and we hope to keep them in that state'. Similarly in Manchester the streets were kept tolerably clear as a result of police action,[87] with the Manchester Vigilance Association claiming it was instrumental in cutting down the number of brothels from 402 in 1882 to 3 in 1892.[88] Liverpool was believed to enjoy an impressive rate of conviction because it had an active Vigilance Committee which worked hard to gain public support, an elected Watch Committee committed to enforcing the law and magistrates determined to back up the police.[89] In Liverpool, if known prostitutes merely spoke to men on the streets they were charged with soliciting and, because the magistrates accepted the uncorroborated evidence of the police, were usually found guilty.

Nevertheless, the police force and social purists in Nonconformist cities were not as compatible as Frank Mort claims. Indeed, social purists had to work hard to convince police authorities of the need to suppress prostitution – only a small number of Liverpool brothels were prosecuted in the first few years after the CLA Act. Initially, rather than suppressing prostitution, the Liverpool police and authorities, like those in London, contained prostitution by monitoring selected districts.

> Four hundred houses were so tolerated and protected, and this policy of protection and toleration, inaugurated by the Chief Constable, had the support of the Watch Committee, and the majority of the members of the City Council. By the Watch Committee, a manifesto, in favour of a stricter administration of the law, was treated with contempt, though it was signed by the Bishop, the Archdeacon, and many leading citizens.[90]

The Chief Constable felt it undesirable to take brothel-owners to court because it drove them into previously respectable areas where it took the police a long time to find them.[91] As a consequence, Liverpool police tended to prosecute brothel-owners only if they opened in a hitherto reputable street, had children living there, were nuisances or had a high incidence of robberies in them.[92] Only after a vigorous campaign by the Liverpool Vigilance Committee, which led to the resignation of the chairman of the Watch Committee, and the election of a Liberal Council in November 1890 did the Liverpool police reverse their policy, thus leading to a dramatic increase in prosecutions.[93] Even so, the police crackdown did not last because when prostitution spread to previously respectable neighbourhoods, the Liverpool Council reversed its policy in 1896 and returned to the 1890 system.[94] Success was also limited in Birmingham and Manchester. By 1904 the Midlands branch of the NVA, despite their previous efforts, was defunct,[95] and prostitution continued unabated.[96] The situation in Manchester was legally sensitive: one of the superintendents was on intimate terms with many prostitutes, informed brothel-owners of imminent police raids and even co-owned a brothel.[97]

Figure 7.2, taken from the *Judicial Statistics for England and Wales*, indicates the number of women tried for prostitution between 1860 and 1914.[98] Fewer prostitutes were prosecuted in the years after the CLA Act 1885 – the numbers fell from 11,830 in 1884 to 7,071 in 1890 – but this may have little to do with the claims of social purists that they had cleared the streets of prostitutes and more to do with a relaxing of police pressure. Indeed, the decrease in prosecutions could be related to police fears of wrongful arrest in the aftermath of the Cass débâcle rather than of a decline in prostitution. Of course, it is important not to read too much into these

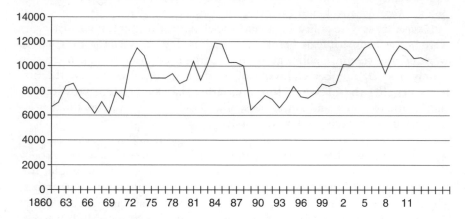

Figure 7.2 Numbers of women tried for prostitution 1860–1914
Source: compiled from *Judicial Statistics of England and Wales* 1860–1914

statistics, as they are indicative only of police response to prostitution rather than the extent of prostitution itself.

Nevertheless these statistics, combined with the other evidence, makes one suppose that not only was co-operation between the police force and social purists not as widespread as Frank Mort has assumed but also social purists were not always as successful as they claimed in curbing prostitution.

Effects on prostitutes and prostitution

Unrepentant prostitutes, Judith Walkowitz argues, were the casualties of the gendered and middle-class ideology of the social purists. She points out, in relation to the Contagious Diseases Acts, that official intervention into the lives of prostitutes may have damaged the fragile social equilibrium that existed between them and the local community in which they lived.[99] As a result of increased police vigilance and middle-class interference, prostitutes may well have become increasingly marginalised, thus facilitating the creation of an outcast group. Repressive police action might also, as in the CD Acts districts, have made the move into prostitution more permanent.[100] The Police Commissioner in London believed that the active suppression of brothels led to such a large increase in street solicitation that London supplanted Paris as the 'City of Pleasure'.[101] Social purists, apparently unconscious of the social dislocation that their actions might generate, appeared unconcerned about the future of women thrown out of the brothels or rented accommodation. As a consequence of social purity action, prostitutes could have been denied access to a safe place in which to work, thus making the working lives of prostitutes more difficult and increasing their physical vulnerability. Indeed, a contemporary observer stated that 'they are hunted from place to place, till no one outside of the criminal class will venture to give them a lodging. But prostitution is in no way lessened by this. The women are brutified, not reclaimed.'[102] In the *City of Dreadful Delight*, Judith Walkowitz argues that such repression made the streets unsafe for women.[103] For example, between August 31st and November 9th 1888 five brutal murders of prostitutes took place in London by an unknown criminal whom the press dubbed 'Jack the Ripper'.

In many cases, the effects of the CLA Act on the working life of prostitutes were hardly catastrophic. Prostitutes who left the brothels and lodgings, and who could not find or afford accommodation elsewhere, appeared to have had few alternatives open to them: they could work on the streets or through a pimp, or else give up their trade, enter a reformatory,[104] or even go into domestic service. However, it was more likely that they moved elsewhere. Social purity workers suspected that brothels often masqueraded as legitimate business. The London Council for the Promotion of Public Morality,[105] for instance, claimed that prostitutes offered their services under the cover of nursing homes, massage parlours or manicure establishments.[106] The National Vigilance Association certainly expressed disquieting concern about massage parlours in St James', Piccadilly and the Haymarket in which

> discipline treatment is now 'run' as a speciality, and there is no doubt that it is too often simply another name for flagellation . . . The much advertised nursing nymphs, who, clad in the flimsiest of costumes, minister to the desire of elderly gentlemen.[107]

Brothels presented themselves as 'schools' offering a certain type of lesson: 'Elocution lessons: Madame Osborne Gray has re-opened her studio for lessons in elocution and deportment; also classes can be arranged to study the art of fencing.'[108] This particular 'school' was raided by the police who took possession of 'two leather bands partly lined with wool; several dog whips, 19 canes, some bearing marks of blood; four birches, a mask, three pairs of handcuffs, three padlocks, and books, many of which were of a grossly obscene character'.[109] Prostitutes circumvented the CLA Act by renting small flats which were not subject to the laws covering brothels. If women used their own homes for prostitution these were not, in legal terms, defined as brothels, so in order to avoid conviction, large houses were divided up and let out as individual flats. In Manchester too women dwelt alone in small houses where they carried 'on their abominable trade in defiance of all law, civil or moral . . . the police are powerless'.[110]

Prostitution may have declined, if indeed it did, for other reasons besides the intervention of social purists. The introduction of free and compulsory education, better job prospects, increased wages and improved working conditions offered women greater opportunities than they had previously enjoyed. In addition the Liberal government elected in 1906 passed a range of measures which alleviated some of the worst excesses of poverty deemed to cause prostitution.

White slavery

By the early twentieth century, possibly influenced by its lack of success
in curbing English prostitution, possibly encouraged by the support of the
women's suffrage movement, the NVA focused attention on the problems
associated with international prostitution called 'white slavery'. This term
enabled social purists to draw parallels between the experiences of white
women and those of black American and British slaves before emancipation.[111] At one and the same time, foreign prostitutes working in England
were viewed both sympathetically and antagonistically. On the one hand,
young women who were abducted from foreign countries (either by force
or else unwittingly) were perceived as victims who needed assistance. On
the other hand, possibly because social purists were receptive to imperial-
istic and eugenic theories, adult foreign prostitutes were held responsible
for much of the continued vice in England and were viewed as criminals
who needed to be restrained. Social purists wanted to rid England of 'foreign
women' who solicited in Piccadilly and the West End, maintaining 'that
if some parts of the West End could be relieved of the German, French
and Belgian women who haunt our streets, it would tend to the purifica-
tion of our city'. Lara Marks points out that Jewish prostitution, which
increased largely because of conditions in Eastern Europe, was viewed particularly unsympathetically.[112] The leading eugenist, Arnold White, believed
that the white slave trade was managed largely by the Jewish community
and campaigned in support of immigration restriction. Along with a number
of preventive organisations and the emerging suffragette movement, the
NVA campaigned to protect young and vulnerable women, put pressure
on the British government to change the law and set up an international
committee to stop the trade world-wide. Once again, the tension between
repression and protection was all too evident.

The NVA devised a number of strategies to combat international prostitution. Largely due to the efforts of British social purists, international conferences were organised from 1899 onwards. The most important diplomatic
conference was held in Paris in 1902 when sixteen countries were represented
by a number of influential delegates: the British government, for instance,
was represented by Judge Snagge, who had drafted the CLA Act 1885. Most
of the great powers ratified an International Convention for the Suppression
of the White Slave Traffic, which was passed at the conference. This convention agreed to the appointment of specially trained officials who would
keep a watchful eye at railway stations and ports for those engaged in the
white slave trade; to question known prostitutes of foreign origin about
the ways in which they were recruited; and to keep a surveillance over
employment agencies professing to find work for women. Committees were
formed in Belgium, Denmark, France, Germany, Holland, Hungary, Italy,
Norway, Russia, Spain, Sweden and Switzerland as well as further afield in
Argentina, Egypt and South Africa to supervise this work. As a result of the

Paris Convention the Home Office in Britain appointed a special branch (called the White Slave Traffic Branch) at New Scotland Yard in the charge of an assistant commissioner of police. A further convention, ratified in 1910, punished those who procured women with a prison sentence.[113]

In England, fifty paid workers were employed to meet young unaccompanied women embarking from continental ships docking in the ports of Hull, Folkestone and Dover and at the major London railway stations. Social purists tried to ensure that these young women had a decent job to go to and sufficient money to travel and find decent lodgings. However, they enjoyed a mixed success. Not all the young women accepted their philanthropic endeavours: the organisation saw 400 at Hull but only 8 accepted help. Nevertheless, between 1903 and 1908 over 12,000 young women had been helped in some way by the social purity network.[114]

Social purists also tried to strengthen the law regarding prostitution. Delegates from the Salvation Army, Church Army, Jewish Association for the Protection of Girls and Women, London Diocesan Council for Preventive, Rescue and Penitentiary Work, Society for the Rescue of Young Women and Children, the NUWW and other associated societies for the protection of women and children sent, under the auspices of the NVA, a number of deputations to the Home Secretary and others expressing concern about the white slave trade and requesting the law be changed.[115]

One of the most important pieces of legislation to be passed as a result of social purity, and indeed eugenic, pressure was the Aliens Act 1905.[116] This, the first of many immigration Acts, was passed mainly to limit the number of Jewish immigrants fleeing from the pogroms of Russia entering Britain. At the time, the Russian tsarist secret police encouraged massacres against the Jewish population in order to deflect criticism of the government: hundreds were killed in these cruel atrocities and many left to live in a more sympathetic environment. Repatriation in general was a cause of great concern, particularly for young women émigrés from countries such as Russia, Romania and Galicia. For Jewish women, who were seen to form a large contingent of the white slave trade,[117] and who were 'suspected to be most numerous in the East End of London, where there is a large population of aliens, chiefly Jews from Russia and Poland',[118] repatriation was doubly dangerous. The Jewish Association for the Protection of Girls and Women, formed in 1885, was particularly alarmed that in some European states young Jewish women were 'driven to vice through physical and mental distress',[119] and if sent back to their native country would be placed at the mercy of unsympathetic (and probably anti-Semitic) frontier officials. Despite these reservations, and the likely outcome of potential abuse should women return to Russia, the NVA advocated repatriation. William Coote, in his evidence to the Royal Commission on Alien Immigration, considered that prostitution was a menace to society and asked that power be given to repatriate immoral women.[120] His views were shared by Herbert Samuel who stated that 'it was some little consolation to our national pride to know that many of the worst offenders were aliens and that in this respect . . . the expulsion clauses in the Aliens Act were of the greatest value'.[121] Largely in response to NVA campaigners, the Aliens Act included a clause that allowed the expulsion of 'improper and scandalous foreigners'. This enabled immigration officials to refuse entry to any women judged to be immoral and gave magistrates the right to expel those convicted of offences such as soliciting, living upon the results of prostitution or of keeping immoral houses. Between 1905 and 1913, 336 women and 168 men were expelled for living on immoral earnings, while 97 women and 153 men were expelled for running brothels.[122] Police constables escorted these women and men to vessels leaving for their respective countries; their fare was paid but they were generally left to fend for themselves. Even though the police were responsible for enacting the law they expressed doubts about its efficacy in eliminating prostitution, since women could – and did – return to England under a different name and/or their place filled by new women.[123] Others married Britons or claimed Canadian, Maltese or Gibraltar citizenship to avoid deportation.

By the First World War, the NVA seemed to be working closely with the government and the police force. In December 1912, a new Criminal Law Amendment Act was passed which tightened up the laws against prostitutes and prostitution still further. This Act, commonly known as the White Slave Act, revoked the 'reasonable cause to believe' clause that allowed men to claim that they thought the girl with whom they had sexual intercourse was over 16 (men aged 23 or under and charged with first offence were exempt from this later amendment); permitted the arrest of suspected procurers without warrant; increased the fine of brothel-owners to £100; required landlords to evict tenants convicted of using their homes for prostitution; and allowed men convicted of procuring young women to be whipped: the 'number of strikes and the instrument with which they shall be inflicted specified by the court in the sentences'. Such a law, supported by an alliance of feminists, social purists and the Liberal government, consolidated the trend towards a punitive legal system. In the same year a White Slave Traffic branch was formed to suppress procuration; to keep watch on trains linked to foreign boats and massage and manicure establishments; to keep an eye on suspicious advertisements; and to provide a home for foreign women charged with soliciting. The governor of Holloway prison instructed prison staff to help 'the ladies' of the NVA in their visits to 'alien' prostitutes.[124] The women of the NVA enquired about the history of every prostitute they visited, the methods they adopted in carrying on prostitution, what friends they had in their own country and whether they would be willing to give up prostitution.

The Metropolitan Police Force, although giving the NVA official support, were more sceptical in private about the existence of the White Slave Traffic. In a confidential memorandum, the Criminal Investigation Department (CID) reported that the White Slave Traffic Branch, which had been in existence for a year, had found little evidence of actual trafficking. It complained that Britain had been aroused by a number of alarming statements made by religious, social and other workers, who spread the belief that there was a highly organised gang of 'White Slave Traffickers' with agents in every part of the civilised world, kidnapping and otherwise carrying off women and girls from their homes to lead them to their ruin in foreign lands.[125]

The White Slave Traffic Branch believed that there was an 'utter absence' of evidence to justify the alarming statements put forward by social purists since every case it investigated proved to be false. As far as they were concerned, white slavery was of such small proportions and so sporadic that it did not justify police attention.

In general, it is perhaps safe to assert that social purists were more repressive than protective in their efforts to curb prostitution. Only those deemed 'innocent' emigrants were extended a helping hand, offered travel assistance, alternative employment opportunities and decent lodging. In contrast, women who persisted in prostitution were condemned, persecuted and, if foreign, deported. However, the social purists enjoyed a limited victory. While it is often supposed that social purists were largely successful in curbing prostitution, the evidence is inconclusive. English social purists, unlike those in Scotland, did not find it easy to control prostitution and had to struggle continuously to win over the support of the judiciary, the police and the state. In fact, officialdom was very much a subordinate partner in effecting moral transformation and this undoubtedly made the work of social purists more difficult.

Notes

1 Mrs Lucas (the suffragist daughter of Jacob Bright) was also a founding member (*The Pioneer*, September 1892, p. 7).
2 *London Council for the Promotion of Public Morality Annual Report* 1910, p. 2.
3 Ellice Hopkins, *Homely Talk on the New Law for the Protection of Girls, Addressed to Fathers* (London: Hatchards, 1886), p. 19.
4 Ellice Hopkins, quoted in J.M. Cole and F.C. Bacon, *Christian Guidance of the Social Instincts* (London: The Faith Press, 1928), p. 10.
5 Ellice Hopkins, quoted in Rosa M. Barrett, *Ellice Hopkins: A Memoir* (London: Wells Gardner, 1907), p. 157.
6 Ellice Hopkins, ibid., p. 158.
7 *Seeking and Saving* (1885), p. 54.
8 Report of the Committee on Purity, February 1890, National Society's Depository, p. 3.
9 The NVA has been heralded as a repressive force in British politics by Judith Walkowitz, *Prostitution and Victorian England* (Cambridge: Cambridge University Press, 1980), pp. 99 and 251–252. In contrast the NVA has been viewed as a feminist-inspired organisation by radical feminists like Margaret Jackson, *The Real Facts of Life* (London: Taylor and Francis, 1994), pp. 29–30, and Sheila Jeffreys, *The Spinster and her Enemies* (London: Pandora, 1985).
10 See Frank Mort, *Dangerous Sexualities* (London: Routledge and Kegan Paul, 1987), pp. 106 and 126–130, and Judith Walkowitz, *City of Dreadful Delight* (London: Virago, 1992), for a discussion of the reasons why the CLA Act was passed.

11 This particularly active regional group was inaugurated at a public meeting held on December 9th 1886 and consisted of the counties of Cheshire, Derbyshire, Gloucestershire, Herefordshire, Leicestershire, Lincolnshire, Northamptonshire, Nottinghamshire, Rutland, Shropshire, Staffordshire, Warwickshire and Worcestershire (*BMCVA Occasional Papers* 1886–1904).

12 NVA Executive Minutes 1885–1914.

13 *BMCVA Occasional Paper* May 1887, p. 4.

14 Lucy Bland has analysed these different tendencies within the NVA. She has suggested that the NVA mixture of repressive and statist ideas combined some-what uneasily with feminism: Lucy Bland, '"Purifying" the Public World: Feminist Vigilantes in Late Victorian England', *Women's History Review*, 1(3), 1992, for further details.

15 As previously mentioned, women were supposed to be both chaste and sexually passive.

16 Mrs Creighton, 'What Woman Can Do for Purity', *NUWW Conference* 1894, p. 9.

17 Lucy Bland suggests that prosecutions of brothels rose dramatically after the CLA Act 1885. From 1885 to 1914 there were over 1,200 prosecutions each year: Lucy Bland, *Banishing the Beast: English Feminism and Sexual Morality 1885–1914* (London: Penguin, 1995), p. 116. In contrast there were only about 86 prosecutions before 1885. However, this is not the case.

18 See Lucy Bland, *Banishing the Beast*, for a discussion of the notion of public women.

19 Letter from T. Elton, Euston Square, to Metropolitan Police (MEPO 2/293).

20 Letter from Clapham Vigilance Association to the Rt Hon. Henry Mathews, Secretary of State, December 4th 1886 (HO 45/9666).

21 Letter from North Kensington Ratepayers' Association (HO 45/10123/B13517/35).

22 *BMCVA Occasional Paper* 1892, p. 5.

23 Letter from James Stock to Metropolitan Police, February 22nd 1892 (MEPO 2/293).

24 Residents of Euston Road to Police Authorities, May 1893 (MEPO 2/293).

25 Complaint to Police Authorities, February 1892 (MEPO 2/293).

26 Petition to Secretary of State from St Anne's Westminster for an Amendment of Law relating to Brothels and Street Prostitution (HO 45/9511/17216).

27 See Lucy Bland, *Banishing the Beast*, p. 109.

28 Frank Mort, *Dangerous Sexualities*, p. 104

29 Special Report, June 9th 1893 (MEPO 2/293).

30 *London Council for the Promotion of Public Morality Annual Reports* 1902–1904.

31 *The Social Gazette* (October 12th 1895), p. 1.

32 Letter from Clapham Vigilance Association to the Rt. Hon. Henry Mathews, Secretary of State, December 4th 1886 (HO 45/9666).

33 Letter from Rural Dean of St Martin-in-the-Fields to Home Office, July 3rd 1896 (HO 45/10123/B13517).

34 Letter from Revd London, Wimbledon, to Metropolitan Police, November 9th 1905 (MEPO 2/293).

35 Synopsis of Replies from Provincial Towns and Cities Respecting the Action Taken to Prevent Solicitation and the Walking of the Streets for Immoral Purposes 1901 (MEPO 2/8835).

36 Synopsis of Replies from Provincial Towns and Cities Respecting the Action Taken to Prevent Solicitation and the Walking of the Streets for Immoral Purposes November 13th 1901 (HO 45/10123/B13517/33).

37 *National Vigilance Association Annual Report* 1888, p. 4.

38 *The Vigilance Record* (November 1887), p. iv.

39 *The Vigilance Record* (July 1891), p. 72.

40 *BMCVA Occasional Papers* 1887–1893.
41 *The Vigilance Record* (November 1893).
42 *The Vigilance Record* (December 1888), p. 124.
43 *The Vigilance Record* (October 1888), p. 99.
44 Ibid., p. 101.
45 Linda Mahood, *The Magdalenes: Prostitution in the Nineteenth Century* (London: Routledge, 1990).
46 Letter from the Vestry of the Parish of Chelsea to Secretary of State, Home Office, August 11th 1887 (HO 45/9678/A47459).
47 Memo M. Pearson, August 13th 1887 (HO 45/9678/A47459). Sir Charles Warren resigned in 1888 after the failure to catch 'Jack the Ripper': Stefan Petrow, *Policing Morals: The Metropolitan Police and the Home Office 1870–1914* (Oxford: Clarendon Press, 1994), p. 135. There were five Police Commissioners during this period.
48 Letter from Sir Charles Warren to Vestry Clerk, Parish of St George's, October 31st 1887 (HO 45/9678/A47459).
49 James Last, Metropolitan Police Papers, W Division, December 19th 1886 (HO 45/9666/A45364).
50 Alfred Easter, Metropolitan Police Papers, W Division, December 19th 1886 (HO 45/9666/A45364).
51 Hunter Street Station Report, January 14th 1900 (MEPO 2/293).
52 Metropolitan Police Reports, W Division, December 27th 1886.
53 *London Council for the Promotion of Public Morality Annual Report* 1908, p. 1.
54 Notes of deputation from the Westminster City Council to Home Office, December 17th 1901; Home Office Memorandum November 27th 1901 (HO 45/10123/B13517/35).
55 Letter from the Home Office to Vestry Clerk, St George's Hanover Square, March 22nd 1888 (HO 45/9678).
56 Letter from Bow Street Police Court to Home Office, May 6th 1881 (HO 45/9615).
57 Anon, *The Police and the White Slave Trade* (London: James Timewell, *c.* 1911), p. 9.
58 Ibid., p. 9.
59 Letter from New Scotland Yard to Home Office, October 26th 1893 (HO 45/10123/B13517).
60 Confidential Memorandum on Prostitution and Solicitation 1906 (MEPO 2/8835).
61 Ibid.
62 Home Office Memorandum November 27th 1901 (HO 45/10123/B13517/33).
63 *The Times* (July 9th 1887), p. 14.
64 Compiled from Metropolitan Police Statistics, 1870–1914.
65 *The Vigilance Record* (July 1891), p. 68.
66 Confidential Memorandum on Prostitution and Solicitation 1906 (MEPO 2/8835).
67 Royal Commission on the Metropolitan Police, Session January 1908–December 1908, vol. L, p. 213.
68 *The Vigilance Record* (July 1906), p. 58.
69 Royal Commission on the Metropolitan Police, Session January 1908–December 1908, vol. L, p. 125.
70 Home Office Memorandum, November 27th 1901 (HO 45/10123/B13517/33).
71 House of Commons July 13th 1900, p. 1,539.
72 *The Vigilance Record* (May 1907), p. 39.
73 *The Vigilance Record* (July 1891), p. 68.

74 *The Vigilance Record* (July 1900), p. 7.
75 It was alleged that police had found diaries and other literature mentioning men in high positions in Queenie Gerald's flat but these were not produced as evidence in court.
76 *The Vigilance Record* (March 1891), p. 24.
77 Metropolitan Police Office Memo sent to Home Office, 16th February 1889 (MEPO 2/209).
78 *London Council for the Promotion of Public Morality Annual Report* 1904, p. 4.
79 St Jude's Vigilance Association (HO 45/9511/17216/50).
80 Frank Mort, *Dangerous Sexualities*, p. 134.
81 Frank Mort, *Dangerous Sexualities*.
82 *BMCVA Occasional Paper* 1893, p. 3.
83 For one example, see *BMCVA Occasional Paper* 1889, pp. 2–3.
84 *BMCVA Occasional Paper* 1891, p. 5.
85 These figures were derived from the NVA Executive Minutes, 1899. Court records registered twelve people convicted for either running or helping to run a brothel during a similar period. Under the CLA Act 1885 brothel-owners could be fined up to £20 or three months' imprisonment. Most brothel-owners in Birmingham were fined £5+ costs or one month's imprisonment. Occasionally they were fined £10. There is no way of knowing whether these were prosecuted as a result of the BMCVA's intervention. It is also impossible to discover how many brothels there were in Birmingham (Register of the Court of Summary Jurisdiction, 1899–1900).
86 *The Vigilance Record* (November 1890), p. 111.
87 Synopsis of Replies from Provincial Towns and Cities Respecting the Action Taken to Prevent Solicitation and the Walking of the Streets for Immoral Purposes 1901 (MEPO 2/8835).
88 *The Vigilance Record* (November 1893).
89 Home Office Memorandum, November 27th 1901 (HO 45/10123/B13517/33).
90 *The Vigilance Record* (October 1892), p. 72.
91 *The Vigilance Record* (August 1890) p. 78.
92 Ibid., p. 78.
93 *The Vigilance Record* (April 1896), p. 45.
94 P. Beck, *Victorian Lancashire* (Newton Abbot: David and Charles, 1974), p. 159.
95 A number of reasons can be suggested for the demise of the BMCVA. First, it did not seem to recover from Revd Wastell's death in 1894. Revd Wastell had been a particularly active and efficient secretary. Second, after Revd Wastell's death the secretaryship was beset with problems. One 'unsatisfactory' secretary resigned in 1894, a second was forced to resign in 1894 because of circumstances related to his private life and in 1902 a third left because he had lied about the number of meetings he had held. Third, by 1904 many of the influential founders of the BMCVA were either extremely old or dead. Fourth, the BMCVA did not recover from its affiliation to the NVA. By 1904 the 'question had therefore arisen as to the advisability of continuing the work in Birmingham or of allowing it to lapse' (NVA Executive Minutes, January 24th 1904). The BMCVA enjoyed a brief respite when a national organiser became involved but when he left to take up a post with Dr Barnardo's, the Birmingham branch collapsed. Social purity therefore disappeared from the moral agenda in early-twentieth-century Birmingham.
96 Birmingham police force were especially unwilling to prosecute prostitutes after 1905 because two police officers had been dismissed for wrongly prosecuting a couple for indecent behaviour.
97 See Edward Mynott, 'Purity, Prostitution and Politics: Social Purity in Manchester 1880–1900' (PhD thesis, University of Manchester, 1995), pp. 401–405, for a full discussion of this.

98 This figure was compiled from *Judicial Statistics* 1860–1914.

99 Judith Walkowitz, *Prostitution and Victorian Society*.

100 Judith Walkowitz suggests that the CD Acts – along with the special police force, the enforced attendance at lock hospitals and the appearances in court – stamped women as prostitutes more firmly than ever before. This marked them out from their local community and thus estranged them from it. As a consequence, women could not engage in part-time prostitution quite so easily: *Prostitution and Victorian Society*, pp. 201–213. Increased police action in non-CD Act areas such as Birmingham could have produced a similar result.

101 Sir Howard Vincent, Police Commissioner, *The Vigilance Record* (May 1907), p. 39.

102 Anon, *Freedom the Fundamental Condition of Morality* (no date), p. 7.

103 Judith Walkowitz, *City of Dreadful Delight*.

104 It can be assumed that very few took up this particular option. Consequently, the NVA did not wipe out prostitution, as Jeffrey Weeks suggests in relation to the CD Acts, but merely changed the way in which it operated: J. Weeks, *Sex, Politics and Society* (London: Longman, 1981).

105 *London Council for the Promotion of Public Morality Annual Report* 1903, p. 2.

106 Ibid., 1910, p. 2.

107 *The Vigilance Record* (May 1897), p. 6.

108 *The Vigilance Record* (December 1913), p. 100.

109 Ibid., p. 100.

110 *The Vigilance Record* (April 1902), p. 5.

111 *The Times* (September 17th 1908), p. 17.

112 Lara Marks, 'Jewish Women and Jewish Prostitution in the East End of London', *Jewish Quarterly* (1987).

113 See Sheila Jeffreys, *The Idea of Prostitution* (Melbourne: Spinifex, 1997), ch. 1, for a discussion of the later campaigns.

114 *The Times* (April 15th 1908), p. 15.

115 *The Times* (February 9th 1904), p. 2.

116 Arnold White, the leading eugenist, supported the Aliens Act.

117 See Marion Kaplan, 'Prostitution, Morality Crusades and Feminism: German-Jewish Feminists and the Campaign against White Slavery', in Elizabeth Sarah (ed.) *Reassessments of 'First Wave' Feminism* (Oxford: Pergamon, 1982), for an examination of the German involvement in white slavery.

118 Mr F. Bullock responding to How the Aliens Act Can Help, speaking at Fifth International Congress for the Suppression of the White Slave Traffic, London, July 1913, p. 282.

119 Fraulein Pappenheim responding to How the Aliens Act Can Help, speaking at Fifth International Congress for the Suppression of the White Slave Traffic, London, July 1913, p. 119.

120 Royal Commission on Alien Immigration 1903, p. 426.

121 *The Times* (March 31st 1909), p. 31.

122 John Pedder (Home Office spokesperson), How the Aliens Act Can Help, speaking at Fifth International Congress for the Suppression of the White Slave Traffic, London, July 1913, p. 113.

123 Aliens Act 1905 (HO 45/10390/171419).

124 Letter from the Prison Commission to the Home Office, October 29th 1913 (HO 45/15041).

125 Special Report, Criminal Investigation Department, November 7th 1913 (MEPO 3/228).

8   Men and morality

Social purists not only tried to repress prostitution but also, in common with other reformers, attempted to tackle what they perceived to be its underlying causes.

> We must strike at the root of the evil . . . Not until it is generally recognised that the man who has wrought a woman's degradation is at least a great an offender against society as the man who has robbed a till or the man who has forged a cheque . . . So long as the violation of purity is condoned in the one sex and visited with shame in the other our unrighteousness and unmanliness must continue to work out its own terrible retribution.[1]

By the 1880s, social purists held that men were equally responsible as women for the continuance of prostitution. It was believed that prostitution could be eliminated only if single men became celibate and married men remained faithful to their wives. Since both sexes shared an equal responsibility for prostitution, the focus changed to improving the morality of men, as well as of women, so that the root cause of prostitution would be destroyed completely.[2] The ideological shift away from blaming women to condemning men resulted in new initiatives to prevent prostitution. This chapter explores the ways in which social purists tried to prevent child sexual abuse, to make men chaste and to improve the moral climate of England. The attitude of social purists towards children and men illuminates the curious asymmetry between protection and punishment, between forgiveness and condemnation, and between toleration and persecution.

Preventing child abuse

Child sexual abuse generated a similar sense of moral outrage as prostitution. Certainly, child abuse and prostitution were thought to be inextricably linked: when Mrs Bramwell Booth examined the family background of prostitutes she found that a large proportion had been sexually abused. However, the connections between paedophilia and prostitution were never fully explored. Nevertheless, social purists, and women in particular, voiced continual anxiety about the extent of child abuse which existed in Victorian and Edwardian England. According to Mrs Edwin Gray, speaking at a NUWW Conference in 1911, the National Society for the Prevention of Cruelty to Children (NSPCC) dealt with 3,910 cases between 1905 and 1910 of which 913 were criminal assaults, 1,126 were indecent assaults and 1,871 were as a consequence of immoral surroundings. More particularly, social purity workers were deeply concerned about the sexual abuse of very young children:

> Incredible though it may appear, assaults are frequently made upon children of tender years. A search through the records of London for the year 1907–8 disclosed that many of the children were less than five years of age. Among others there was a girl of four assaulted by her father. Another of three and a half outraged in the street. An offence committed in a field on a little girl of four. Attempted carnal knowledge of a girl child only two years and ten months old. These are given as illustrations of the inhuman depravity that sees nothing sacred in youth, and that gratifies its desires on the defenceless.[3]

Child abuse was associated with young girl children who had been abused by older men.[4] Louise Jackson points out that 98 per cent of defendants in London court trials between 1890 and 1914 were male while 92 per cent of victims were young girls.[5] Social purists claimed that most child sexual abuse remained hidden since the majority were never reported,[6] and complained that men shielded their paedophilic tendencies behind a respectable, and sometimes a religious, façade. For example, Philip Lyne from Dulwich, accused of living 'one life, honourable in appearance, towards his friends, and the other life as an utter hypocrite, in polluting the minds of young children',[7] was eventually indicted and imprisoned for two years with hard labour for improperly assaulting four girls aged between 10 and 13 years. Similarly, in 1887, one Stafford man, who presented himself as deeply religious, was gaoled for five years for assaulting a young child – and this was believed to have been but one of a long series of similar events.[8] Government statistics also demonstrated that few sexual abuse cases were reported to the police and even fewer prosecuted.[9]

Both Margaret Jackson and Sheila Jeffreys suggest that the prosecution of, and campaigns against, child sexual abuse broke the conspiracy of silence and protected young women from aggressive male behaviour.[10] This proactive policy, they claim, raised general questions about the abuse of male power. Not only did the NVA seek to defend young girls from sexual abuse, thereby espousing a sexual politics based upon protection, but also it was willing to use the law against the perpetrators of such crimes. Here, gender and class appear to be more harmonious categories than antagonistic ones as middle-class power was utilised in support of gender politics. The coercive mechanisms of the state were targeted at the protection of the weak, women and young children, since there was enormous concern that male adults were sexually assaulting young girls. Cases were reported of abuse ranging from indecent exposure to rape. Offenders were prosecuted:

> the case of indecent behaviour to little girls, which was heard at the Aston Police Court, yesterday, and which resulted in the prisoner, JOHN HAMMERSLEY, being sentenced to two months imprisonment with hard labour, without the option of a fine, was of considerable importance. These degrading and disgusting offences are becoming increasingly common ... It has evidently become the practice of a certain class of persons, whom a brutal lust has deprived of all sense of decency and manliness, to entice little children into a public park and to attempt by promises or threats to induce them to submit to outrage.[11]

The above extract appears to be a clear-cut case whereby class and gender power (the law)[12] was exercised in support of class and gender politics (protecting working-class women) and supports the ideas of Margaret Jackson[13] and Sheila Jeffreys.[14] Yet while initiatives around child sexual abuse were welcomed, the prosecutions of child abusers were not always secure since the NVA wielded a doubled-edged moral sword in the fight against sexual impurity. Certainly, there are a number of weaknesses in viewing gender and class politics as complementary. First, social purists were motivated by a repressive anti-sensual ideology – as much as a gendered one – to prosecute offenders. No distinction was ever made between the abuse of the paedophile and the sexual activities of adult consenting partners: all sexual activity outside the conventional framework of marriage was considered unacceptable.

Second, and perhaps more importantly, young girls were penalised for crimes that older men might, at some future date, commit. Girls were advised not to play in the playgrounds or the streets and were thus punished by being denied access to public areas because of the fear of potential abuse. At no time was it suggested that a curfew be extended to men walking alone in these areas. Social purists assumed that sexually abused children posed a moral danger to other children since they had been morally contaminated.[15] As a result, young children who suffered abuse were sent away from their families to a home:[16] 'half witted girl interfered with by several men. Taken to a Home.'[17] Indeed, there were several homes (for example, the Church Penitentiary Association Home in Wolverhampton; the Nest in Clapton, London; the Agnes Cotton Home in Leytonstone; and the Waifs and Strays Home at Shrewsbury) where abused children were consigned. Some, like the Agnes Cotton Home, which sanctioned corporal punishment for youngsters who misbehaved, were little better than penitentiaries. Children who were the victims of abuse must have blamed themselves for their violation since they were removed from their families, placed in an institution and, in effect, given a custodial sentence.

Third, the focus on child abuse centred on the crowded living conditions of the working classes that were seen to lead to acts of indecency.[18] Moreover, the working class was often considered to be more physical, and thus more sexually promiscuous, than the other classes. There was little mention in the literature about the possibility of middle- and upper-class children suffering from sexual abuse; indeed, immorality always seemed to be considered a working-class crime.

Finally, the NVA was not always successful in obtaining a conviction or a lengthy sentence. Judges appeared reluctant to pass heavy sentences and juries were unwilling to convict. Louise Jackson shows that only three out of six NVA London prosecutions ended in conviction in 1890.[19] Criminal statistics overall demonstrated the weakness of the judicial system. In 1907 only 232 out of 327 cases examined actually went to court. Of these 145 were convicted, 5 cases were thrown out and 82 were acquitted. Sentencing was generally lenient: 23 were given penal servitude for terms varying from 1 to 20 years; 1 was flogged; the remaining 121 received sentences of imprisonment varying from 14 days to 2 years.[20] Such results led Mrs Bramwell Booth to criticise magistrates whose 'names have become a positive byword in the courts of wickedness, and it is almost impossible to secure a verdict before them against the perpetrators of these dastardly outrages'. Despite the efforts to prosecute child abusers many men remained unconvicted and young girls left unprotected:

> In April last an intimation was made to us . . . that a man (Ollerenshaw) in that parish had been guilty of an indecent assault upon a little girl of 7 years of age; and that there was evidence of assault upon other little girls . . . he had escaped on a former occasion through the evidence not being properly worked up . . . and on July 28th was sentenced to six months imprisonment.[21]

Two years later, Ollerenshaw was still abusing children. He was found guilty again in 1894 for abusing an 8-year-old girl and sentenced to eighteen months' imprisonment with hard labour.[22] According to Assize Records many other men were discharged or else served a light sentence. Similarly at Oxford, two cases, one for an indecent assault and the other for an attempted rape, were brought before magistrates but the men involved were ultimately acquitted. In Bournemouth too an alleged rapist had his case quashed by the judge because of a legal technicality, which prompted the prosecuting NVA barrister to complain that he 'can only bewail the imperfections of human justice'.[23]

This failure to convict and to obtain long sentences, of course, was not the fault of the NVA but of an ineffective judicial process. Social purists prosecuted known offenders but, largely because judges and magistrates were unsympathetic to their cause, most of the accused were not convicted. In some respects, this provides evidence of the tensions between the judiciary and social purists and, yet again, undermines the belief that a homogeneous and middle-class state exercised its power coherently.[24]

Social purists turned their attention towards reforming the legal system since they believed that inadequate legislation resulted in grave social injustice for the children concerned. For example, men who abused children between the ages of 13 and 16 could not be prosecuted if three months had elapsed since the initial offence.[25] Social purists protested that children of 13 or 14 were frequently intimidated or bribed to say nothing to any one else about the abuse: 'I can tell you of a case where a man wronged his own daughter, a child of fourteen, threatened to kill her and her mother too if she said a word to anyone about what had occurred.'[26] In many instances, child abuse was discovered only when girls were obviously pregnant, by which time it was too late to take the case to court. Eventually, in 1904, the time limit for prosecutions was raised to six months.

Social purists criticised the fact that if men swore they had reasonable cause to suppose that the girls they abused were 16 or over, they escaped punishment. In addition, the law did not accept the personal testimony of abused children, but demanded corroborative evidence that was largely impossible to obtain. Finally, there was no effective penalty for incest in civil law so offenders had to be tried under either existing laws against rape or the Offences against Minors Act.[27] As Anthony Wohl points out, the question of incest was raised in the House of Lords Select Committee on the Protection of Young Girls in 1882, the Royal Commission on the Housing of the Working Class in 1884–5 and the House of Lords Select Committee on the Sweating System in 1888 but to little avail.[28] Eventually, after considerable campaigning, the Punishment of Incest Act was passed in 1908, which instituted a punishment for incest in civil law by stating that

> any male person who has carnal knowledge of a female person known to be his grand daughter, daughter, sister or mother is guilty of a misdemeanour and liable to penal servitude of not less than 3 years and not more than 7 years.

For the first time, male biological relatives could be put on trial for child abuse. Even so, social purists claimed that proving incest was difficult as mothers often acquiesced in the abuse and, because the offence was committed in the home, everything was hushed up. Tragically, for both the young victim and the NVA, the following case, which involved an alleged abuser who was let off because the magistrates considered there was not enough evidence to convict, was all too typical:

> I was at the court the other day with the child, and I wondered how much evidence was required in a case like this. It was heart-breaking

to sit there and hear the little girl of seven recite the transactions that had taken place between her father and herself. She told the Magistrate that on one occasion the father had bought her a halfpenny balloon because she cried so, and he was afraid her mother would see her. The wife also gave evidence as to the condition she had found the child in – told how she had had to keep her in bed from school, because she could not walk for two or three days.[29]

The National Union of Women Workers, believing that it was 'so often the father, step father or master who commits the offence',[30] along with social purity workers, called for much more severe punishment for male abusers in control of children.

Making men chaste

By the 1880s social purists came to believe that it was wiser to stop the demand for prostitutes rather than curtail its supply. They tended to assume that prostitution was the logical consequence of masculine sexual 'incontinence' rather than female impropriety. To some extent they saw prostitution as a crime against women as well as a crime by them. It was perhaps the increasing willingness of social purists to blame men, rather than women, for the sins of prostitution that has led to their restoration in the annals of sexual progress by Margaret Jackson and Sheila Jeffries. However, one must remain sceptical of this perspective as the move towards attributing blame to men also led to an increasing emphasis on an anti-sensual approach to sexuality. Sex outside marriage was viewed as 'spiritual suicide'.[31] Once again, the ideology and practice of social purists exhibited both progressive and conventional tendencies.

Social purists were nevertheless critical of the emphasis on reform and preventive work among women because, by blaming women for prostitution rather than the men who used them, it attacked the problem the wrong way round. 'We have been talking about work amongst girls. We have all these years been taking hold of the wrong end of the skein . . . the right end of this question is not the girl, but the man.'[32] Social purists wanted to make men as equally responsible as women in the alleged crime of prostitution. Penitentiaries, reformatories and other curative agencies were seen to be quite powerless to

> stem the torrent of misery and vice. We must strike at the root of the evil . . . So long as the violation of purity is condoned in the one sex and visited with shame in the other, our unrighteousness and unmanliness must continue to work out its own terrible retribution.[33]

Men, it was thought, should be taught that they were the root cause of all the prostitution in the world and that they could no longer exist in another parallel world where different moral rules applied.[34] 'Prostitution is a terrible stain upon civilisation but the demand creates the supply. If the vicious tendencies of our young men can be removed or prevented, we are striking at the root of this and other grievous evils.'[35] The Church of England Purity Society aimed to 'purify the foul stream at the fountain head',[36] with the White Cross Obligations stating its intention:

(I)   To treat all women with respect, and endeavour to protect them from wrong and degradation

(II) To endeavour to put down all indecent language and coarse jests

(III) To maintain the law of purity as equally binding upon men and women

(IV) To endeavour to spread these principles among my companions, and to try and help my younger brothers

(V)   To use every possible means to fulfil the command 'Keep thyself pure'.

Purity workers, like the Ladies' Associations before them, deplored the incongruity of the double moral sexual standard which, they argued, was to blame for the continuance of prostitution. In particular, they thought it iniquitous that if women solicited men they were liable to be sent to prison whereas men were able to solicit as many women as they wished without being prosecuted.[37] Prostitution, it was alleged, would end only if men adopted the same moral principles that were expected of women like Thomas Hardy's Tess of the D'Urbervilles or Wilkie Collins' Mercy Merrick.

> Too long has society maintained a double standard of morals – a severe one for women, a very lenient one for men. A man may have been a rake, but he is not in society's view thereby unfitted for marriage . . . whereas a girl who has once forgotten her modesty is never pardoned by society.[38]

The same law of purity was advocated for both men and women,[39] as the whole moral atmosphere was thought to be poisoned by the influence of that 'old and chartered lie that that which is sin and degradation and shame for woman is but a light and venial offence, if offence at all, in man'.[40] Social purists condemned the fact that in the upper classes of society, the fallen woman was proclaimed an alien and an outcast.

> She is condemned, reproached, despised. Neither repentance nor amendment condones her sin and a black mark is upon her, and water applied for half a lifetime will not wash it out; a man, on the contrary, known to be profligate in his conduct, may hold in society very much the same position as the innocent . . . The body of the man is not less sacred than that of the woman, and not less designed to be a temple of the Holy Spirit.[41]

Even language was criticised for perpetuating the double standard. The fact that there were two languages for sexual conduct – men sowed their 'wild oats', were considered 'fast', 'gay' and 'men of the world', whereas women were 'fallen' or 'outcast' and called 'sluts', 'trollops', 'strumpets' and 'harlots' – was condemned.[42]

The Social Purity Alliance, the more radical of the social purity groups, went further by opposing prostitution on the grounds of social justice. Prostitution, it was believed, was based on fundamental gender inequalities since men, because of their economic superiority, were able to exploit women who were in dire financial need. No man, they argued, had the right to purchase a woman's body under such conditions.[43] Prostitution was thought to humiliate all women since 'the man who enslaves one woman implicitly tells every other woman that she is entitled only by accident, not by right, to be spared the same degradation'.[44] Accordingly, men were judged guilty of the moral ruin of women and of buying the 'sacrifice of bodily honour and spiritual life from others . . . with them lies the responsibility for the social degradation of prostitutes'.[45]

Men, social purists generally believed, should not be allowed to shelter behind their private and closed domestic doors but should be punished for 'sexual incontinence'. Public morality was considered to be of greater importance than personal privacy: indeed, the NVA consistently upheld the view that if moral principles were transgressed then punishment must be meted out to male and female alike whether they were working or middle class and that men who sought to buy sexual favours should be punished, as nearly as possible, in the same way as women who sold them.[46] Both the White Cross Society and the NVA focused their attention on men in high public office who undermined morality but who escaped moral censure. Concern was expressed that the most respectable men in society were often the ones who offended against the moral code for 'there were men of position and influence who deliberately sacrificed other men's sisters and daughters to life-long disgrace and eternal ruin for the satisfaction of their own lusts'.[47] Men who posed as pillars of society, building churches and endowing universities, were utterly condemned when they were found to 'pollute innocence and then fling it forth as a withered flower'.[48] Because men in authority were thought to colour the moral tone of the whole community, so social purists demanded that 'aspirants for municipal, or other honours of the kind, shall not only be personally free from reproach, but shall have healthy moral sympathies'.[49] Men in positions of power, it was believed, should be expected to be paragons of virtue in order to set a good example to the rest of society. Immoral men should be shunned:

I wish, that the higher classes of society treated this matter as it ought to do. Men of loose morals should be banished from all good society. In the past their evil deeds have been very much condoned. I cannot see why a man who infringes God's law in this way should not be treated as you would treat a man who commits some other crime.[50]

Men who were known to be sexually profligate were cautioned not to hold offices of public trust and influence.[51] In the municipal elections of November 1892 social purity workers tried to stop allegedly licentious men from seeking and winning office.

> Our friends all over the provinces should see to it that . . . strong effort is made to keep out of the Town Councils, the men who have no regard for the moral questions in which we are interested, and who by their lives evince a practical sympathy with vice.[52]

In 1889 the Midland Counties formed a standing committee to oppose the candidature of men of immoral character for either town or county councils.[53] Time after time annual reports stressed the need to keep out those men from municipal or parliamentary office who had a moral stain on their character. The Midland Counties membership wished to exclude debauched men from the homes and social circles they frequented:

> I would remorselessly exclude from all honourable office, either municipal or parliamentary, any man with any taint whatever upon his moral life . . . until you make it impossible for a man whose reputation has been sullied, to seek as a candidate for any honour whatever in public life, we shall have to fight with this vice continuously and for ever.[54]

Similarly the Church of England Purity Society suggested that men known to be leading a dissolute life ought not to be received in Christian society,[55] and declared that men should be punished for sexual crimes:

> Only one difference can be tolerated: men do not need to be sent to an adult reformatory to learn how to support themselves . . . But all men can go fourteen days to prison, and therefore, if found soliciting women on the street, or found in brothels, low class or high class, by the moral police, off to prison they must go, or pay the alternative fine.[56]

However, these worthy sentiments were largely rhetorical: when the Revd H.G. Wakefield, a member of the Shropshire Vigilance Association, was accused of writing 'the most revoltingly obscene letters that it has ever been our misfortune to peruse' to local servant girls, the Bishop of Lichfield refused to take action against him because he had a previously irreproachable character.[57] Only when a local newspaper published the story did the vicar confess his guilt and resign his post.

The promotion of a single standard probably had more to do with religious fervour, middle-class suspicion of the upper class, and conservative ideas

about gender identity than with radical politics. Undeniably, the philosophy
of the double standard was thought to be incompatible with Jesus Christ's
teachings that there was One Moral Law applicable alike to both men and
women. The body, it was argued, was sanctified by God and thus should
not be desecrated.[58] St Paul's Letters to the Corinthians (1 vi 18) were
published as evidence that 'he that committeth fornication sinneth against
his own body'.[59] Marriage was seen to be the only arena in which sexual
relations could legitimately take place since 'he prostitutes to the indul-
gence of sensual inclination the obligations of that holy marriage state which
was designed to accomplish the noblest purposes of God'.[60]

Social purity was not only religiously inspired but also informed by ideas
about class and race. At first it appeared that the establishment of a sound
moral base cut, unequivocally, across boundaries. In establishing a moral code
which encompassed all classes, social purists could be seen not only to erode
class barriers but also to forge links across them. The rhetoric of a uniform
chastity, however, obscured the hierarchical nature of the enterprise. Moral
reform never was, and was never meant to be, a relationship of equals, for the
notion of one sexual moral standard for all classes was to be a standard decided
by a certain section of the middle class. Its application was ultimately coercive
because this middle class imposed its own sexual ethos of sexual abstinence
before marriage and faithfulness within it upon others.[61]

In addition, social purists, like the Ladies' Associations before them,
tended to view women as victims, and men as perpetrators, of immorality.
The next extract epitomises the gender and class attitudes of the social
purists. The assumptions, both explicit and implicit, reflect the notions of
women as victims and men as hunters, of women as passive and men as
aggressive and of women as subservient and men as superordinate. It uses
traditional images of sexual conquest and narrates the story of a poor,
extremely young innocent victim who has been preyed upon by older, world-
lier wise married, richer men, plied with drink and seduced. Step by slow
step the unwilling, unsuspecting and gullible young woman was deflow-
ered by a disreputable character.[62] Punishment swiftly followed for the male
offender while the blameless casualty was offered protection:

> L aged sixteen was employed in a small manufactory. B aged 25 (a
> married man and son of L's employer) with the assistance of C, a young
> woman engaged in the same business, gained L's consent to go with
> them to a place of public amusement. Finding that C was accompanied
> by a young man, L was induced to accept the companionship of B.
> Instead, however, of proceeding to the proposed place of amusement,
> they walked about until after midnight. L became alarmed and begged
> C to go home with her and make it right with her parents; to which
> C replied 'You cannot go home now, it's too late; I am going to sleep
> at a friend's house; come with me and I will take you home early in
> the morning.' Unfortunately, L who had for some time previously been

a total abstainer, accepted the proffered intoxicants, and thus became an easy prey to the seducer. The house of C's friend proved to be a disreputable lodging house, and there B committed a criminal offence on L.[63] A summons was duly served upon him, to which he did not appear. Thereupon a warrant was issued, and he speedily fled the country. Meantime, with the consent of the distressed parents, L was taken under the care of the Ladies Association for the Care and Protection of Young Girls; was placed in their training home, and is now duly qualified for domestic service.[64]

The White Cross Army saw women both as victim and temptress. At times it asked that men extend a helping hand to those weaker than themselves and protect women and children.

> It is the first impulse of all brave and manly spirits to prevent women or children from stepping heedlessly into danger, or to rescue them if they have already done so . . . There is no man who ought not to feel that these weaker ones are committed to his care.[65]

The elimination of impurity was thought to depend on men. In particular, the reform of prostitutes and the prevention of prostitution was impossible if men did not practise self-restraint.[66] At other times, the Old Testament image of Eve the Temptress and Adam the seduced was used to illustrate the dangers of female sexual allurement.[67] Men, considered morally superior, were thus exhorted to protect women against their baser instincts rather than give into them.[68]

Purity in men was considered not only a religious duty but also a social and nationalistic necessity: purity of self was directly equated with purity of nation. Xenophobic, and racist, fears underpinned the drive for male chastity. Men were encouraged to be chaste at all times lest they contribute to the decline not only of moral standards but also of England itself, for 'if impurity in the woman destroys the family, impurity in the man destroys the nation'.[69] Men were viewed as the moral standard bearers of England and were reminded that

> all history teaches us that the welfare and very life of a nation is determined by moral causes; and that it is the pure races – the races that respect their women and guard them jealously from defilement – that are the tough prolific, ascendant races.[70]

The low standard of purity among men was held to be responsible for the 'Eurasian' population in India and of the 'half-caste' in general, both of which were regarded as anti-social, possessing 'the vices of both parent races, and the virtues of neither . . . with a tendency to be a liar, cowardly, licentious and without self-respect'.[71]

Ultimately, social purists condemned masturbation as well as sexual inter-course since the former inevitably led to the latter. In particular the White Cross Society campaigned fervently for the complete rest of the sexual organs during childhood and boyhood as

> nothing takes away our energy of body and clearness of mind as the waste of this seminal fluid – Far better would it be for you to lose blood than this substance . . . it is absolutely necessary that these sexual organs or private parts should be kept entirely free from any rubbing, handling or anything whatsoever that causes excitement in them or change of appearance or the passing of any fluid besides the urine whether done by ourselves or others . . . Many thousands of happy boys have become miserable and ruined men, moral and mental wrecks, idiots, lunatics and suicides entirely through this vile habit called by names such as Onanism, self-abuse and pollution, unnatural crime, sodomy and masturbation.[72]

The writer of this piece blamed masturbation for the physical ailments of lack of energy, indigestion, sore throats, colds and consumption as well as the social problems of business failure, intemperance and alcoholism. One of the best defences against impurity, the White Cross suggested, was to keep busy so that the body became healthily tired at the end of the day and ready for sleep. It recommended that young men eat plain food and avoid stimulants because a pampered body was necessarily open to evil. Young men were further exhorted to keep the teaching of the scripture on the sanctity of their body before them at all times and parents were urged to warn their children against the 'misuse of their bodily organs'.[73]

The social purist emphasis on masculine responsibility did not reconfig-urate nineteenth- and early-twentieth-century ideas about sexuality but was just another way of forbidding any sexual relationship outside the confines of marriage. Based on a Christian doctrine of chastity, it was ultimately inhibiting for both sexes since the only sexual pleasure permitted was that which was firmly rooted in marriage. Overall, the social purists advocated a sexuality that was anti-sensual in its approach towards conjugal relation-ships. Nevertheless, in focusing on men as much as women, it undermined both the biological theory that men were naturally promiscuous and the conventional dichotomous image of women as either virgin or whore.

Censoring obscenity

Social purists not only wanted to repress prostitutes and control immoral men but also wished to change the face of society by promoting a high standard of public morality which would, in turn, help eliminate prostitution. The Church of England condemned immorality in thought, word and deed: the thought and the word were believed to precede action. In the words of

Christ, 'whosoever looketh on a woman to lust after her hath committed adultery with her already in his heart'.[74] The battle of purity was thus seen to be lost or won in the mind as much as in the body and so

> evil pictures which are suggested through our own depravity, or by means of the words or deeds of others, or by some sensual engraving or photograph must be thrust down again as soon as they rise. All the wickedness of the world is first enacted in the imagination.[75]

Church of England social purists were against the popular press, cheap novelettes, sensational periodicals and 'penny dreadfuls'. Some illustrated journals were thought morally disgraceful and thus a peril to young men since their pictures gave them too many profane ideas. Popular novels were thought to be largely impure and consequently were condemned. The sale and distribution of immoral literature was seen to work immense harm – not only books and papers that were obtrusively and thoroughly obscene, but also those which hinted at immorality.[76]

Hostility to censorship may well once have been the defining characteristic of the liberal intelligentsia but the NVA, abandoning any vestiges of sympathy with J.S. Mill's philosophy, shared the opinions of the Church of England. Although the liberty of the press was seen to be a precious national asset, it was argued that there were limits beyond which liberty became licence.[77] Words, as well as deeds, the NVA believed, undermined morality.[78] Obscene literature, indecent advertising and immoral plays were linked, in their mind, with moral turpitude. Exposure to such literature, it was believed, encouraged sexual incontinence and augmented the pervasive corruption of the day because it created the climate in which immorality thrived.[79] Indecent advertisements, for example, were blamed for inciting immoral thoughts in the minds of impressionable young people which in turn led to immoral actions. There was decisive proof, according to the NVA, that immoral literature and advertising encouraged licentious behaviour. In the minds of the committee, a definite link was established between language and action: indecent literature fostered indecent behaviour.

This reductionist approach, whereby 'indecent' literature and theatre directly contributed to immorality, was never questioned. Nonetheless, there was never an agreed definition about what constituted indecency. The Chief Constable of Birmingham, concerned that there might be some confusion among his men as to what was indecent or obscene, sent out extracts from *Webster's Dictionary* as a guide to his superintendents:

> *Indecent*
> Not Decent; unfit to be seen or heard; offensive to modesty and delicacy
> *Synonymous* terms
> Unbecoming; indecorous; indelicate; unseemly; immodest; gross; shameful; impure; improper; obscene; filthy

Obscene
Offensive to chastity or modesty; expressing or presenting to the mind or view something which delicacy, purity and decency forbid to be exposed; impure; foul; filthy; disgusting
Synonymous terms
Impure; immodest; indecent; unchaste; lewd[80]

Similarly, the London Council for the Promotion of Public Morality set up a committee to draw up a definition of what was indecent but there is no evidence that its conclusions were ever published.[81]

No distinction was ever made between pornography and informative sexual literature; it was all condemned as indecent.[82] Any public portrayal of sexuality was deemed to be degrading to humanity. The London Council for the Promotion of Public Morality agreed with them and wanted birth control literature[83] and advertisements for medicines which produced abortions to be banned because they implied that sex outside of marriage was not to be feared.[84] The NVA kept 'a strict eye upon one form of evil, which took the form of the sale of indecent literature and pictures';[85] it advocated a robust prosecution – and somewhat persecutory – policy based on the damage that such literature posed to the general public. The London police raided a house in the West End and 'made an extensive seizure of indecent pictures and books, which, judging from the price at which they were sold, could only have been bought by the wealthy people in Society',[86] as well as prosecuting street hawkers who sold indecent photographs.[87] Sometimes, they were imprisoned, as in the case of one Mr Vizetelly who was gaoled for three years for publishing 'indecent literature'.[88] This included Emile Zola's *La Terre*, 'the obscenity of which is so revolting and brutal' that it was condemned, ultimately banned,[89] and destroyed.[90] Similarly, men were prosecuted for giving lectures on health, biology and science because they were considered 'full of obscene language, unfit to be given in public'.[91] With monotonous predictable regularity, even to a nation being weaned on moral indignation, the Midlands branch successfully prosecuted men who produced and sold improper prints,[92] made immodest speeches,[93] posted indecent advertisements,[94] or sold objectionable Christmas cards.[95] The Birmingham police were instructed to look out for any indecent or obscene theatrical or music hall poster.[96] In Oxfordshire, two men were prosecuted for selling indecent photographs at St Giles' Fair: in one case the photographs were destroyed by order of the magistrates and in the other the offender was committed to the Quarter Sessions and was discharged only when he consented to destroy the photographs.[97]

The NVA even investigated incidents in board schools and public lavatories. On one occasion indecent cards circulated by a board schoolboy were destroyed after an investigation.[98] The London Council was urged to purge the indecent inscriptions in some of their lavatories;[99] similarly police constables in Birmingham were instructed to look into public lavatories each time they passed in order to stamp out indecent posters.[100] Both the London Council for the Promotion of Public Morality and the NVA led a successful campaign to drive out Living Statuary, that is nude poses on the stage,[101] largely because they objected to 'the inhumanity in the use and abuse of these women'.[102] 'Low' concert halls were targeted since they allegedly encouraged vice among young people. It was argued that the crowds who left them late at night used 'the most vile and obscene language, indulging in the grossest indecency, and proceeding to acts of immorality in the open street'.[103] Indeed, 'immoral' performances were held responsible for child sexual abuse.

> Possibly it was nothing more than a sad coincidence but it is never-theless a fact that during the recent performances of semi-nude dances in places of public entertainment assaults on little girls in different parts of the country became more or less epidemic.[104]

Even some plays, such as Oscar Wilde's *Salomé*, performed by Sarah Bernhardt, were condemned as indecent and thus seen only in France.[105] The Birmingham police were exhorted to exercise careful supervision over the performances that took place at music halls and other theatres 'so that nothing improper or offensive should be permitted to be exhibited'.[106] The London Council attempted to reform public behaviour. In certain parks and other places such as Epping Forest (which was seen as a moral plague spot as young couples used it for their courting at night) nightly patrols by the council ensured that young people behaved themselves. In Hyde Park – sometimes known as Jekyll and Hyde Park – men and women were prohib-ited from mixing together when they dressed and undressed by the Serpentine Lake.[107] Women's public lavatories were closed at night because they feared immoral women loitered in them.

Any public portrayal of sexuality was deemed to be degrading to humanity so educational leaflets, erotica and pornography were indiscriminately condemned and ultimately censored:[108]

> Novels exhaling its stygian stench burden news-stands and book agents' baskets. Papers teeming with salaciousness obtain readers by the hundreds of thousands, and drive out of the market self-respecting and decent publications. Painting and sculpture reveal the human form in hideous suggestiveness. Theatrical posters . . . are to our young people unmistakable object lessons in lasciviousness; and the stage . . . not unfrequently becomes the panderer to lowest passions.[109]

Class power exercised through the legal system was used to implement their ideas. This was characterised by the NVA's willingness, like the Ladies' Associations, to use the emerging interventionist – and middle-class – state to regulate the private behaviour of its citizens. Certainly the local branches used the regulatory powers of the state to institute proceedings against those who offended their distinctively middle-class moral code. Nevertheless, because of the absence of a clear legal definition of what was considered to be immoral, obscene and indecent, the actions of magistrates throughout England differed.

> In one town a publisher is successfully prosecuted and convicted for the sale of a certain book or paper, in another town, copies of the same book or paper, prosecuted under the same Act, are not held to be indecent, and the person prosecuted is acquitted.[110]

The NVA, often out of touch with the sentiments of the majority of the population, did not escape public censure. The *Punch* cartoon of Mrs Ormiston Chant, defined as a prying prude, was one of the most famous parodies. *The Town Crier* pilloried the zeal with which social purists sought to reform public morals:

> That worthy and excessively dull body of ultra good and impossibly good-doing persons who call themselves the Birmingham and Midland Vigilance Association had an Annual Meeting on Monday. If they want the support of the general public – they must leave off twiddle twaddle ... Does the worthy chairman wish boys to associate only with boys, and girls only with girls. Imagine a dance where only girls were present, they would not have a really jolly time. This is not the way to put an end to immorality.[111]

As shown by the evidence in this chapter, social purity groups, like the reform and preventive movements before them, were a complex mixture of radicalism and moral conservatism. Unquestionably, their response to child abuse and the double standard was ambiguous. They may have raised awareness of child sexual abuse and helped to change the laws to protect young children from paedophiles but children, as well as adults, were punished for sexual transgressions which were clearly not their fault.

Similarly, the challenge to the double moral standard was both innovatory and inhibiting. On the one hand, social purists rejected the view that women should be held solely responsible for sexual misdemeanours. Men, they asserted, should be held equally responsible for maintaining Christian moral values. On the other hand, their beliefs were centred within an anti-sensual sexual politics that were largely indistinguishable from an orthodox repressive moral code. Social purists were unequivocal, and overwhelmingly repressive, in their response to prostitution and alleged obscenity: prostitutes were condemned, ejected from their homes and subjected to general harassment while literature and the arts were subjected to heavy censorship.

Historians have often assumed that the social purity movement was largely successful in diminishing prostitution and its associated offences but the evidence is inconclusive. What emerges is that social purists did not find it easy either to control prostitution or to curb child abuse, sexual immorality and obscene literature. Indeed, they had to struggle constantly to win over the support of the judiciary, the police and the state. Moreover, social purists, largely because of official reluctance to convict prostitutes and men who abused children, were unsuccessful in eliminating prostitution and were ineffectual in getting children's testimony believed. They may well have tried to use the power of the state to implement their moral beliefs but they were ultimately unsuccessful and failed to make a significant impact on social policy. More importantly, of course, prostitution continued.

Notes

1 Bishop of Durham, quoted in Rosa M. Barrett, *Ellice Hopkins: A Memoir* (London: Wells Gardner, *c.* 1907), p. 160.
2 Church of England Purity Society, *Seeking and Saving* (April 1885), p. 77.
3 Miss Mary Burrs, *International Congress of Nurses* 1909.
4 The BMCVA was equally opposed to homosexuality, although never named it as such. It is interesting to note that the word, coined in the mid-nineteenth century (J. Weeks, *Sex, Politics and Society* (London: Longman, 1981), pp. 99–100), was never used by the BMCVA. Nevertheless, it was aware of the practice and condemned it: 'the offence would be inconceivable but for the fact that it was well known to all students of history, being charged especially against the worst of the Roman Emperors' (*BMCVA Occasional Paper* 1891, p. 4). However, this theory was rarely practised: only one prosecution was ever reported in the annual reports and occasional papers.
5 Louise Jackson, 'Child Sexual Abuse and the Law: London 1870–1914' (PhD thesis, University of Surrey, 1997), p. 12. This excellent PhD examines the extent of child sexual abuse during this period from a number of perspectives.
6 Mrs James Gow, *NUWW Conference* 1910, p. 4.
7 Prosecutions by the Associate Institution for Improving and Enforcing the Laws for the Protection of Women 1876.
8 *BMVCA Occasional Paper* 1887, p. 12.
9 Miss Mary Burrs, *International Congress of Nurses* 1909.
10 See Margaret Jackson, *The Real Facts of Life* (London: Taylor and Francis, 1993) and Sheila Jeffreys, *The Spinster and her Enemies* (London: Pandora, 1985).
11 *BMCVA Occasional Paper* 1887, pp. 3–4.
12 Presuming of course that the law in this instance was the manifestation of middle-class male power.
13 Margaret Jackson, *The Real Facts of Life*.
14 Sheila Jeffreys, *The Spinster and her Enemies*.
15 Revd T.J. Cree, Homes for Morally Defective Children, *NUWW Conference* 1913, p. 16.
16 The following is a typical account of what happened to abused girls: 'Aged 12. Alleged outrage by man of whom complainant gave description. Efforts to trace him unsuccessful. Police rendered invaluable help. Girl sent to a Home out of town by Ladies connected with a kindred Association' (*BMCVA Annual Report* 1888, p. 10).
17 *The Vigilance Record* (December 1897), p. 4.
18 *Oxford Vigilance Association Annual Report c.* 1889, p. 2.
19 Louise Jackson, 'Child Sexual Abuse and the Law', p. 128.
20 Miss Mary Burrs, *International Congress of Nurses* 1909.

21 *BMCVA Occasional Paper* 1892, p. 6.
22 *BMCVA Occasional Paper* 1894, p. 6.
23 *The Vigilance Record* (February 1890), p. 9.
24 Linda Mahood, for example, suggests that the bourgeoisie and police officials co-operated to impose a strict moral code onto working-class women: *The Magdalenes: Prostitution in the Nineteenth Century* (London: Routledge, 1995), pp. 199–253.
25 *The Vigilance Record* (May 1906), p. 38.
26 Mrs Henry Fawcett, *NUWW Conference* 1885, p. 5.
27 Sheila Jeffreys, *The Spinster and her Enemies*, p. 77.
28 Anthony Wohl, *The Victorian Family* (London: Croom Helm, 1978), p. 200.
29 Mrs Booth, *NUWW Conference* 1910, p. 12.
30 Miss Steer, *NUWW Conference* 1885, p. 17.
31 Dr Arthur Sibly, *Private Knowledge for Boys* (London: 1908), p. 3.
32 Head-Deaconess Gilmore, *NUWW Conference* 1898, p. 17.
33 Bishop of Durham, in Ellice Hopkins, *The White Cross Army* (London: Hatchards, 1883), p. 6.
34 *The Pioneer* (September 1892), p. 6.
35 *The Pioneer* (February 1890).
36 *Seeking and Saving* (December 1884), p. 273.
37 *The Vigilance Record* (April 1895), p. 10.
38 *The Pioneer* (February 1890).
39 Mrs Creighton, 'What Women Can Do for Purity', *NUWW Conference* 1894, p. 6.
40 Catharine Mary Whitehead, *The Pioneer* (1894), p. 5.
41 Revd Professor Milligan, *The White Cross Movement* (London: MacNiven and Wallace, 1887), p. 122.
42 *The Vigilance Record* (April 1887), p. 18.
43 Address by R.A. Bullen, *Social Purity Alliance, c.* 1900, p. 15.
44 Ibid., p. 18.
45 Ibid., p. 20.
46 *BMCVA Occasional Paper* 1893.
47 *BMCVA Occasional Paper* 1891, p. 1.
48 *The Vigilance Record* (January 1895), p. 34.
49 *The Leamington, Warwick, Rugby and County Chronicle* in *The Vigilance Record* (October 1888), p. 100.
50 *BMCVA Occasional Paper* 1889, p. 2.
51 *BMCVA Occasional Paper* 1891, p. 2.
52 *The Vigilance Record* (October 1892), p. 72.
53 *BMCVA Annual Report* 1889, p. 8.
54 *BMCVA Occasional Paper* 1893, p. 2.
55 The Lambeth Conference on Purity, quoted in *The Lancet* (October 13th 1888), p. 736.
56 *The Pioneer* (January 1894), p. 4.
57 *The Vigilance Record* (February 1888), p. 9.
58 Revd Professor Milligan, *The White Cross Movement*, p. 111; *Derbyshire Advertiser and Journal* (February 20th 1885), p. 2.
59 Revd Professor Milligan, *The White Cross Movement*, p. 114.
60 Ibid., p. 115.
61 *BMCVA Occasional Papers* 1887–1893.
62 The language used in many of these reports was highly colourful. As Judith Walkowitz has pointed out, the 'narratives of sexual danger' produced by the *Maiden Tribute* influenced the language of others: *City of Dreadful Delight* (London: Virago, 1992), pp. 81–135.
63 Either L was under the legal age of consent when B seduced her or the criminal offence was for rape rather than seduction.

64 *BMCVA Annual Report* July 1887, p. 13.
65 Revd Professor Milligan, *The White Cross Movement*, p. 120.
66 Ibid., p. 117.
67 Ibid., p. 117.
68 Ibid., p. 112.
69 Ellice Hopkins, *The White Cross Army*, p. 21.
70 Ellice Hopkins, *The Power of Womanhood*, p. 161.
71 Olive Schreiner, quoted by Ellice Hopkins, *The Power of Womanhood*, p. 167.
72 Anon, *A Private Letter to Some Friends at School by a Member of the White Cross Union Upon a Subject of the Most Vital Importance to Those Who Would Prosper in Both Worlds*, 1890.
73 *The Pioneer* (February 1890).
74 *The Pioneer* (January 1894), p. 2.
75 Ibid., p. 2.
76 Ibid., p. 15.
77 *The Vigilance Record* (September 1902), p. 3.
78 *BMCVA Occasional Papers* 1887–1893.
79 *BMCVA Annual Reports* 1887–1893; *BMCVA Occasional Papers* 1887–1893.
80 Police Orders, Birmingham City Police, October 1910.
81 *London Council for the Promotion of Public Morality Annual Report* 1903, p. 4.
82 *BMCVA Occasional Papers* 1887–1893.
83 *London Council for the Promotion of Public Morality Annual Report* 1905, p. 5.
84 *The Lancet* (September 19th 1896), p. 835.
85 *The Vigilance Record* (April 1892), p. 25.
86 *The Vigilance Record* (October 1892), p. 76.
87 *The Vigilance Record* (March 1893), p. 12.
88 *The Christian* (June 7th 1889); *The Pioneer* (August 1889).
89 M. Emile de Laveleve, 'How Bad Books May Destroy States', *The Vigilance Record* (December 1888), p. 123.
90 *The Vigilance Record* (October 1902), p. 2.
91 *The Vigilance Record* (April 1900), p. 10.
92 *NVA Occasional Papers* 1891, pp. 4–5.
93 *The Vigilance Record* (April 1900), p. 10.
94 *The Vigilance Record* (April 1902), p. 4.
95 *The Vigilance Record* (January 1902), p. 6.
96 Letter from Birmingham Chief Constable to Superintendents, Police Orders, Birmingham City Police, February 10th 1911.
97 *Oxford Vigilance Association Annual Report c.* 1880, p. 2.
98 NVA Executive Committee Minutes, March 29th 1898.
99 *The Pioneer* (1890).
100 Letter from Birmingham Chief Constable to Superintendents, February 10th 1911.
101 *London Council for Promoting Public Morality Annual Report* 1907, p. 3.
102 *The Vigilance Record* (April 1895), p. 15.
103 *The Vanguard* (April 1893), p. 49.
104 *NUWW Conference* 1910, p. 7.
105 *The Pioneer* (September 1891), p. 4.
106 From Birmingham Chief Constable to Superintendents, Police Orders, October 20th 1910.
107 *London Council for Promoting Public Morality Annual Report* 1911, p. 4.
108 *BMCVA Occasional Papers* 1887–1893.
109 *The Pioneer* (January 1894), p. 14.
110 *London Council for the Promotion of Public Morality Annual Report* 1909, p. 5.
111 *Town Crier* (February 1890), p. 10.

Conclusion: from *fin de siècle* to the millennium

On Monday December 15th 1997 the London *Evening Standard* published an article alleging that young women from Thailand were lured to London with the promise of domestic work and forced into prostitution. In response to this fear, Scotland Yard's Vice Squad raided various saunas, massage parlours and private homes in order to help stamp out this trade. Both the tone and the message of the article – with its images of young, unsuspecting, poverty-stricken female victims duped by moral degenerates into a world of vice – mirrored that of the white slavery movement reported in the *Pall Mall Gazette* over a hundred years ago. Today, just as in the past, reformers called for the governments involved to set up international agreements to stop the trade in women.[1]

It is perhaps not surprising that parallels can be drawn between the two episodes for, despite the moral coercion of the late nineteenth century and the so-called sexual liberalism of the late twentieth, prostitution is still in evidence. All in all, prostitution remains a problem yet to be settled and, as with most unresolved dilemmas, similar issues emerge time and time again. What is more, the moral values and motivations of those involved in the debates around and approaches to prostitution continue to be complex and contradictory.

Today, as in the earlier period, women are the objects of scrutiny. Although prostitution itself has never been a criminal offence prostitutes nonetheless remain criminalised. Moreover, prostitution continues to be considered *mainly* a female – not a male – problem. In nineteenth- and early-twentieth-century England some attention was paid to men who paid prostitutes or who were 'sexually incontinent' by attempting to exclude them from public office and general society but ultimately women bore the brunt of the blame. At the start of the new millennium, the focus of law, policing and community activity (apart from a few *causes célèbres* when well-known men have been caught kerb-crawling and recent police initiatives in Nottingham and Wolverhampton) remains on women even though statistically, as Barbara Gwinnett has shown, far more men are involved – as punters, pimps and landlords – in prostitution.[2] There are still serious shortcomings in the way the justice system views and treats prostitute women:

women remain defined as 'common' prostitute – a label not applied to any other category of offender (such as common thief or common murderer). It is an adjective resonant with meaning – vulgar, cheap, coarse, inferior and low class – which reveals in linguistically significant ways the underlying attitudes of the law enforcers.

However, the latter years of the nineteenth century were quite different from those of the late twentieth and it is important not to oversimplify attitudes towards prostitutes by imagining a seamless continuity between the past and the present. For those concerned more directly with prostitution, there have been some marked changes. There may well be some underlying similarities in the response to prostitution, but the practical outcome and the moral underpinnings are very different. In the past, largely because of Christian religious beliefs, prostitutes were regarded either as sinners who needed to be saved from everlasting fire or as victims who needed safeguarding. Prostitution, reformers believed, was morally indefensible. In contrast, possibly because of the secularisation of morality and the declining importance of religion, prostitutes today are viewed by feminists either as sex-workers or as victims of patriarchy rather than women who have broken God's moral laws. Those who regard prostitutes as sex-workers consider prostitution to be legitimate work and believe that prostitutes have made some sort of choice to work in the 'sex industry'. Prostitutes are equivalent to shop assistants, the only difference being the exclusivity of the product: whereas prostitutes sell sexual services, the rest of the retail trade offers a variety of goods. Others argue that the sexual nature of prostitution distinguishes it from other forms of work as it is 'the only form of labour constructed solely from the oppression of women'.[3] In this analysis, prostitutes are defined as 'prostituted women' rather than sex-workers and prostitution regarded as a crime against women. However, the feminists who adopt this latter perspective perhaps share more in common with those Victorian and Edwardian reformers who blamed men for the continuation of prostitution than with their modern counterparts.

Another important distinction to be made in attitudes towards prostitution is that in the nineteenth and early twentieth centuries, middle-class female reformers felt a deep concern for the moral salvation of women working as prostitutes and aimed to rescue and reform them. Here emphasis was placed on reforming the individual prostitute (by placing them in an institution for two years) whereas at present this is no longer recognised as a solution. Today, only one order of nuns – the Sisters of the Good Shepherd Order – engage in rescue work. In 1995 they established the only refuge in Britain in Manchester for women who wished to leave prostitution.[4] Such groups are definitely exceptional as most express scant concern for the moral or spiritual welfare of women working on the streets. On the contrary, there is a dilemma as to whether one should work for the elimination of prostitution or for the amelioration of the conditions of prostitution, to regulate it, to decriminalise it and make it physically safer for women.[5] There are also calls for prostitutes to be unionised.

There has been a shift away from focusing on the causes of prostitution to a concern about its consequences. Reformers in the nineteenth century, partly due to a redemptive Christian theology, shared a belief that they could, by tackling the causes of prostitution, eradicate it. As a consequence, moral reformers developed a multi-pronged attack on prostitution: they trained those perceived to be at risk for jobs as domestic servants; they set up support networks for single mothers; they built homes for the 'feeble-minded'; they petitioned Parliament to pass protective legislation; they tried to censor literature and the arts; and above all tried to make men chaste and improve the moral tone of Britain. The motivations of moral reformers may have been complex but they shared a confidence that prostitution could be eliminated if enough effort was made. This optimism has been super-seded by a newer, and secular, cynicism: the majority of English feminists seem little interested in tackling the causes of prostitution. Indeed, there is a tacit acceptance of its inevitability and, apart from the work of radical feminists like Sheila Jeffreys,[6] links are rarely made between prostitution and other social problems. Nevertheless, the reasons why women prostitute themselves have remained remarkably similar: money, homelessness and lack of self-esteem. Cocaine and heroin may have replaced alcohol but the relationship between prostitution and drugs remains.

The way in which the regulation of prostitution has been implemented differs across the centuries. In many respects, because the church has significantly less influence in setting a moral agenda, the state has replaced it as moral monitor. Even so, it took some time before the requisite legal mechanisms were in place: in the *fin-de-siècle* period, a national legal framework was perhaps still, if not in an embryonic state, at least in its infancy but today a comprehensive fully fledged legal system has emerged. Social purity groups in Victorian and Edwardian England, conscious of the legal limitations surrounding the question of prostitution, pressurised the government to change the law and legal powers to implement those changes. Interestingly, it has been, and still is, local community groups – not the church or the state – which have usually instigated complaints against prostitutes.

One of the points made about prostitution in this book was that, despite the protestations of women like Ellice Hopkins, it attributed good and bad labels to women. Good women were wives and mothers who conformed to social norms about the role of women in society whereas bad women were women who continued to work as prostitutes even after reformers had attempted to rescue them. This dichotomy was very pronounced in the nineteenth century and continues to be so today despite the attempts by some feminists to promote prostitution as another form of work. The social upshot of these beliefs, whether occurring in the past or present, makes the gap between the prostitute and other women widen further, and confirms the existence of an outcast group and an underclass. Social purists, by persecuting prostitutes and forcing women out of brothels, reinforced, if not invented, the image of the streetwalker as prostitute and with it an image of the street as the province of the prostitute rather than the 'good' woman. Today, those who come into contact with prostitution generally just want it removed from their district and appear unconcerned that it may cause a problem elsewhere. Barbara Gwinnett points out that, in Balsall Heath, any woman alone on the streets is viewed as a potential prostitute. Women have spoken of verbal assaults, attacks on their cars and other forms of intimidation. Not surprisingly, such actions inevitably create a mutual atmosphere of suspicion between women, thus undermining any potential solidarity between them.

In the past, those prostitutes who refused the administrations of the rescue movement were incarcerated into homes on the judgement of the middle-class rescuers and denied the freedoms and autonomy associated with citizenship. Today, prostitutes who break the law daily by soliciting for business on the streets of red light areas may not be incarcerated in institutions but they are viewed as an underclass, imprisoned in their own drug dependency and their own impoverishment. Women working on the streets are criminalised and harassed by police and local residents. The actions of the pickets in Balsall Heath have driven them from the streets, not only reinforcing their status as an underclass but sometimes forcing them to work in more dangerous locations. Recent initiatives in Nottingham and Wolverhampton, whereby police and social workers target young prostitutes and their clients, may mark a new shift in policing strategies and community politics. In Nottingham the police force view male punters as the problem, so they organise mounted patrols in known red light areas, take down the car numbers of kerb crawlers and send police letters to private residences. In contrast, they consider young prostitutes to be 'victims of abuse and coercion',[7] and refer them to social workers rather than prosecute them. Although social workers reject comparisons with nineteenth-century rescue work 'because it implies something immediate',[8] they share more in common with their historical antecedents than perhaps they realise.

There were, of course, as many differences *between* and *within* Victorian and Edwardian groups as between the past and the present. Certainly, this book has tried to illuminate the tensions inherent in the earlier approaches to managing prostitution, thereby revealing uncertainties in what is often perceived to be an age of certainty. Victorian and Edwardian reformers may have shared the belief that prostitution was a problem but, because of different attitudes, various measures were advocated to eradicate it. These responses, the book has argued, were underpinned by class, gender, race and religious attitudes, values and assumptions that could never be simply categorised or hierarchically arranged. Similarly, even among feminists today, responses to prostitution are diverse, as there is no single perspective on the causes, continuation and consequences of prostitution. In terms of the dynamics of class, gender, religion and race, the West Midland town of Walsall has an explosive mixture: white working-class young women, often with African-Caribbean 'boyfriends', are used by a predominantly

Asian male clientele. In this situation one can legitimately wonder who is the oppressor, who the oppressed.

Consequently, one is led to believe that more vestiges of the past survive than have been lost, reminding women who have inherited the privileges associated with emancipation that others have been, and continue to be, denied them. Prostitution remains unacceptable in most circles and, regardless of the rise of feminism, a collectivist ideology, a 'sexual revolution' and an awareness that prostitution involves at least two people, emphasis is still placed on persecuting prostitutes rather than examining – and eliminating – the underlying economic and social causes of its continuation.

Notes

1 This chapter is based on a joint paper given by myself and Barbara Gwinnett at the *Women and Human Rights, Social Justice and Citizenship Conference* of the International Federation for Research in Women's History held in Melbourne, Australia, July 1998.
2 Joint paper delivered by Paula Bartley and Barbara Gwinnett, ibid.
3 Sheila Jeffreys, *The Idea of Prostitution* (Melbourne: Spinifex, 1997), p. 184.
4 *The Independent* (October 22nd 1995), p. 3.
5 *The Independent Magazine* (March 27th 1999), p. 53.
6 Sheila Jeffreys, *The Idea of Prostitution*. The Josephine Butler Society also continues to point out the links between prostitution and other social problems. In March 1999 it organised a conference on modern juvenile prostitution to which the police were invited. This conference aimed to establish and extend joint policies to help young prostitute women and others who were perceived to be in moral danger.
7 *Guardian* (December 29th 1998), p. 5.
8 Ibid., p. 5.

Appendix: major laws concerning prostitution

1824 Vagrancy Act punished any common prostitute wandering the public streets or highways or in any place of public resort who behaved in a riotous or indecent manner with one month imprisonment or on subsequent convictions imprisonment for a longer period.

1839 Metropolitan Police Act fined any common prostitute or night-walker loitering or being in any thoroughfare or public place for the purposes of prostitution or solicitation to the annoyance of the inhabitants or passers-by, 40s.

1847 Town Police Act fined any common prostitute or night-walker loitering and importuning passers-by for the purpose of prostitution, 40s.

1864 Contagious Diseases Act provided for the medical inspection of prostitutes working in certain army garrison towns and naval ports.

1866 Contagious Diseases Act repealed and replaced.

1869 Contagious Diseases Act amended and extended.

1880 Industrial Schools Act allowed local authorities to remove children thought to be in moral danger from their homes.

1885 Criminal Law Amendment Act increased police powers of prosecution. Brothel-keepers and their agents could be fined up to £20 or sentenced to three months' imprisonment with hard labour for the first offence and £40 or four months for subsequent convictions.

1886 Contagious Diseases Act repealed.

1898 Amendment to 1824 Vagrancy Act made living on the earnings of prostitutes an offence.

1905 Aliens Act provided for the repatriation of known foreign prostitutes.

1908 Children's Act excluded children from known brothels.

1910 Licensing Consolidation Act prohibited licensees from 'knowingly permitting' premises to be the 'habitual resort' of reputed prostitutes or allowing premises to be used as a brothel.

1912 Criminal Law Amendment Act increased the penalty for brothel-owners to £100 or twelve months' imprisonment.

1913 Mental Deficiency Act gave authorities powers to incarcerate women believed to be 'feeble-minded'.

Bibliography

Primary sources: manuscripts

Personal papers

All papers with reference numbers (e.g. A/FWA) are in the Public Record Office, London. All other personal papers are to be found in the places identified in the source.

Correspondence and assorted papers of the National Society for the Protection of Young Girls, 1893–1914 (A/FWA/C/D56/1).
Correspondence of the Homes of Hope, 1884–1898 (A/FWA/C/D23/2).
Correspondence of the London Lock Hospital and Asylum, 1876–1916 (A/FWA/C/D78/1).
Correspondence of the National Vigilance Association, 1886–1914 (A/FWA/C/D150/1).
Diaries of Elizabeth Taylor Cadbury, Birmingham, 1880–1914.
Letter from Dovers Green, Reigate, to Female Mission to the Fallen, Bristol, November 20th 1894.
Letter from Dovers Green, Reigate, to Female Mission to the Fallen, Manchester, 1894.
Letter from Florence Kitson (Honorary Secretary of Leeds Ladies' Association for the Care and Protection of Friendless Girls) to unknown person/s, c. 1910.
Letter from Josephine Butler to Lord Mayor of Liverpool, June 1st 1867.
Letter from Royal Philanthropic Society to Oxford Ladies' Association, September 1910.
Letters concerning Miss Stride's Home, London (A/FWA/C/D18).
Letters from Wilhelmine Albright to her aunt, Agatha Stacey, Birmingham, 1872.
Letters of Elizabeth Taylor Cadbury, Birmingham, 1902–1956.
Letters to Dorothy Cadbury and others concerning Police Court work, Uffcolme and holidays, Birmingham.
Letter to Royal Albert Hospital, Plymouth, from C. Buttick, G. Hubbard and T. Coney, April 16th 1883.

Official papers

All these papers are in the Public Metropolitan Record Office, London, unless otherwise stated.

Birmingham Board of Guardians Poor Law Minutes, 1885.
Bristol Penitentiary Trustees Minute Books, 1870–1890.
Calendar of Prisoners Tried at the Autumn Assizes in Birmingham, 1892–1904.
Case Books of Southwell House, Nottingham, 1886–1914.
Devonport Female Orphan Asylum Minute Book, 1869–1889.
Homes of Hope papers (A/FWA/C/D23/2).
Hysom Green Home, Nottingham, Minute Books, 1890–1909.
King's Norton Board of Guardians Poor Law Minutes, 1885.
Leeds Ladies' Association for the Care and Protection of Friendless Girls, Minute Books, 1884–1914.
Liverpool Female Penitentiary Minute Books of the Gentlemen's Committee, 1850–1914.
Liverpool Rescue Society and House of Help Minute Books, 1901–1914.
Miscellaneous papers and leaflets on Rescue Work (ACC2201/B22/2/1–5).
National Union of Women Workers' Minute Book, 1895–1914.
National Vigilance Association, Executive Minutes, 1886–1914.
Norfolk and Norwich Ladies' Association for the Care of Friendless Girls, 1884–1914.
Notes on the founding of Leeds Ladies' Association for the Care and Protection of Friendless Girls, *c*. 1890.
Police Orders, Birmingham City Police, 1860–1914.
Proceedings of the Plymouth Watch Committee, 1850–1914.
Record of Girls in Service in Leeds Ladies' Association for the Care and Protection of Friendless Girls, 1885–1914.
Register of the Court of Summary Jurisdiction sitting at the Police Court, Victoria Courts, November 28th 1899–May 24th 1900.
Reports of the Leeds House Committee for the Care of Friendless Girls, 1888–1900.
Rescue Stations of the Church Army, 1911–1916.
Rochester Diocesan Association for the Care of Friendless Girls, 1893–1914 (ACC2201/H9/1).
Society of Friends Minute Books of Women's Monthly Meetings, 1880–1914.
Southwark Diocesan Association for the Care of Friendless Girls, 1904–1910.
Southwell House Management Meetings, Nottingham, 1893–1897.
Special Committee for Feeble-Minded, Epileptic, Deformed and Crippled, 1890–1892.
Sydenham Friendless Girls (ACC2201/J1/1).

Public Record Office, London

HO refers to Home Office files; MEPO refers to Metropolitan Police files.

Aliens Act (HO 45/10390/171419).
Children: Juvenile Offenders: Reformatory and Industrial Schools; Traffic in Girls; Memorandum, 1877–1892 (HO 347/5).
Complaint re immoral conduct and lack of police action on Clapham Common, 1886–1887 (HO 45/96666/A45364).

Confidential Report: The Law Relating to the Protection of Young Girls: Recommendations of the Select Committee of the House of Lords on This Subject (HO 45/9547/593431).

Conspiracy to procure women under 21 for carnal connection, 1891–1902 (HO 45/9724/A52012C).

Efforts of Police to Eradicate Prostitution in the Haymarket, 1869–1885 (HO 45/9511/17216).

Memorandum on Prostitution and Solicitation in London (MEPO 2/8835).

Metropolitan Police Office Police Orders (MEPO 3/1764).

Police observation on disorderly houses and brothels, 1887–1896 (HO 45/9678/ A47459).

Prosecution of brothel-keepers by parish authorities. Proposed transfer of police, 1882 (HO 45/9546/59343G).

Prostitutes: Police action, Magisterial comments, legal opinion, 1887–1896 (MEPO 2/209).

Prostitution: complaints about houses and behaviour in Euston Road area, 1891–1901 (MEPO 2/293).

Prostitution: Criminal Law Amendment Bill and Act of 1885 (HO 45/9547/ 593431).

Prostitution in London, 1893–1907 (HO 45/10123/B13517).

Prostitution in London: request from local authorities for police to take more action, 1901–1906 (MEPO 2/8835).

St George's Vigilance Society, 1887 (HO 45/9963/X14891).

White Slave Traffic: Alleged Complicity between Belgian Police and Brussels Brothel Keepers (HO 45/9599/98018).

Primary sources: published material

Addresses and speeches

Addresses to the Birmingham School Board by Chairman, 1888–1902.

Elizabeth Blackwell, 'Rescue Work in Relation to Prostitution and Disease', a speech given at the Conference of Rescue Workers held in London, June 1881.

Elizabeth Taylor Cadbury, Addresses, 1885–1949.

Ellen Pinsent, Presidential Address of the Birmingham Ladies' Literary Debating Society, 1904–1905.

Ellen Pinsent, Speech given at Annual Conference Meeting of the Girls' Night Shelter, Council House, November 19th 1903.

King's Norton School Board Chairman's Annual Addresses, 1888–1902.

Mrs Lance, 'The Teachers' Responsibility in Creating and Sustaining a High Moral Standard in the Class', a paper read by Mrs Lance of the Ladies' Association for the Care of Friendless Girls, at the Conference in connection with the Sunday School Centenary, July 6th 1880.

R.A. Bullen, Address to the Social Purity Alliance, c. 1900.

Annual reports

The annual reports are mostly located in the archives of the town or city named.

Agatha Stacey Homes for the Feeble-Minded, Knowle, 1892–1914.
Albion Hill Home, Brighton, 1890–1911.
Association for the Care and Training of Unmarried Mothers and their Babies, 1919–1930.
Birmingham and Midland Counties Vigilance Association (BMCVA), 1887–1893.
Birmingham Diocesan Council for Rescue and Preventive Work, Seventh Annual Report, 1915.
Birmingham Ladies' Association for the Care and Protection of Young Girls (BLACPYG), 1887–1914.
Birmingham Ladies' Association for the Care of Friendless Girls (later Mrs Rogers' Memorial Home), 1891–1914.
Birmingham Magdalen Asylum and Refuge, 1861–1914.
Birmingham Medical Mission, 1875–1897.
Birmingham School Board, 1886–1902.
Birmingham Society for Women's Suffrage, 1880–1900.
Brighton Police Court and Rescue Mission, 1896.
Bristol Female Penitentiary, 1870–1904.
Bussage House of Mercy, Gloucester, 1861.
Cheetham Hill Institute, Manchester, 1892–1904.
Church Army Blue Book, London, 1901–1918.
Church of England Purity Society, 1887–1889.
Clewer House of Mercy, 1849.
Cumnor Rise, Oxford, 1910.
Eastern Counties' Asylum for Idiots, Imbeciles and the Feeble-Minded, 1910–1912.
Edgbaston Mendicity Society, 1871.
Essex Diocesan House of Mercy, Great Maplestead, Essex, 1884.
Girls' Night Shelter, Birmingham, 1888–1914.
Greenwich and Deptford Workhouse Girls' Aid Committee, 1895.
Homes of Hope, London.
Hysom Green Club, Nottingham, 1906.
Ladies' Rescue Association, 1877–1878.
Leeds Guardian Society, 1860–1908.
Leeds House of Rescue, 1895–1900.
Leeds Ladies' Association for the Care and Protection of Friendless Girls, 1885–1914.
Liverpool Female Penitentiary, 1860–1914.
Liverpool Magdalen Institution, 1906.
Liverpool Rescue Society and House of Help, 1892–1913.
London Council for the Promotion of Public Morality, 1902–1914.
London Lock Hospital and Rescue Home, 1876–1914.
Magdalen Asylum, Gloucester, 1894–1914.
Manchester and Salford Asylum, 1860–1914.
Manchester and Salford Central Association of Societies for Girls and Women, 1883–1897.
Manchester and Salford Wesleyan Mission, 1893–1909.
Manchester Ladies' Association for the Care of Friendless Girls, 1883–1897.
Metropolitan Police Home, 1913–1914 (ACC201/B22/1–6).
Midnight Meeting Movement, London, 1898–1899.
National Association for Promoting the Welfare of the Feeble-Minded (NAPWFM), 1897–1901.

National Vigilance Association, London.
Norfolk and Norwich Ladies' Association for the Care of Friendless Girls, 1892–1900.
Oxford Diocesan Council for Preventive and Rescue Work, 1921–1923.
Oxford House of Refuge, 1879–1911.
Oxford Ladies' Association for the Care of Friendless Girls, 1893–1914.
Oxford Vigilance Association, 1888–1890.
Plymouth, Devonport and Stonehouse Female Penitentiary and Home, 1907–1918.
Queen Charlotte's Lying-In Hospital, London, 1870–1880.
Rescue Society, London.
Rochester Diocesan Association for the Care of Friendless Girls, 1895–1906.
St James' Home, 1858.
St Mary's Home for Working Women (Feeble in Body or Mind), Painswick, 1910–1913.
St Mary's Home of Refuge and Penitentiary, Manchester, 1882–1902.
Society for the Protection of Women and Children, London, 1872–1886.
Society for the Rescue of Young Women and Children, London, 1898.
Society for the Suppression of Vicious Practices, Liverpool, 1868.
Southwark Diocesan Association for the Care of Friendless Girls, 1905.
Southwell House, Nottingham, 1884–1900.
White Cross League, London.
Worcester Diocesan Annual Reports, 1884–1914.
Worcester Houses of Mercy, 1884–1902.

Books

Acton, William, *Prostitution* (London: MacGibbon and Kee, 1968).

Auden, George (ed.), *A Handbook for Birmingham and the Neighbourhood* (Birmingham: Cornish Brothers, 1913).

Barrett, Rosa M., *Ellice Hopkins: A Memoir* (London: Wells Gardner, 1907).

Booth, William, *In Darkest England and the Way Out* (London: Salvation Army, 1890).

Burdett-Coutts, Angela, *Woman's Mission* (London: Samson, Low, Marston, 1893).

Chappell, Jenny, *Four Noble Women and their Work: Sketches of the Life-Work of Frances Willard, Agnes Weston, Sister Dora and Catherine Booth* (London: S.W. Partridge, 1898).

Cole, J.M. and Bacon, F.C., *Christian Guidance of the Social Instincts* (London: Faith Press, 1928).

Collins, Wilkie, *The New Magdalen* (London: Alan Sutton, 1998, first published 1873).

Compston, H.F.B., *The Magdalen Hospital* (London: Society for Promoting Christian Knowledge, 1917).

Coote, William, *A Vision and its Fulfilment* (London: National Vigilance Association, c. 1910–1911).

Dale, A.W.W., *The Life of R.W. Dale of Birmingham* (London: Hodder and Stoughton, 1899).

Dickenson, Willoughby Hyatt, *The Treatment of the Feeble-Minded* (London: Westminster, 1903).

Duncan, Peter Martin, *A Manual for the Classification, Training and Education of the Feeble-Minded, Imbecile and Idiotic* (London: Longmans, Green, 1866).

Fawcett, Mrs Henry, *Some Eminent Women of Our Time* (London: Macmillan, 1889).

Freeman, Flora Lucy, *Work Amongst Girls* (London: Skeffington and Son, 1901).
Freeman, Flora Lucy, *Our Working-Girls and How to Help Them* (London: A.R. Mowbray, 1908).
Goddard, H.H., *Feeble-Mindedness: Its Causes and Consequences* (London: Macmillan, 1920).
Haggard, Rider, *Regeneration* (London: Longmans, Green, 1910).
Hemmens, H.L., *Such Has Been My Life* (London: Carey Kingsway Press, 1953).
Higgs, Mary, *Three Nights in Women's Lodging Houses* (privately published, 1905).
Higgs, Mary, *Glimpses into the Abyss* (London: Bradbury, Agnew, 1906).
Higgs, Mary, *Where Shall She Live?* (London: P.S. King, 1910).
Higgs, Mary, *How To Start a Women's Lodging Home* (London: P.S. King, 1912).
Hill, Georgiana, *Women in English Life* (London: Richard Bentley and Son, 1886).
Hooper, James, *Norwich Charities: Short Sketches of their Origin and History* (Norwich: Norfolk News, 1898).
Leckie, William, *History of European Morals* (1905).
Leppington, Blanche, *Public Morals and the Public Health* (1903).
Lloyd, Anna, *A Memoir, 1837–1925* (Birmingham: Cayme Press, 1928).
Lynn, E., *The Girl of the Period* (London: J.G. Berger, 1868).
Mearns, Andrew, *The Bitter Cry of Outcast London* (London: James Clarke, 1883).
Miller, James, *Prostitution Considered in Relation to its Cause and Cure* (Edinburgh: 1859).
Money, A.L., *History of the Girls' Friendly Society* (1911).
Ryan, Michael, *Prostitution in London* (London: H. Baillière, 1839).
Sherlock, E.B. and Donkin, Sir H.B., *The Feeble-Minded* (London: Macmillan, 1911).
Shuttleworth, G.E. and Potts, W.A., *Mentally Deficient Children* (London: H.K. Lewis, 1922).
Taylor, William J., *The Story of the Homes* (London: London Female Preventive and Reformatory Institution, 1907).
Tredgold, A.F., *Mental Deficiency* (London: Baillière, Tindall and Cox, 1908).

British Parliamentary Papers

Annual Report of Chief Inspector of Factories and Workshops 1896–1913.
Judicial Statistics of England and Wales 1860–1914.
Minority Report of the Poor Law Commission 1909.
Royal Commission on the Care and Control of the Feeble Minded 1908.
Royal Commission on the Poor Laws and Relief of Distress 1909.
Select Committee, House of Lords, State of Law Relating to the Protection of Young Girls 1881, 1882.

Calendars, directories and handbooks

Birmingham Congregational Year Handbook 1902.
Birmingham Congregational Year Handbook 1914.
Crockford's Clerical Directory 1860–1914.
Directories for Birmingham, Bristol, Leeds, Liverpool, Manchester, Newcastle upon Tyne, Norwich, Oxford, Plymouth, Torquay, Wolverhampton, Worcester.
Edgbastonia Directory 1893–1914.
Worcester Diocesan Calendar 1879–1899.

Conference reports

Association for Moral and Social Hygiene 1912.
House of Laymen for the Province of Canterbury, Report of the Committee on Purity 1890.
International Congress for the Suppression of the White Slave Traffic 1913.
National Association for Promoting the Welfare of the Feeble-Minded Conference Reports 1901–1911.
National Union of Women Workers' Conference Reports 1888–1914.
Penitentiary Work in the Church of England, Papers for Discussion at the Anniversary Meeting of the Church Penitentiary Association, 1873 (London: Harrison and Sons, 1873).
Poor Law Conference Reports 1898–1911.
Public Morals Conference, London 1910.

Miscellaneous published primary sources

Constitution and Rules for the Formation of Lodges and Branches of the Woman's League for Mothers and Women in Positions of Responsibility, Nottingham, c. early twentieth century.
The Guide to Schools, Homes and Refuges in England for the Benefit of Girls and Women (London: Longmans, Green, 1888).
List of Members of Society of Friends, Warwickshire North Monthly Meeting, 1885–1891.
Metropolitan Police Office, Police Orders 1909 (MEPO 3/1764).
Mothers' Union Handbook and Central Report 1903.
Oxford Ladies' Association for the Care of Friendless Girls leaflet.
Oxford Vigilance Association leaflet.
Proceedings of the Centenary Celebrations of the Monthly Meeting of the Protestant Dissenting Ministers of the Warwickshire and Neighbouring Counties, Broomhall, Stourbridge, 1882.
Some Account of the House of Mercy for Penitent Women at Bussage, in Two Letters by the Lord Bishop of Graham's Town and by the Revd T. Keble, Gloucester, 1865.

Newspapers and journals

Annual Monitor.
Birmingham Daily Gazette.
Birmingham Daily Post.
Birmingham Faces and Places.
Bristol Times and Mirror.
The British Friend.
Charity Organisation Review.
The Christian.
Church Army Gazette.
Church Army Quarterly.
Church Army Review.
Daily Telegraph.
The Deliverer.

Derbyshire Advertiser and Journal.
Edgbastonia.
Englishwoman's Review.
Eugenics Review.
Evening Standard (Derby and Nottingham).
The Friend.
The Friends Quarterly Examiner.
Journal of the Workhouse Visiting Society.
Lady's Pictorial.
The Lancet.
Liverpool Citizen.
The Magdalen's Friend.
The Malthusian.
Mothers' Union Journal.
Mothers' Union Leaflet.
National Union of Women Workers' Quarterly Magazine.
Norfolk Chronicle and Norwich Gazette.
Occasional Papers of the Midland Counties Vigilance Association for the Repression of Criminal Vice and Public Immorality.
The Owl.
The Pioneer.
Refuge and Reformatory Journal.
Rochester Diocesan Chronicle.
St George the Martyr Parish Magazine.
Seeking and Saving.
The Sentinel.
The Shield.
The Snowdrop.
The Southwell Diocesan Magazine.
Stroud News.
Town Crier.
The Vanguard.
The Vigilance Record.
The War Cry.
William Acton's Social Purity Collection.
The Woman's Herald.
The Worcestershire Chronicle.

Pamphlets

Abstract of the Report of the Royal Commission on the Care and Control of the Feeble-Minded (London: P.S. King, 1909).

Anon, *An Interesting Account of an Inmate of the Liverpool Penitentiary* (1835).

Anon, *Report of the Workhouse Visiting Committee* (London: Longman, Brown, Green, Longman and Roberts, 1860).

Anon, *Both Sides of the Question* (c. 1879).

Anon, *How Fresh Victims are Obtained to Recruit the Ranks of the Fallen* (c. 1880).

Anon, *The London Female Guardian Society* (c. 1880).

Anon, *A Message of Love to Fallen Females* (1884).

Anon, *Evil Results of Impurity* (London: Church of England Purity Society, 1885).

Anon, *Letter to a Lad of 15* (London: Church of England Purity Society, 1885).

Anon, *A Culpable Silence by a Watchman* (London: Moral Reform Union, *c*. 1889).

Anon, *A Private Letter to Some Friends at School by a Member of the White Cross Union Upon a Subject of the Most Vital Importance to Those Who Would Prosper in Both Worlds* (1890).

Anon, *Betrayers and Betrayed* (*c*. 1896).

Anon, *Carr's Lane Meeting House: A Retrospect* (Birmingham: Hudson and Son, 1898).

Anon, *How to Help the Feeble-Minded* (London: National Association for Promoting the Welfare of the Feeble-Minded, 1899).

Anon, *The Evils of Prostitution* (*c*. 1900).

Anon, *To Young Ladies Going Abroad, A Friendly Warning* (London: National Vigilance Association, *c*. 1900).

Anon, *A Collection of Papers for Men* (London: White Cross League, 1903).

Anon, *Homeless by Night, being the History of the Open All Night Refuge* (London: Female Preventive and Reformatory Institution, 1908).

Anon, *In the Grip of the White Slave Trader* (London: MAP, *c*. 1910).

Anon, *The Police and the White Slave Trade* (London: James Timewell, *c*. 1911).

Anon, *Leaflets to Liverpool Social Workers, Rescue Work in Liverpool* (August 1915).

Anon, *Prostitution: The Moral Bearings of the Problem* (London: Catholic Social Guild, 1917).

Anon, *Freedom the Fundamental Condition of Morality* (no date).

Anon, *Statutes of the Diocesan House of Mercy, Great Maplestead, Essex*.

Armstrong, Revd J., *An Appeal for the Formation of a Church Penitentiary* (London: J.H. Parker, 1904).

Bickmore, A., *Industries for the Feeble-Minded and Imbecile: A Handbook for Teachers* (London: Alard and Son, 1914).

Carter, Revd, *The First Ten Years of the House of Mercy* (London: Joseph Masters, 1861).

Clorice, *The Evils of Prostitution* (London: National Union Publishing, *c*. 1900).

Edwards, Henry, *Cardinal Archbishop, Lost Sheep Found* (London: Burns and Oates, 1889).

Everitt, Lieut-Colonel, *Your Duty* (London: Church of England Purity Society, 1885).

Fallowes, Arthur, *Moral Teaching in the Board Schools* (Birmingham: Birmingham Socialist Centre, 1900).

Family Welfare Association, *The Feeble-Minded Child and Adult* (1893).

Herbert, Louise, *A Few Suggestions for Rescue Workers* (London: Longhurst, *c*. 1889).

Hopkins, Ellice, *The Visitation of Dens* (London: Hatchards, 1874).

Hopkins, Ellice, *Notes on Penitentiary Work* (London: Hatchards, 1879).

Hopkins, Ellice, *The Power of Womanhood* (London: Hatchards, *c*. 1880).

Hopkins, Ellice, *Grave Moral Questions* (London: Hatchards, 1882).

Hopkins, Ellice, *Village Morality* (London: Hatchards, 1882).

Hopkins, Ellice, *The White Cross Army* (London: Hatchards, 1883).

Hopkins, Ellice, *Drawn unto Death* (London: Hatchards, 1884).

Hopkins, Ellice, *How to Start Preventive Work* (London: Hatchards, 1884).

Hopkins, Ellice, *God's Little Girl* (London: J.F. Shaw, 1885).

Hopkins, Ellice, *A Practical Suggestion to Clergy and Lay Worker* (London: Hatchards, 1885).

Hopkins, Ellice, *Homely Talk on the New Law for the Protection of Girls, Addressed to Fathers* (London: Hatchards, 1886).

Hopkins, Ellice, *The National Purity Crusade* (London: Morgan and Scott, 1904).

Karishka, Paul, *The Underworld and its Women* (*c.* 1900).

Maddison, Arthur J., *Hints on Rescue Work: A Handbook for Missionaries* (London: Reformatory and Refuge Union, *c.* 1888).

Milligan, Revd Professor *The White Cross Movement* (London: MacNiven and Wallace, 1887).

Nokes, Harriet, *Twenty-Three Years in a House of Mercy* (London: Swan, Sonnenschein, 1888).

Richardson, H.M., *The Outcasts* (London: National Union of Women's Suffrage Societies (NUWSS), 1909).

Sibly, Dr Arthur, *Private Knowledge for Boys* (London: 1908).

Sims, George, *Behind Brick Walls* (London: Female Guardian Society, *c.* 1908).

Trenholme, Edward, *Rescue Work* (London: Society for Promoting Christian Knowledge, 1927).

Wallis, Mrs Ransome, *Back to the Source* (London: P.S. King, 1912).

Weigall, Mrs Arthur, *Seeking and Saving* (Manchester: Rescue Work of the Manchester City Mission, 1889).

Whitehead, C.M.A., *Question of the Day* (London: Moral Reform Union, 1883).

Sermons

A Sermon preached at St James' Church, Piccadilly before the Church Penitentiary Association, April 26th 1853, by Samuel Lord Bishop of Oxford (London: Spottiswoode and Shaw, 1853).

Two Sermons preached at West Ham Church by Revd Thomas Leigh and Revd Thomas Scott, August 12th 1873, on behalf of the House of Mercy at Great Maplestead (London: Rivingtons, 1873).

A Sermon preached by Revd P.L.D Acland in the Church of the Holy Trinity, Exeter, December 10th 1848, on behalf of the Devon and Exeter Female Penitentiary (Exeter: Trewman, 1848).

A Sermon preached by Richard, Lord Bishop of Chichester, in St Pauls Church, Knightsbridge for the Church Penitentiary Association, May 4th 1871 (London: Spottiswoode, 1871).

Secondary sources

Articles

Barker, D., 'How to Curb the Fertility of the Unfit: The Feeble-Minded in Edwardian Britain', *Oxford Review of Education*, 9, 1983, pp. 197–211.

Bartley, P., 'Preventing Prostitution: The Ladies' Association for the Care and Protection of Young Girls in Birmingham, 1887–1914', *Women's History Review*, 7, 1998, pp. 37–60.

Bennett, J., 'Women's History: A Study in Continuity and Change', *Women's History Review*, 2, 1993, pp. 173–184.

Bland, L., 'Purifying the Public World: Feminist Vigilantes in Late Victorian England', *Women's History Review*, 1, 1992, pp. 397–411.

Cale, M., 'Working for God? Staffing the Victorian Reformatory and Industrial School System', *History of Education*, 21, 1992, pp. 113–127.

Davin, A., 'Imperialism and Motherhood', *History Workshop Journal*, 5, 1978, pp. 9–57.

Gomersall, M., 'Ideals and Realities: The Education of Working-Class Girls, 1800–1870', *History of Education*, 17, 1988, pp. 37–53.

Gorham, D., '"The Maiden Tribute of Modern Babylon" Re-examined: Child Prostitution and the Idea of Childhood in Late Victorian England', *Victorian Studies*, 21, 1978, pp. 353–379.

Harrison, B., 'Philanthropy and the Victorians', *Victorian Studies*, 9, 1966, pp. 353–374.

Harrison, B., 'For Church, Queen, and Family: The Girls' Friendly Society 1874–1920', *Past and Present*, 61, 1973, pp. 107–138.

Horn, P., 'The Education and Employment of Working-Class Girls, 1870–1914', *History of Education*, 17, 1988, pp. 71–82.

Humphries, Jane, 'Protective Legislation, the Capitalist State and Working Class Men: The Case of the 1842 Mines Regulation Act', *Feminist Review*, 1, 1981, pp. 1–34.

Jeffreys, S., '"Free from All Uninvited Touch of Man": Women's Campaigns around Sexuality, 1880–1914', *Women's Studies International Forum*, 3, pp. 629–644, reprinted in L. Coveney (ed.) *Explorations in Feminism: The Sexuality Papers* (London: Hutchinson, 1984).

L'Esperance, J., 'The Work of the Ladies' National Association for the Repeal of the Contagious Diseases Acts', *Bulletin for the Study of Labour History*, spring, 1973, pp. 14–16.

Levine, P., 'Love, Friendship, and Feminism in Later 19th-Century England', *Women's Studies International Forum*, 13, 1990, pp. 63–77.

Levine, P., 'Consistent Contradictions: Prostitution and Protective Labour Legislation in Nineteenth-Century England', *Social History*, 19, 1994, pp. 17–35.

Lewis, J., 'Gender, the Family and Women's Agency in the Building of the "Welfare States": the British Case', *Social History*, 19, 1994, pp. 37–56.

Littlewood, B. and Mahood, L., 'Prostitutes, Magdalenes and Wayward Girls: Dangerous Sexualities of Working Class Women in Victorian Scotland', *Gender and History*, 3, 1991, pp. 160–175.

Lloyd, S., '"Pleasure's Golden Bait": Prostitution, Poverty and the Magdalen Hospital in Eighteenth-Century London', *History Workshop Journal*, 41, 1996, pp. 51–72.

Lowe, R., 'Eugenicists, Doctors and the Quest for National Efficiency: An Educational Crusade, 1900–1939', *History of Education*, 8, 1979, pp. 293–306.

Lowe, R., 'Eugenics and Education: A Note on the Origins of the Intelligence Testing Movement in England', *Educational Studies*, 6, 1980, pp. 1–8.

Luddy, M., 'An Outcast Community: The "Wrens" of the Curragh', *Women's History Review*, 3, 1992, pp. 341–356.

Luddy, M., '"Abandoned Women and Bad Characters": Prostitution in Nineteenth Century Ireland', *Women's History Review*, 6, 1998, pp. 485–503.

Mahood, L., 'The Magdalene's Friend', *Women's Studies International Forum*, 13, 1990, pp. 49–61.

Mark-Lawson, J. and Witz, A., 'From "Family Labour" to "Family Wage"? The Case of Women's Labour in Nineteenth-Century Coalmining', *Social History*, 13, 1988, pp. 150–173.

Marks, L., 'Jewish Women and Jewish Prostitution in the East End of London', *Jewish Quarterly*, 34, 1987, pp. 6–10.

Mumm, S., '"Not Worse than Other Girls": The Convent-Based Rehabilitation of Fallen Women in Victorian Britain', *Journal of Social History*, 29(3), 1996, pp. 527–564.

Nash, S., 'Prostitution and Charity: The Magdalen Hospital, a Case Study', *Journal of Social History*, 17, 1984, pp. 617–628.

Prochaska, F., 'Female Philanthropy and Domestic Service in Victorian England', *Bulletin of the Institute of Historical Research*, 1981, pp. 79–85.

Prochaska, F., 'A Mother's Country: Mothers' Meetings and Family Welfare in Britain, 1850–1950', *History*, 74, 1989, pp. 379–399.

Seccombe, W., 'Patriarchy Stabilized: The Construction of the Male Breadwinner Wage Norm in Nineteenth-Century Britain', *Social History*, 11, 1986, pp. 53–74.

Simmons, H.G., 'Explaining Social Policy: The English Mental Deficiency Act of 1913', *Social History*, 11, 1978, pp. 387–403.

Smith, F.B., 'Labouchere's Amendment to the Criminal Law Amendment Bill', *Historical Studies*, 17, 1976, pp. 118–135.

Smith, F.B., 'The Contagious Diseases Act Reconsidered', *The Society for the Social History of Medicine*, 3, 1990, pp. 197–215.

Soloway, R., 'Counting the Degenerates: The Statistics of Race Deterioration in Edwardian England', *Journal of Contemporary History*, 17, 1982, pp. 137–164.

Thane, P., 'Women and the Poor Law in Victorian and Edwardian England', *History Workshop Journal*, autumn, 1978, pp. 28–51.

Thompson, F.M.L., 'Social Control in Victorian Britain', *Economic History Review*, 34(2), 1981, pp. 192–195.

Valverde, Mariana, '"Giving the Female a Domestic Turn": The Social, Legal and Moral Regulation of Women's Work in British Cotton Mills, 1827–1850', *Journal of Social History*, 21, 1988, pp. 619–634.

Walkowitz, J., 'Male Vice and Feminist Virtue: Feminism and the Politics of Prostitution', *History Workshop Journal*, 13, 1982, pp. 77–93.

Weiner, M., 'New Women vs Old Men? Sexual Danger and Social Narratives in Later Victorian England', *Journal of Victorian Culture*, autumn, 1997.

Werth, P.W., 'Through the Prison of Prostitution: State, Society and Power', *Social History*, 19, 1994, pp. 1–16.

Woodhouse, J., 'Eugenics and the Feeble Minded: The Parliamentary Debates of 1912–1914', *History of Education*, 2, 1982, pp. 127–137.

Wright, D., 'Getting Out of the Asylum: Understanding the Confinement of the Insane in the Nineteenth Century', *The Society for the Social History of Medicine*, 10, 1997, pp. 137–155.

Books

Abercrombie, Nicholas, Hill, Stephen and Turner, Bryan, *The Dominant Ideology Thesis* (London: George Allen and Unwin, 1980).

Adam, Pearl, *Women in Council* (Oxford: Oxford University Press, 1945).

Adams, Margaret, *Mental Retardation and its Social Dimension* (New York: Columbia University Press, 1971).

Anon, *Macalpine Maternity Home* (Manchester, no date but *c.* 1950).

Anon, *Rescue, Relief and Preventive Work of the Manchester and Salford Mission* (Manchester: Hall and Son, no date but *c.* 1950).

Banks, Olive, *Faces of Feminism* (Oxford: Basil Blackwell, 1986).

Barnes, Cyril, *Army Without Guns* (London: Salvation Army, 1983).

Barnsby, George, *Birmingham Working People* (Birmingham: Integrated Publishing Services, 1989).

Barret-Ducrocq, Françoise, *Love in the Time of Victoria* (London: Verso, 1991).

Barrett, Michèle (ed.), *Ideology and Cultural Production* (London: Croom Helm, 1979).

Behlmer, George K., *Child Abuse and Moral Reform in England, 1870–1908* (Stanford, CA: Stanford University Press, 1982).

Beisel, Nicola, *Imperiled Innocents* (Princeton, NJ: Princeton University Press, 1997).

Bell, Peter (ed.), *Victorian Lancashire* (Newton Abbot: David and Charles, 1974).

Benson, John, *The Rise of Consumer Society in Britain, 1880–1980* (London: Longman, 1994).

Bland, Lucy, *Banishing the Beast: English Feminism and Sexual Morality 1885–1914* (London: Penguin, 1995).

Bonham, Valerie, *A Place in Life* (Windsor: privately published, 1992).

Bradley, Ian, *The Call to Seriousness* (London: Jonathan Cape, 1976).

Bramwell Booth, Catherine, *Catherine Booth* (London: Hodder and Stoughton, 1970).

Briggs, Asa, *History of Birmingham* (Oxford: Oxford University Press, 1952).

Briggs, Asa, *Victorian Cities* (London: Odhams, 1963).

Bristow, Edward, *Vice and Vigilance: Purity Movements in Britain since 1700* (Dublin: Gill and Macmillan, 1978).

Bryman, Alan (ed.), *Religion in the Birmingham Area: Essays in the Sociology of Religion* (Birmingham: Institute for the Study of Worship and Religious Architecture, University of Birmingham, 1975).

Burman, Sandra (ed.), *Fit Work for Women* (London: Croom Helm, 1979).

Burnett, John, *Plenty and Want* (London: Methuen, 1966).

Cannadine, David, *Lords and Landlords: The Aristocracy and the Towns 1774–1967* (Leicester: Leicester University Press, 1980).

Chinn, Carl, *They Worked All their Lives* (Manchester: Manchester University Press, 1988).

Cohen, S., *The Evolution of Women's Asylums since 1500* (Oxford: Oxford University Press, 1992).

Cohen, S. and Scull, A. (eds), *Social Control and the State* (Oxford: Martin Robertson, 1983).

Collier, Richard, *The General Next to God* (London: Fontana, 1965).

Cooter, Roger (ed.), *In the Name of the Child* (London: Routledge, 1992).

Coutts, General Frederick, *No Discharge in This War* (London: Hodder and Stoughton, 1974).

Coutts, General Frederick, *Bread for my Neighbour: The Social Influence of William Booth* (London: Hodder and Stoughton, 1978).

Coveney, L. (ed.), *Explorations in Feminism: The Sexuality Papers* (London: Hutchinson, 1984).

Cox, Caroline and Mead, Adrienne, *A Sociology of Medical Practice* (London: Collier-Macmillan, 1975).

LIVERPOOL
JOHN MOORES UNIVERSITY
AVRIL ROBARTS LRC
TEL. 0151 231 4022

Crowther, M.A., *The Workhouse System, 1834–1929* (London: Metheun, 1981).

Davidoff, L. and Hall, C., *Family Fortunes* (London: Hutchinson, 1987).

D'Cruze, Shani, *Crimes of Outrage* (London: UCL Press, 1998).

Donajgrodzki, A.P. (ed.), *Social Control in Nineteenth Century Britain* (London: Croom Helm, 1977).

Douglas, Mary, *Purity and Danger* (London: Routledge and Kegan Paul, 1976).

Driver, Arthur H., *Carrs Lane 1748–1948* (Birmingham: Swan Press, 1948).

Dyhouse, Carol, *Girls Growing Up in Late Victorian and Edwardian England* (London: Routledge and Kegan Paul, 1981).

Farrall, Lyndsay, *The Origins and Growth of the English Eugenics Movement, 1865–1925* (London: Garland, 1985).

Finnegan, Frances, *Poverty and Prostitution: A Study of Victorian Prostitutes in York* (Cambridge: Cambridge University Press, 1979).

Foldy, Michael, *The Trials of Oscar Wilde* (New Haven, CT: Yale University Press, 1997).

Foucault, Michel, *Madness and Civilization* (London: Tavistock, 1961).

Foucault, Michel, *Discipline and Punish* (London: Penguin, 1977).

Foucault, Michel, *The History of Sexuality*, vol. 1 (London: Allen Lane, 1979).

Gauntlett, S. Carvosso, *Knight Errant's Crusade* (London: Salvationist Publishing and Supplies, 1960).

Gordon, E. and Breitenbach, E. (eds), *The World is Ill Divided* (Edinburgh: Edinburgh University Press, 1990).

Hall, M. Penelope and Howe, Ismene V., *The Church in Social Work* (London: Routledge and Kegan Paul, 1965).

Hammond, J.L. and Hammond, Barbara, *James Stansfeld: A Victorian Champion of Sex Equality* (London: Longmans, Green, 1932).

Heasman, Kathleen, *Evangelicals in Action* (London: Geoffrey Bles, 1962).

Heath-Stubbs, Mary, *Friendship's Highway, Being the History of the Girls' Friendly Society, 1875–1925* (London: Girls' Friendly Society, 1926).

Hennock, E.P., *Fit and Proper Persons* (London: Edward Arnold, 1973).

Henriques, I., *Prostitution and Society* (London: MacGibbon and Kee, 1968).

Hollis, Patricia (ed.), *Pressure from Without in Early Victorian England* (London: Edward Arnold, 1974).

Hollis, Patricia, *Women in Public: The Women's Movement 1850–1900* (London: George Allen and Unwin, 1981).

Hollis, Patricia, *Ladies Elect: Women in English Local Government, 1865–1914* (Oxford: Clarendon Press, 1987).

Horn, Pamela, *The Rise and Fall of the Victorian Servant* (Dublin: Gill and Macmillan, 1975).

Humphries, Steve, *A Secret World of Sex* (London: Sidgwick and Jackson, 1988).

Impey, E. Adair, *About the Impeys* (Worcester: Ebenezer Baylis, 1963).

Jackson, Margaret, *The Real Facts of Life* (London: Taylor and Francis, 1994).

Jeffreys, Sheila, *The Spinster and her Enemies* (London: Pandora Press, 1985).

Jeffreys, Sheila, *The Idea of Prostitution* (Melbourne: Spinifex, 1997).

John, Angela V., *By the Sweat of their Brow* (London: Croom Helm, 1980).

John, Angela V. (ed.), *Our Mothers' Land* (Cardiff: University of Wales Press, 1991).

Johnson, George and Johnson, Lucy (eds), *Josephine E. Butler: An Autobiographical Memoir* (Bristol: J.W. Arrowsmith, 1928).

Koven, Seth and Michel, Sonya, *Mothers of a New World* (London: Routledge, 1993).

Kunzel, Regina G., *Fallen Women, Problem Girls* (New Haven, CT: Yale University Press, 1993).

Langan, Mary and Schwarz, Bill (eds), *Crises in the British State, 1880–1930* (London: Hutchinson, 1985).

Larsson, Flora, *My Best Men are Women* (London: Hodder and Stoughton, 1974).

Levine, Philippa, *Victorian Feminism, 1850–1900* (London: Hutchinson, 1987).

Levine, Philippa, *Prostitution in Florida* (Tallahassee, FL: Policy Studies, Florida State University, 1988).

Levine, Philippa, *Feminist Lives in Victorian England* (Oxford: Basil Blackwell, 1990).

Luddy, Maria and Murphy, Cliona (eds), *Women Surviving: Studies in Irish Women's History in the 19th and 20th Centuries* (Dublin: Poolbeg Press, 1990).

McHugh, P., *Prostitution and Victorian Social Reform* (London: Croom Helm, 1980).

McLaren, Angus, *Birth Control in Nineteenth-Century England* (London: Croom Helm, 1978).

McNay, Lois, *Foucault and Feminism* (Cambridge: Polity Press, 1992).

Magnuson, Norris, *Salvation in the Slums: Evangelical Social Work, 1865–1920* (Metuchen, NJ: Scarecrow Press and American Theological Library Association, 1977).

Mahood, Linda, *The Magdalenes: Prostitution in the Nineteenth Century* (London: Routledge, 1990).

Malcolmson, Patricia, *English Laundresses* (Chicago: University of Illinois Press, 1986).

Malmgreen, Gail (ed.), *Religion in the Lives of English Women, 1760–1930* (London: Croom Helm, 1986).

Marcus, Steven, *The Other Victorians: A Study of Sexuality and Pornography in Mid-Nineteenth-Century England* (London: Weidenfeld and Nicolson, 1966).

Marwick, Arthur, *The Nature of History* (London: Macmillan, 1970).

Mason, Michael, *The Making of Victorian Sexual Attitudes* (Oxford: Oxford University Press, 1994)

Mason, Michael, *The Making of Victorian Sexuality* (Oxford: Oxford University Press, 1995).

Mendus, Susan and Rendall, Jane (eds), *The Rights and Wrongs of Women* (London: Penguin, 1976).

Midgley, Clare, *Women against Slavery* (London: Routledge, 1992).

Morris, R.J., *Class, Sect and Party* (Manchester: Manchester University Press, 1990).

Mort, Frank, *Dangerous Sexualities* (London: Routledge and Kegan Paul, 1987).

Mowat, Charles, *The Charity Organisation Society 1869–1913* (London: Methuen, 1961).

Mumm, Susan, *Stolen Daughters, Virgin Mothers: Anglican Sisterhoods in Victorian Britain* (London: Leicester University Press, 1999).

Nead, Lynda, *Myths of Sexuality: Representations of Women in Victorian Britain* (Oxford: Basil Blackwell, 1988).

O'Connor, N. and Tizard, J., *The Social Problem of Mental Deficiency* (London: Pergamon, 1956).

Offen, K., Pierson, R.R. and Rendall, J. (eds), *Writing Women's History* (London: Macmillan, 1991).

Parsons, Gerald (ed.), *Religion in Victorian Britain* (Manchester: Manchester University Press with the Open University, 1988).

Payne, Edward, *The Charity of Charles Dickens: His Interest in the Home for Fallen Women and a History of the Strange Case of Caroline Maynard Thompson* (London: privately printed for Charles E. Goodspeed, no date).

Pearson, Michael, *The Age of Consent: Victorian Prostitution and its Enemies* (London: David and Charles, 1972).

Penrose, L., *Mental Defect* (London: Sidgwick and Jackson, 1933).

Petrow, Stefan, *Policing Morals: The Metropolitan Police and the Home Office 1870–1914* (Oxford: Clarendon Press, 1994).

Phillips, Anne, *Divided Loyalties* (London: Virago, 1987).

Porter, Roy and Hall, Lesley, *The Facts of Life* (London: Yale University Press, 1995).

Powell, Cyril, *Catherine Booth* (London: Epworth Press, 1951).

Prochaska, Frank, *Women and Philanthropy in Nineteenth Century England* (Oxford: Clarendon Press, 1980).

Redwood, Hugh, *God in the Slums* (London: Hodder and Stoughton, 1930).

Reilly, John, *Policing Birmingham* (Birmingham: West Midlands Police, 1990).

Rendall, Jane (ed.), *Equal or Different* (Oxford: Basil Blackwell, 1987).

Rendall, Jane, *Women in an Industrializing Society: England 1850–1880* (Oxford: Basil Blackwell, 1990).

Rose, Sonya, *Limited Livelihoods* (London: Routledge, 1992).

Rosen, M., Clark, G. and Kivitz, M. (eds), *The History of Mental Retardation* (Baltimore, MD: University Park Press, 1976).

Rover, Constance, *Love, Morals and the Feminists* (London: Routledge and Kegan Paul, 1970).

Sandall, Robert, *The History of the Salvation Army* (London: T. Nelson, 1947–1986).

Sarah, Elizabeth (ed.), *Reassessments of 'First Wave' Feminism* (Oxford: Pergamon, 1982).

Scion, A., *Prostitution and the Law* (London: Faber and Faber, 1977).

Scott, George Ryley, *A History of Prostitution from Antiquity to the Present Day* (London: T. Werner Laurie, 1936).

Scott, Richenda, *Elizabeth Cadbury* (London: George Harrap, 1955).

Searle, G.R., *Eugenics and Politics in Britain 1900–1914* (Leyden: Noordhoof International, 1976).

Showalter, Elaine, *The Female Malady: Women, Madness and English Culture, 1830–1980* (London: Virago, 1987).

Showalter, Elaine, *Sexual Anarchy* (London: Bloomsbury, 1991).

Skultans, Vieda, *English Madness: Ideas on Insanity, 1580–1890* (London: Routledge and Kegan Paul, 1979).

Smart, Carol, *Regulating Womanhood* (London: Routledge, 1992).

Smart, Carol and Smart, Barry (eds), *Women, Sexuality and Social Control* (London: Routledge and Kegan Paul, 1978).

Smith-Rosenberg, Carroll, *Disorderly Conduct* (New York: Alfred A. Knopf, 1985).

Snitow, Ann, Stansell, Christine and Thompson, Sharon (eds), *Desire: The Politics of Sexuality* (London: Virago, 1984).

Spongberg, Mary, *Feminizing Venereal Disease* (London: Macmillan, 1997).

Stafford, Ann, *The Age of Consent* (London: Hodder and Stoughton, 1963).

Strauss, Sylvia, *'Traitors to the Masculine Cause': The Men's Campaigns for Women's Rights* (Westport, CT: Greenwood Press, 1982).

Symondson, A. (ed.), *The Victorian Crisis in Faith* (London: Society for the Promotion of Christian Knowledge, 1970).

Terrot, Charles, *The Maiden Tribute* (London: Frederick Muller, 1959).

Thompson, F.M.L. (ed.), *Cambridge Social History of Britain, 1750–1950* (Cambridge: Cambridge University Press, 1990).

Thomson, Mathew, *The Problem of Mental Deficiency: Eugenics, Democracy and Social Policy c. 1870–1959* (Oxford: Clarendon Press, 1998).

Tilly, Louise and Scott, Joan, *Women, Work and Family* (New York: Holt, Rinehart and Winston, 1978).

Trudgill, Eric, *Madonnas and Magdalens* (London: Heinemann, 1976).

Turner, E.S., *Roads to Ruin* (London: Penguin, 1966).

Unsworth, Madge, *Maiden Tribute* (London: Salvationist Publishing and Supplies, 1949).

Vicinus, Martha (ed.), *A Widening Sphere: Changing Roles of Victorian Women* (London: Methuen, 1977).

Vicinus, Martha (ed.), *Independent Women* (London: Virago, 1985).

Walkowitz, Judith, *Prostitution and Victorian Society* (Cambridge: Cambridge University Press, 1980).

Walkowitz, Judith, *City of Dreadful Delight* (London: Virago, 1992).

Wallace, Ryland, *Organise! Organise! Organise!* (Cardiff: University of Wales Press, 1991).

Walton, Ronald G., *Women in Social Work* (London: Routledge and Kegan Paul, 1975).

Weeks, Jeffrey, *Sex, Politics and Society* (London: Longman, 1981).

Whitney, Arthur, *The Control of Feeble-Mindedness* (1929).

Wilson, Elizabeth, *The Sphinx in the City* (London: Virago, 1991).

Wohl, Anthony, *The Victorian Family* (London: Croom Helm, 1978).

Woodroofe, Kathleen, *From Charity to Social Work* (London: Routledge and Kegan Paul, 1962).

Wright, David and Digby, Anne (eds), *From Idiocy to Mental Deficiency: Historical Perspectives on People with Learning Difficulties* (London: Routledge and Kegan Paul, 1996).

Zedner, Lucia, *Women, Crime, and Custody in Victorian England* (Oxford: Clarendon Press, 1991).

Chapters

Bland, Lucy, 'The Married Woman, the New Woman and the Feminist: Sexual Politics of the 1890s', in Jane Rendall (ed.) *Equal or Different* (Oxford: Basil Blackwell, 1987).

Englander, David, 'The Word and the World: Evangelicalism in the Victorian City', in G. Parsons (ed.) *Religion in Victorian Britain* (Manchester: Manchester University Press, 1988).

Higginbotham, Ann, 'Respectable Sinners: Salvation Army Rescue Work with Unmarried Mothers, 1884–1914', in Gail Malmgreen (ed.) *Religion in the Lives of English Women, 1760–1930* (London: Croom Helm, 1986).

Ignatieff, M., 'State, Civil Society and Total Institutions: A Critique of Recent Social Histories of Punishment', in S. Cohen and A. Scull (eds) *Social Control and the State* (Oxford: Martin Robertson, 1983).

Kaplan, Marion, 'Prostitution, Morality Crusades and Feminism: German-Jewish Feminists and the Campaign against White Slavery', in Elizabeth Sarah (ed.) *Reassessments of 'First Wave' Feminism* (Oxford: Pergamon, 1982).

Kerlin, N., 'Moral Imbecility', in M. Rosen, G. Clark and M. Kivitz (eds) *The History of Mental Retardation* (Baltimore, MD: University Park Press, 1976), originally published 1889.

Mort, Frank, 'Purity, Feminism and the State: Sexuality and Moral Politics, 1880–1914', in M. Langan and B. Schwarz (eds) *Crises in the British State, 1880–1930* (London: Hutchinson, 1985).

Scull, Andrew, 'The Social History of Psychiatry in the Victorian Era', in Andrew Scull (ed.) *Madhouses, Mad Doctors, and Madmen* (London: Athlone Press, 1987).

Showalter, Elaine, 'Victorian Women and Insanity', in Andrew Scull (ed.) *Madhouses, Mad Doctors, and Madmen* (London: Athlone Press, 1987).

Storch, Robert, 'The Problem of Working-Class Leisure: Some Roots of Middle-Class Moral Reform in the Industrial North, 1825–1850', in A.P. Donajgrodzki (ed.) *Social Control in Nineteenth Century Britain* (London: Croom Helm, 1977).

Theses

Bartley, Paula, '"Seeking and Saving": the reform of prostitutes and the prevention of prostitution in Birmingham, 1860–1914' (PhD thesis, University of Wolverhampton, 1995).

Bland, Lucy, 'Banishing the Beast: English Feminism and Sexual Morality' (PhD thesis, University of Birmingham, 1994).

Cale, Michelle, '"Saved from a Life of Vice and Crime": Reformatory and Industrial Schools for Girls, *c.* 1854–*c.* 1901' (DPhil thesis, University of Oxford, 1993).

Jackson, Louise, 'Child Sexual Abuse and the Law: London 1870–1914' (PhD thesis, University of Surrey, 1997).

Morgan, Susan, 'Ellice Hopkins' (PhD thesis, University of Bristol, 1997).

Mynott, Edward, 'Purity, Prostitution and Politics: Social Purity in Manchester 1880–1900' (PhD thesis, University of Manchester, 1995).

Walkowitz, Judith, '"We are not Beasts of the Field": Prostitution and the Campaign Against the Contagious Diseases Acts' (PhD thesis, University of Rochester, 1974).

Ware, Helen, 'Prostitution and the State: The Recruitment, Regulation, and Role of Prostitution in the Nineteenth and Twentieth Century' (PhD thesis, University of London, 1969).

Index